Best Jobs For Ex-Offenders

101 Opportunities to *Jump-Start* Your New Life

Second Edition

Ronald L. Krannich, Ph.D.

IMPACT PUBLICATIONS
Manassas Park, VA

ISBNs: 978-1-57023-360-9 (paperback); 978-1-57023-374-6 (eBook)

Library of Congress: 2015902085

Publisher: For information on Impact Publications, including current and forthcoming publications, authors, press kits, online bookstore, newsletters, downloadable catalogs, and submission requirements, visit the left navigation bar on the front page of www.impactpublications.com.

Publicity/Rights: For information on publicity, author interviews, and subsidiary rights, contact the Media Relations Department: Tel. 703-361-7300 or query@impactpublications.com.

Sales/Distribution: All special sales inquiries should be directed to the publisher: Sales Department, IMPACT PUBLICATIONS, 9104 Manassas Drive, Suite N, Manassas Park, VA 20111-5211, Tel. 703-361-7300, Fax 703-335-9486, or email: query@impactpublications.com. All bookstore sales go through Impact's trade distributor: National Book Network, 15200 NBN Way, Blue Ridge Summit, PA 17214, Tel. 1-800-462-6420.

Quantity Discounts: We offer generous quantity discounts on bulk purchases. Please review our discount schedule for this book at www.impactpublications.com, refer to the discounts listed on the inside back cover of this book, or contact the Special Sales Department, Tel. 703-361-0255.

The Author: Ronald L. Krannich, Ph.D., is one of today's leading career and travel writers who has authored more than 100 books, including several bestsellers for ex-offenders: *The Ex-Offender's New Job Finding and Survival Guide, 99 Days to Re-Entry Success Journal, Best Resumes and Letters for Ex-Offenders, The Ex-Offender's Job Interview Guide, Best Jobs for Ex-Offenders, The Ex-Offender's Re-Entry Success Guide, The Ex-Offender's Quick Job Hunting Guide, The Ex-Offender's 30/30 Job Solution, The Re-Entry Employment and Life Skills Pocket Guide, The Re-Entry Start-Up Pocket Guide, The Anger Management Pocket Guide,* and *The Re-Entry Personal Finance Pocket Guide*. He can be contacted at ron@impactpublications.com.

Acknowledgments: Special thanks goes to the many correctional educators, ex-offenders, and community leaders who shared their insights into the employment issues facing ex-offenders, especially the transitional employment experiences (Chapter 2) and barriers to employment (Chapter 3) incorporated into this book. Most of the individual job descriptions (Chapters 4-10) are based on the U.S. Department of Labor's authoritative 2014-2015 edition of the biannual *Occupational Outlook Handbook* (www.bls.gov/ooh). Please visit their website for additional details on these and hundreds of additional jobs.

Contents

1

Find the Best Job for You!

"You're largely on your own in navigating a job market that is not-so-friendly to ex-offenders. Knowing the best jobs in general, and those for ex-offenders in particular, can help you quickly jump-start your new life in the free world."

WELCOME TO THE FREE WORLD that's anything but free. Let's talk about the realities of money and jobs – that's what will make or break you on the outside. What's in your pockets right now? It's probably not money. After all, you haven't had to handle money in awhile, because you've lacked a real job for making money. Indeed, you've been the property of the government, which has taken care of all your very limited needs. And what little money you may have made behind bars won't go far.

Now you need to make some serious money in order to support yourself in a much more independent and costly lifestyle. Let's face it – you need a **good job**. What will this job and your work look like in the weeks and months ahead? In the following pages I want to introduce you to some attractive job and career opportunities for ex-offenders. Above all, I want to **spark** some new thinking about what you want to do with the rest of your life, beginning on Day One. I want you to experience the "Wow!" of finding an exciting job that will literally **change your life for the better!**

The Cost of Sunlight

After collecting your $100 to $200 in gate money, putting on your new street clothes, walking through the gates, and heading into the sunlight of freedom, everything will now cost more from here on. Much of your newfound freedom will center around **people and money** – who you know and how to get money, spend it, save it, invest it, borrow it, and find more of everything. How will you get money to eat, acquire shelter, buy stuff, establish credit, and pay bills? There's not much "free stuff" for you in the free world unless you decide to become homeless and live a tough hand-to-mouth existence on the streets where you are likely to encounter low-lifers and a not-so-friendly criminal justice system that prefers to keep its streets free from people like you.

> *Much of your new-found freedom will center around people and money.*

While friends and family may help you get back on your feet, you really need to get a good paying and steady job that will enable you to live independently and move ahead with your life. Without such a job, your future will remain uncertain, and you may be in danger of falling through the cracks and becoming another recidivism statistic. Now is the time to identify jobs that are most appropriate for someone with your background.

1

That's my purpose in the following pages – help you identify some great jobs you should consider pursuing in order to change your life for good. I'm not talking about physically demanding, dead-end jobs, such as climbing up and down hot roofs, digging ditches, or hauling trash. As you will quickly discover, the **right first job** out can well transform your life and put you on the road to lifelong career success.

A Failed But Hopeful System

Spending time in a cage is no way to prepare for successful re-entry. You most likely experienced a combination of fear, distress, hopelessness, boredom, distrust, grief, and depression. But you're a survivor who managed to get through an often crazy and dangerous maze. While you're older and maybe wiser, you're not the same after this questionable experience with the American way of punishment. And if you're now jobless with a rap sheet that documents red flags in your background, few employers will want to hire you. As you'll quickly discover, you face several barriers to employment.

It's well documented – and not surprising to most observers familiar with America's sprawling criminal justice and correctional systems – that ex-offenders face numerous difficulties in finding and keeping jobs. Given the widespread use of background criminal and credit checks, there's no place to lie or hide these days. Unfortunately, most ex-offenders become re-offenders. In fact, we do a relatively mediocre job of managing our corrections system – from arresting, and convicting, to locking up criminals – and a very poor job in changing mindsets and behaviors to ensure that offenders don't become repeat offenders after release from prisons, jails, and detention centers. It's a costly, incendiary, and mind-numbing "lock-up and control" program that often promotes more failures and collateral damage. An amazing system, it seems to work against everyone's best interests.

> *The whole process of getting arrested, jailed, convicted, and incarcerated is often a ticket to purgatory as well as a big red flag for employers.*

America's annual correctional and recidivism statistics are staggering. We truly live in an "arrested society" – 707 of every 100,000 citizens behind bars; 2.2 million people locked up in state and federal prisons (up from 330,000 in 1960) at the cost of $55+ billion a year; 10-12 million people circulating in and out of jails and detention centers; over 5 million people on parole and probation; and over 77 million with an arrest record. Because of the "war on drugs" and tough sentencing laws and practices since the 1980s, it's not surprising to learn that the majority of today's prisoners are nonviolent drug offenders. But, as their rap sheets state, they engaged in "crimes" as defined by an overreaching legal system.

The whole process of getting arrested, jailed, convicted, and incarcerated is often a ticket to purgatory as well as a big red flag for employers. Yes, mother was right – getting sent to prison or jail can ruin your life (it can even kill you) – or at least make your future more difficult and challenging. But it's even worse. Just getting arrested and released – not copping a plea bargain or getting convicted or incarcerated – often serve as red flags and knock-outs for employers who prefer not hiring potential "troublemakers" and re-offenders. After all, nearly two-thirds of all incarcerated ex-offenders return to prison within three years (usually for minor parole violations or the failure to pay child support in a timely manner).

From all objective indicators, we live in a very dangerous society where public safety is a major concern. But the truth is closer to this reality: we live in an over-criminalized society that creates numerous self-fulfilling prophecies – it inflicts serious long-term damage on those who come into contact with the criminal justice system, starting with an appalling juvenile intake justice system that continues to snatch school truants into its dreadful clutches and then turns them into offenders, outcasts, and outlaws. Locking them in cages, authorities and do-gooders in the system try to "fix" offenders by dumbing down and regimenting daily life (correctional officers), jacking with minds (psychologists and therapists), harvesting souls (faith-based operators), and telling sorry stories about ugly sociopaths behind bars (media). The end result of such incarceration is often a chilling and costly experience for prisoners, predictably punctuated with fear, distrust, fragile hope, boredom, grief, and depression (for details on the incarceration experience, see Ned Rollo, *A Map Through the Maze: A Guide to Surviving the Criminal Justice System,* Impact Publications, 2016). And no one seems to agree on what to do to change this dysfunctional system. Apparently, few things work in this system. Simply amazing!

> *This system is very costly when it produces negative results for everyone involved – victims, offenders, and taxpayers. The direct and collateral costs are astounding.*

If this system were a business, it would have been declared bankrupt and closed long ago. But it's not a business – it's a classic government growth program preoccupied with expanding facilities, hiring personnel, and acquiring technology in order to warehouse more bodies mandated by the courts. It simply doesn't work beyond temporarily keeping some offenders off the streets, locking them up for a while, and extracting retribution. Not surprisingly, after serving time and tasting freedom, the "clients" most likely will be back for more costly retribution!

While getting tough on crime may make for great photo opps for politicians and public officials, in reality this system is very costly when it produces negative results for everyone involved – victims, offenders, and taxpayers. The direct and collateral costs – probably over $200 billion a year – are astounding. If taxpayers knew the true costs of this "get-tough-on-crime" system, they might become outraged and cynical about those who claim to be trusted and cost-effective gatekeepers. For example, it costs $208,000 per year to jail someone in New York City and $210,000 per year to house a juvenile offender in California. Some observers say it costs $25,000 a year to incarcerate a young person and $70,000 a year to imprison someone 50 years of age or older. Don't believe such numbers. It's most likely much, much more, especially when you factor in the costs of collateral damage and lost opportunity costs.

Many people have lots of good ideas on what needs to be done, and several experimental re-entry programs with strong employment components have demonstrated excellent "lessons learned." Indeed, there is hope for a better day when this system begins to get serious about the whole **re-entry employment process** by developing re-entry programs that really work. In the meantime, most ex-offenders are on their own in navigating a challenging job market that is not too receptive to their backgrounds. After all, who wants to hire and nurture an ex-offender?

Believe it or not, many employers do hire ex-offenders. As you will see throughout this book, certain jobs are very ex-offender-friendly. Knowing what jobs are best suited for ex-offenders can get you started in the right direction as you re-enter the free world.

Jobs and Re-Offending

The failure to find steady and rewarding employment, along with decent and affordable housing, is one of the key factors explaining why so many ex-offenders don't make it on the outside. Unable to support themselves, many ex-offenders return to old habits that initially got them into trouble. Within three years, nearly two-thirds of the more than 650,000 ex-offenders who are released into society each year return to prison. Both the human and economic costs of such a high recidivism rate are horrendous.

As I've documented in *The Ex-Offender's New Job Finding and Survival Guide*, on www. exoffenderreentry.com, and on pages 21-26, ex-offenders face many barriers to employment.

Some are legal, such as the prohibition from working in certain occupations, but most relate to knowledge, skills, education, and training. Many ex-offenders lack basic literacy skills – unable to read, write, and communicate at satisfactory workplace levels. Others have little work experience and few job skills. And still others don't have a clue as to what types of jobs best fit their interests, skills, and abilities. Their biggest barriers tend to be their own attitudes and mindsets – **things they can change**.

Knowing various job options should help you better develop a pre-release resume as well as target your job search in the days ahead.

It's this latter group that this book is primarily aimed at – those who have basic workplace skills but who need more **information** on the types of jobs that are most appropriate for their present level of interests, skills, and abilities as well as their red flag background. They need a **spark** to get them motivated to change their lives in a new direction. For example, it's not true that ex-offenders should primarily seek out hard labor jobs in construction, landscaping, moving, and other trades. There are many other more rewarding jobs and careers awaiting ex-offenders who plan their lives accordingly. Knowing various job options available for someone with their backgrounds should help them better develop a pre-release resume as well as target their job search in the days ahead.

On Your Own on the Outside

Being on the inside often means being divorced from **reality**. In fact, what you hear and believe on the inside often has no relationship to reality on the outside. That's prison noise – a toxic mix of rumors, falsehoods, illusions, delusions, paranoia, and wishful thinking. If you want to make it on the outside for good, you need useful knowledge about the realities on the outside – especially on how to find a rewarding job, decent housing, and a good support system. Put aside any **illusions** about the free world. You need to become job-smart by identifying jobs and employers that best fit your interests, skills, and abilities. If you lack education, training, and basic workplace skills, you'll need to start somewhere – perhaps in a low-paying entry-level position – and work your way up by getting more education, training, and work experience.

You'll have to take a great deal of **initiative** to make it on the outside – no one else can do it better than you. You need knowledge about the best jobs for ex-offenders to quickly jump-start your new post-prison life . . . for good!

Consider New Options

If you have been incarcerated for more than a year, this is a good time to reassess what you want to do with the rest of your work life. Do you want to go back to what you were once doing, or do you feel there may be other things you would like to do? Perhaps you would like to pursue one of today's fastest growing or hottest jobs. For example, the U.S. Department of Labor's Bureau of Labor Statistics every two years updates its employment outlook for the coming decade and publishes the results in the November issue of the ***Monthly Labor Review*** as well as in the latest edition of the biannual ***Occupational Outlook Handbook***. For the latest statistics and projections relating to several tables presented in this chapter, please visit the website of the Bureau of Labor Statistics: http://stats.bls.gov. You also can access online the complete text of the popular ***Occupational Outlook Handbook*** through this website: www.bls.gov/ooh.

Assuming a moderate rate of economic growth in the decade ahead – not boom-and-bust cycles – the U.S. Department of Labor projects a growth rate of 10.8% for all occupations in the coming decade from 145.4 million to 161 million jobs. Technical and service occupations will grow the fastest, as indicated the following tables:

Fastest Growing Occupations, 2012-2022*
(Numbers in thousands of jobs)

Occupational Title	Employment 2012	2022	Percent % change	Median annual wage, 2012
Total, All Occupations	**145,355.8**	**160,983.7**	**10.8**	**$34,750**
Industrial-organizational psychologists	1.6	2.5	3.4	$83,580
Personal care aides	1,190.6	1,771.4	48.8	$19,910
Home health aides	875.1	1,299.3	48.5	$20,820
Insulation workers, mechanical	28.9	42.4	46.7	$39,170
Interpreters and translators	63.6	92.9	46.1	$45,430
Diagnostic medical sonographers	58.8	85.9	46.0	$65,860
Helpers – brickmasons, blockmasons, stonemasons, and tile and marble setters	24.4	34.9	43.0	$28,220
Occupational therapy assistants	30.3	43.2	42.6	$53,240
Genetic counselors	2.1	3.0	41.2	$56,800
Physical therapist assistants	71.4	100.7	41.0	$52,160
Physical therapist aides	50.0	70.1	40.1	$23,880
Skincare specialists	44.4	62.0	39.8	$28,640
Physician assistants	86.7	120.0	38.4	$90,930
Segmental pavers	1.8	2.4	38.1	$33,720
Helpers – electricians	60.8	83.3	36.9	$27,670
Information security analysts	75.1	102.5	36.5	$86,170
Occupational therapy aides	8.4	11.4	36.2	$26,850
Health specialties teachers, postsecondary	190.0	258.6	36.1	$81,140
Medical secretaries	525.6	714.9	36.0	$31,350
Physical therapists	204.2	277.7	36.0	$79,860
Orthotists and prosthetists	8.5	11.5	35.5	$62,670
Brickmasons and blockmasons	71.0	96.2	35.5	$46,440
Nursing instructors/teachers, postsecondary	67.8	91.8	35.4	$64,850
Nurse practitioners	110.2	147.3	33.7	$89,960
Audiologist	13.0	17.3	33.6	$69,720
Dental hygienists	192.8	256.9	33.3	$70,210
Meeting, convention, and event planners	94.2	125.4	33.2	$45,810
Market research analysts/market specialists	415.7	547.2	31.6	$60,300
Substance abuse and behavioral disorder counselors	89.6	117.7	31.4	$38,520

* Compiled by the Occupational Employment Statistics program,

   U.S. Department of Labor, U.S. Bureau of Labor Statistics

Occupations With the Largest Job Growth, 2012-2022
(Numbers in thousands of jobs)

2012 National Employment Matrix title and code		Employment 2012	2022	Change, 2012-22 Number	Percent	Median annual wage, 2012[1]
Total, All Occupations	00-0000	145,355.8	160,983.7	15,628.0	10.8	$34,750
Personal care aides	39-9021	1,190.6	1,771.4	580.8	48.8	19,910
Registered nurses	29-1141	2,711.5	3,238.4	526.8	19.4	65,470
Retail salespersons	41-2031	4,447.0	4,881.7	434.7	9.8	21,110
Home health aides	31-1011	875.1	1,299.3	424.2	48.5	20,820
Combined food preparation and serving workers, including fast food	35-3021	2,969.3	3,391.2	421.9	14.2	18,260
Nursing assistants	31-1014	1,479.8	1,792.0	312.2	21.1	24,420
Secretaries and administrative assistants, except legal, medical, and executive	43-6014	2,324.4	2,632.3	307.8	13.2	32,410
Customer service representatives	43-4051	2,362.8	2,661.4	298.7	12.6	30,580
Janitors and cleaners, except maids and housekeeping cleaners	37-2011	2,324.0	2,604.0	280.0	12.1	22,320
Construction laborers	47-2061	1,071.1	1,331.0	259.8	24.3	29,990
General and operations managers	11-1021	1,972.7	2,216.8	244.1	12.4	95,440
Laborers and freight, stock, and material movers, hand	53-7062	2,197.3	2,439.2	241.9	11.0	23,890
Carpenters	47-2031	901.2	1,119.4	218.2	24.2	39,940
Bookkeeping, accounting, and auditing clerks	43-3031	1,799.8	2,004.5	204.6	11.4	35,170
Heavy and tractor-trailer truck drivers	53-3032	1,701.5	1,894.1	192.6	11.3	38,200
Medical secretaries	43-6013	525.6	714.9	189.2	36.0	31,350
Childcare workers	39-9011	1,312.7	1,496.8	184.1	14.0	19,510
Office clerks, general	43-9061	2,983.5	3,167.6	184.1	6.2	27,470
Maids and housekeeping cleaners	37-2012	1,434.6	1,618.0	183.4	12.8	19,570
Licensed practical and licensed vocational nurses	29-2061	738.4	921.3	182.9	24.8	41,540
First-line supervisors of office and administrative support workers	43-1011	1,418.1	1,589.6	171.5	12.1	49,330
Elementary school teachers, except special education	25-2021	1,361.2	1,529.1	167.9	12.3	53,400
Accountants and auditors	13-2011	1,275.4	1,442.2	166.7	13.1	63,550
Medical assistants	31-9092	560.8	723.7	162.9	29.0	29,370
Cooks, restaurant	35-2014	1,024.1	1,174.2	150.1	14.7	22,030
Software developers, applications	15-1132	613.0	752.9	139.9	22.8	90,060
Landscaping and groundskeeping workers	37-3011	1,124.9	1,264.0	139.2	12.4	23,570
Receptionists and information clerks	43-4171	1,006.7	1,142.6	135.9	13.5	25,990
Management analysts	13-1111	718.7	852.5	133.8	18.6	78,600
Sales representatives, wholesale and manufacturing, except technical and scientific products	41-4012	1,480.7	1,612.8	132.0	8.9	54,230

(1) Data are from the Occupational Employment Statistics program, U.S. Department of Labor, U.S. Bureau of Labor Statistics.

Source: Employment Projections program, U.S. Department of Labor, U.S. Bureau of Labor Statistics

The Fastest Growing and Declining Industries, 2012-2022

(Numbers in thousands of jobs)

Industry Description	Sector	2007 NAICS	Thousands of Jobs 2012	2022	Change, 2012-22	Compound Annual Rate of Change 2012-22
Fastest Growing						
Home health care services	Health care and social assistance	6216	1,198.6	1,914.3	715.7	4.8
Individual and family services	Health care and social assistance	6241	1,311.4	2,022.9	711.5	4.4
Outpatient, laboratory, and other ambulatory care services	Health care and social assistance	6214 6215 6219	1,151.4	1,673.7	522.3	3.8
Management, scientific, and technical consulting services	Professional and business services	5416	1,121.1	1,577.1	456.0	3.5
Computer systems design and related services	Professional and business services	5415	1,620.3	2,229.0	608.7	3.2
Cement and concrete product manufacturing	Manufacturing	3273	161.6	218.9	57.3	3.1
Office administrative services	Professional and business services	5611	426.4	571.3	144.9	3.0
Offices of health practitioners	Health care and social assistance	6211 6212 6213	3,968.0	5,193.8	1,225.8	2.7
Veneer, plywood, and engineered wood product manufacturing	Manufacturing	3212	63.8	83.5	19.7	2.7
Facilities support services	Professional and business services	5612	125.8	164.4	38.6	2.7
Construction	Construction	23	5,640.9	7,263.0	1,622.1	2.6
Commercial and industrial machinery and equipment rental and leasing	Financial activities	5324	132.2	167.1	34.9	2.4
Software publishers	Information	5112	286.0	359.1	73.1	2.3
Other professional, scientific, and technical services	Professional and business services	5419	609.5	761.0	151.5	2.2
Employment services	Professional and business services	5613	3,147.9	3,929.6	781.7	2.2
Junior colleges, colleges, universities, and professional schools	Educational services	6112 6113	1,763.2	2,196.6	433.4	2.2
Nursing and residential care facilities	Health care and social assistance	623	3,193.5	3,954.2	760.7	2.2
Other educational services	Educational services	6114-7	671.5	830.3	158.8	2.1
Funds, trusts, and other financial vehicles	Financial activities	525	86.8	107.3	20.5	2.1
Child daycare services	Health care and social assistance	6244	855.5	1,052.0	196.5	2.1
Securities, commodity contracts, and other financial investments and related activities	Financial activities	523	814.4	1,001.0	186.6	2.1

(Continued on next page)

The Fastest Growing and Declining Industries, 2012-2022 (Continued)

Industry Description	Sector	2007 NAICS	Thousands of Jobs		Change, 2012-22	Compound Annual Rate of Change 2012-22
			2012	2022		
Most Rapidly Declining						
Apparel manufacturing	Manufacturing	315	148.1	62.3	− 85.8	− 8.3
Leather and allied product manufacturing	Manufacturing	316	29.4	18.5	− 10.9	− 4.5
Communications equipment manufacturing	Manufacturing	3342	109.5	78.6	− 30.9	− 3.3
Postal Service	Federal government	491	611.2	442.1	− 169.1	− 3.2
Computer and peripheral equipment manufacturing	Manufacturing	3341	158.6	118.7	− 39.9	− 2.9
Spring and wire product manufacturing	Manufacturing	3326	41.6	31.3	− 10.3	− 2.8
Newspaper, periodical, book, and directory publishers	Information	5111	451.8	346.8	− 105.0	− 2.6
Hardware manufacturing	Manufacturing	3325	25.0	19.4	− 5.6	− 2.5
Textile mills and textile product mills	Manufacturing	313, 314	234.6	183.1	− 51.5	− 2.4
Other miscellaneous manufacturing	Manufacturing	3399	268.4	211.1	− 57.3	− 2.4
Glass and glass product manufacturing	Manufacturing	3272	80.0	64.0	− 16.0	− 2.2
Sugar and confectionery product manufacturing	Manufacturing	3113	66.8	53.5	− 13.3	− 2.2
Pulp, paper, and paperboard mills	Manufacturing	3221	108.2	86.8	− 21.4	− 2.2
Pesticide, fertilizer, and other agricultural chemical manufacturing	Manufacturing	3253	36.8	29.8	− 7.0	− 2.1
Manufacturing and reproducing magnetic and optical media	Manufacturing	3346	21.0	17.2	− 3.8	− 2.0
Pipeline transportation	Transportation and Warehousing	486	43.9	36.1	− 7.8	− 1.9
Audio and video equipment manufacturing	Manufacturing	3343	19.9	16.4	− 3.5	− 1.9
Natural gas distribution	Utilities	2212	109.7	92.1	− 17.6	− 1.7
Other chemical product and preparation manufacturing	Manufacturing	3259	80.8	67.9	− 12.9	− 1.7

Source: Employment Projections Program, U.S. Department of Labor, U.S. Bureau of Labor Statistics

Median Annual Earnings for Fastest Growing Occupations, 2012-2022

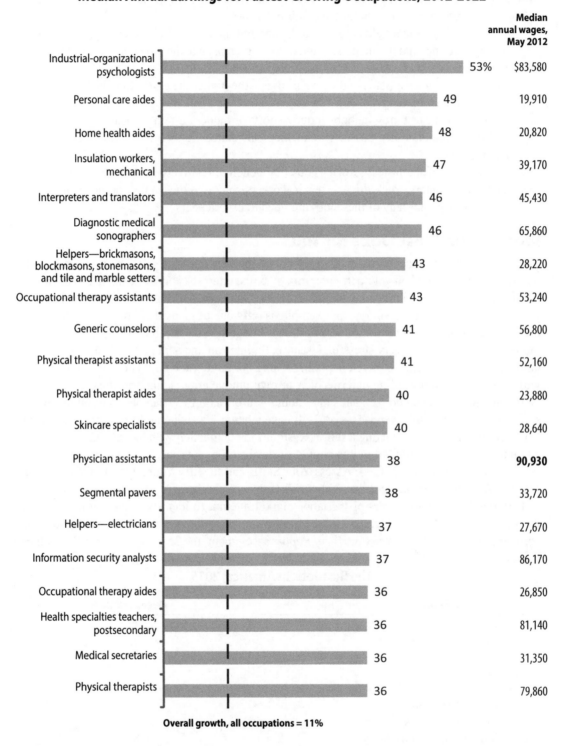

		Median annual wages, May 2012
Industrial-organizational psychologists	53%	$83,580
Personal care aides	49	19,910
Home health aides	48	20,820
Insulation workers, mechanical	47	39,170
Interpreters and translators	46	45,430
Diagnostic medical sonographers	46	65,860
Helpers—brickmasons, blockmasons, stonemasons, and tile and marble setters	43	28,220
Occupational therapy assistants	43	53,240
Generic counselors	41	56,800
Physical therapist assistants	41	52,160
Physical therapist aides	40	23,880
Skincare specialists	40	28,640
Physician assistants	38	**90,930**
Segmental pavers	38	33,720
Helpers—electricians	37	27,670
Information security analysts	37	86,170
Occupational therapy aides	36	26,850
Health specialties teachers, postsecondary	36	81,140
Medical secretaries	36	31,350
Physical therapists	36	79,860

Overall growth, all occupations = 11%

Projected percent growth in employment measures how fast an occupation is expected to add jobs. The 20 occupations in the chart are projected to grow the fastest over the 2012–22 decade. Many of these fast-growing occupations are related to health care.

Source: Occupational Outlook Quarterly, U.S. Department of Labor, U.S. Bureau of Labor Statistics

Similar to the past decade, certain patterns are clearly evident from the U.S. Department of Labor's employment projections for the coming decade:

1. The hot occupational fields are in health care and the STEM fields (science, technology, engineering, and mathematics) and involve increased technical education and training on an ongoing basis.
2. Education is closely associated with earnings – the higher the education, the higher the average annual earnings.
3. Many of the fastest growing jobs require short- or moderate-term education.
4. Two-year associate degrees in several medical-related fields offer some of the best-paying jobs.
5. Nearly 50% of the fastest growing jobs that generate relatively high median earnings, such as carpenters, truck drivers, repair workers, and auto mechanics, do not require a four-year degree. Many of these jobs are open to ex-offenders.

Identify the "Best" Jobs for You

The fastest growing occupational fields may not be the best ones for you. The best job and career for you will depend on your particular mix of skills, interests, and work and lifestyle values. At the same time, certain jobs may be off-limits to you because of legal restrictions relating to your criminal background. Money, for example, is only one of many determiners of whether or not a particular job or career would be a desirable one to pursue. A job may pay a great deal of money, but it also may be very stressful, insecure, found in an undesirable location, involve long hours, and require extensive travel, including a long commute each day. The "best" job for you will be one you find rewarding in terms of your own unique criteria and priorities.

If you know what you do well and enjoy doing – information you can obtain through various self-assessment tests and exercises – you will have a better idea which jobs best fit you. Indeed, I strongly recommend conducting a **self-assessment** in conjunction with the information included on the various jobs profiled in this book. For details on how to identify your best fit, see the self-assessment section ("STEP 4: Assess Your Skills and Identify Your MAS") of *The Ex-Offender's New Job Finding and Survival Guide* (Impact Publications, 2016, pages 73-100).

Periodically some observers of the labor market attempt to identify what are the best, the worst, the hottest, the most lucrative, or the most promising jobs and careers of the decade. According to the annual *U.S. News & World Report* assessment, the 25 best jobs for 2015 include the following:

The Best Jobs in America, 2015

Job title	Overall rank
• Dentist	1
• Nurse Practitioner	2
• Software Developer	3
• Physician	4
• Dental Hygienist	5
• Physical Therapist	6
• Computer Systems Analyst	7
• Information Security Analyst	8
• Registered Nurse	9
• Physician Assistant	10
• Web Developer	11
• Diagnostic Medical Sonographers	12

- Occupational Therapist   13
- Market Research Analyst   14
- Marketing Manager   15
- Accountant   16
- School Psychologist   17
- Mechanical Engineer   18
- Occupational Therapy Assistant   19
- Operations Research Analyst   20
- IT Manager   21
- Civil Engineer   22
- Cost Estimator   23
- Esthetician   24
- Financial Advisor   25

According to CareerCast.com, which produces the annual Jobs Rated report of 200 top jobs, the 25 top jobs for 2015 include the following:

25 Top Jobs in America, 2015

Rank	Job title	Income
1	Actuary	$94,209
2	Audiologist	$71,133
3	Mathematician	$102,182
4	Statistician	$79,191
5	Biomedical Engineer	$89,165
6	Data Scientist	$124,149
7	Dental Hygienist	$71,102
8	Software Engineer	$93,113
9	Occupational Therapist	$77,114
10	Computer Systems Analyst	$81,150
11	Speech Pathologist	$71,144
12	Dietitian	$56,132
13	Network and Computer Systems Administrator	$74,160
14	Human Resources Manager	$101,200
15	Economist	$93,216
16	Optometrist	$101,256
17	Physical Therapist	$81,256
18	Meteorologist	$87,165
19	Petroleum Engineer	$132,258
20	Medical Records Technician	$35,148
21	Physicist	$110,231
22	Financial Planner	$75,467
23	Computer Programmer	$76,180
24	Technical Writer	$68,165
25	Astronomer	$110,227

CareerCast.com also identified the 10 worst jobs in America for 2015 – an interesting mix of jobs that don't pay particularly well, lack a very promising future, or may be dangerous to perform:

The Worst Jobs in America, 2015

Rank	Job title	Income
1	Newspaper Reporter	$36,300
2	Lumberjack	$34,100
3	Enlisted Military Personnel	$44,300
4	Head Cook	$42,200
5	Broadcaster	$29,300
6	Photojournalist	$29,300
7	Corrections Officer	$39,200
8	Taxi Driver	$23,100
9	Firefighter	$45,300
10	Mail Carrier	$41,100

Look for Exciting New Occupations

In the early 1980s the auto and related industries – steel, rubber, glass, aluminum, railroads, and auto dealers – accounted for one-fifth of all employment in the United States. Today that percentage continues to decline as service occupations further dominate America's occupational structure.

New occupations for the decade ahead will center around information, energy, high-tech, health care, and financial industries. Today we have blue-collar and white-collar jobs. Tomorrow we are likely to have more and more green-collar jobs related to promising new jobs and careers in the alternative energy industries. We should see a new occupational structure and vocabulary relating to green technologies, computers, the Internet, robotics, biotechnology, nanotechnology, lasers, and fiber optics. By 1999, for example, the Internet reportedly was responsible for 1.3 million new jobs within a four-year period that generated more than $300 billion in business. Those numbers have more than tripled in the past nine years. And as these fields begin to apply new technologies to developing innovations, they in turn will generate other new occupations in the decades ahead. While most new occupations are not major growth fields – because they do not initially generate a large number of new jobs – they will present individuals with fascinating new opportunities to become leaders in pioneering new fields and industries.

Futurists agree that most new occupations in the coming decade will have two dominant characteristics:

- **They will generate fewer new jobs** in comparison to the overall growth of jobs in hundreds of more traditional service fields, such as sales workers, office clerks, truck drivers, and janitors.

- **They require a high level of education and skills** for entry into the fields as well as continuing training and retraining as each field develops and transforms itself into an additional growth field.

If you plan to pursue an emerging occupation, expect to first acquire highly specialized skills which may require years of higher education and training.

Implications of Future Trends for You

Most growth industries and occupations require training and experience. Moving into one of the health care or STEM career fields will require knowledge of job qualifications, the nature of the work, and sources of employment. Fortunately, the U.S. Department of Labor publishes several useful sources of information available online and in most libraries to help you. These include the *O*NET Dictionary of Occupational Titles*, which identifies over 1,100 job titles. The *Occupational Outlook Handbook* provides an overview of current labor market conditions and projections, as well as discusses nearly 250 occupations that account for 107 million jobs, or 87% of the nation's total jobs, according to several useful informational categories: nature of work; working conditions; employment; training, other qualifications, and achievement; job outlook; earnings; related occupations; and sources of additional information.

During the past 15 years, the U.S. Department of Labor overhauled its traditional job classification system, which was based on an analysis of the U.S. job market of the 1960s, 1970s, and 1980s. This system had generated over 13,000 job titles as outlined in the *Dictionary of Occupational Titles* and numerous related publications. Known as the O*NET project (The Occupational Information Network), this new occupational classification system more accurately reflects the structure of today's new job market; it condenses the 13,000+ job titles into over 1,100 job titles.

Anyone seeking to enter or re-enter the job market or change careers should initially consult the U.S. Department of Labor publications as well as the O*NET (www.onetcenter.org). The Department of Labor only makes this data available online (http://onetonline.org). A commercial version of this system, published in book form, also is available. You should be able to find it in your local library. If not, the *O*NET Dictionary of Occupational Titles* can be acquired through Impact Publications's resource section at the end of this book or through its online bookstore: www.impactpublications.com.

However, remember that labor market statistics are for industries and occupations **as a whole**. They tell you little about the shift in employment emphasis **within the industry**, and nothing about the outlook of particular jobs for you, **the individual.** For example, employment for farmers, ranchers, and other agricultural managers is projected to decline by 19.1% between 2012 and 2022, but the projected decline consists of an important shift in employment emphasis within the industry: fewer self-employed workers but more wage and salary earners in the service end of agriculture. The employment statistics also assume a steady state of economic growth with consumers having more and more disposable income to stimulate a wide variety of service and trade industries.

Therefore, be careful how you interpret and use this information in making your own job and career decisions. If, for example, you want to become a substance abuse counselor, and the data tells you there will be a 10% decline in this occupation during the next 10 years, this does not mean you would not find employment, as well as advance, in this field. It merely means that, on the whole, competition may be keen for these jobs, and that future advancement and mobility in this occupation may not be very good – **on the whole**. At the same time, there may be numerous job opportunities available in a declining occupational field as many individuals abandon the field for more attractive occupations. In fact, you may do much better in this declining occupation than in a growing field depending on your interests, motivations, abilities, job search savvy, and level of competition. And if the decade ahead experiences more boom-and-bust cycles, expect most of these U.S. Department of Labor statistics and projections to be invalid for the economic realities of this decade.

Use this industrial and occupational data to expand your awareness of various job and career options. By no means should you make critical education, training, and occupational choices based upon this information alone. Such choices require additional types of information about you, the individual, based upon an assessment of your interests, skills, and values. If identified and used properly, this information will help clarify exactly which jobs are best for you.

Your Hopeful First Job Out

As an ex-offender trying to survive on the outside with little money, a spotted past, and an official record, you face many challenges most other job seekers take for granted. You may, for example, lack housing, transportation, appropriate clothing, a phone, Internet access, and other basic resources for conducting an effective job search. Despite the fact that many states have recently "banned the box" on job applications, you still need to disclose your criminal record – a big red flag that may quickly knock you out of the competition when employers do background checks or raise the issue at the job interview and job offer stages. In fact, compared to other groups with difficult backgrounds, employers are least likely to risk hiring an ex-offender. Maybe such discrimination is unfair in your special case, but that's just a fact of life you must deal

> *Despite the fact that many states have recently "banned the box" on job applications, you still need to disclose your criminal record.*

with. After all, life in general is unfair. Don't get angry – deal with it by presenting your best self. You've got to move on to other opportunities of which there are many.

Needing immediate employment upon release, many ex-offenders look for low-skill and low-paying jobs with employers who ask few questions about their backgrounds. Not surprisingly, these jobs also tend to be high-turnover positions as janitors, cleaners, lawn maintenance workers, construction laborers, roofers, movers, warehouse workers, home health care workers, food preparers and servers, packers, car washers, and retail salespeople. The construction trades, manufacturing, transportation, and lodging and food industries tend to be most receptive to hiring ex-offenders. While many such positions are actually dead-end jobs, they are at least a **starting point** for acquiring experience and establishing a work record. They offer one of the most important ingredients in your new life – **hope**. While difficult and sometimes depressing (see our "Worst Jobs" on page 12), nonetheless, such jobs can be key stepping stones to a brighter and more rewarding future. In the end, you may discover that there was actually a **purpose** in taking such a **first job out** – it leads to a more promising second and third job out!

If you want to find a job with a good future, you may need to acquire additional education and training. Try to quickly land your first job out in order to get work experience. Demonstrate that you are an excellent worker who has been rehabilitated and who is very productive. But also keep an eye on some of the promising jobs outlined in this book. A few may become your second and third job out – ones that have a future for those who have the necessary education, training, experience, motivation, and drive to move ahead in their careers.

Late-Breaking Education News for Inmates

The federal government will soon (2016) allow some inmates in federal and state prisons to once again gain access to federal Pell grants, which enable them to take college courses and pursue degrees while incarcerated. Suspended in 1994 through one of the dumbest and most counterproductive moves in congressional history, Pell grants were critical to turning around many ex-offenders' lives. With this new Pell grant "experiment," the federal government may finally be getting smart about dealing with the high costs and devastating consequences of mass incarceration by providing renewed access to higher education. As you'll see throughout this book, education is a key to successful re-entry!

2

Transitional Employment Experiences

*"Employers want recent **proof of performance** as well as **evidence of rehabilitation** relevant to the workplace. Transitional employment experiences are excellent ways to present the character and work sides of yourself to potential employers."*

WOULDN'T IT BE GREAT if you could leave prison and jail with a piece of paper or diploma that literally certifies that you're rehabilitated and ready for productive employment? Employers would then snap you up as a very desirable future employee who poses few risks, and you could go on to achieving a very successful career.

Well, this is not going to happen, because no one wants to get into such a sticky business. To do so would create new liabilities for those in charge of certifying so-called rehabilitated ex-offenders. Remember, you're largely on your own in a very competitive job market where applicants normally receive numerous **rejections** regardless of whether or not they have a rap sheet and other red flags in their background. Indeed, rejections are part of the job search game. People with little work experience and weak communication skills are more likely to experience rejections than those with demonstrated work performance and who can clearly communicate what they want to do, can do, and will do for the employer. So, don't just assume you'll be rejected because you're an ex-offender. Life in the job market is much more complicated.

Taking Initiative, Encountering Reality

Since many ex-offenders lack a stable work history, you are well advised to acquire some type of transitional employment experience while incarcerated or while participating in a work release program. In fact, employers who hire ex-offenders are more impressed with such transitional work experiences than with work experiences that took place three, five, or 10 years ago. The most recent work experiences give employers some immediate proof of performance as well as evidence of rehabilitation relevant to the workplace.

But let's also be very frank about what you are likely to encounter in the outside employment world, especially when it comes to transitional jobs. If you have a similar background to many other ex-offenders – low education level, few work skills, language and cognitive problems, anger and substance abuse issues, part of a dysfunctional street culture, and few job- or career-related goals – you'll be drawn toward very low-level, unstable, and temporary jobs that may only

15

pay minimum wages and offer few benefits. You'll gravitate toward **hard jobs** no one else may want, such as a day laborer, roofer, mover, or trash hauler. These are heavy lifting and hot physical jobs best suited for young and strong people who can best tolerate the demands of such jobs. These are not happy jobs. They will eventually wear you down. Some may even drive you to substance abuse!

If you have higher level skills appropriate for the health care, fiber optics, and biotech industries, you may end up working in an **underground economy** with subcontractors who offer few if any benefits. Even jobs in the promising hospitality industry may be limited to back-of-the-house positions, which involve few direct contacts with customers and the public.

> *Take that transitional job and run with it. There is a purpose to all of this, and it too shall pass.*

But you **must** find work and embrace it as the **first** of many stepping stones on a path to re-entry, recovery, and renewed career success. Since you must start somewhere, at least from the bottom you can look up and dream of a much brighter future. My advice: take that transitional job and run with it. Make the most of what may not seem to be a very interesting or worthwhile job at the time. It's **experience** you are getting. As you may eventually discover, there is a **purpose** to all of this, and it too shall pass as you move toward re-entry success. Impress upon the employer that you are someone who is very special. You have the motivation, enthusiasm, drive, and skills to become a highly desirable employee. Above all, you want to start creating a **new record** of success that employers will find most attractive.

Employers Want Proof of Performance

Regardless of how much you believe you can do a job and become a trusted employee, employers want evidence that you can do a job well. In addition to possessing specific work skills, employers also are looking for many of these major characteristics when they hire someone new:

■ Accurate	■ Fair	■ Purposeful
■ Adaptable	■ Focused	■ Reliable
■ Careful	■ Good-natured	■ Resourceful
■ Competent	■ Happy	■ Respectful
■ Considerate	■ Helpful	■ Responsible
■ Cooperative	■ Honest	■ Self-motivated
■ Dependable	■ Intelligent	■ Sensitive
■ Determined	■ Loyal	■ Sincere
■ Diligent	■ Nice	■ Skilled
■ Discreet	■ Open-minded	■ Tactful
■ Educated	■ Patient	■ Team player
■ Efficient	■ Perceptive	■ Tenacious
■ Empathic	■ Precise	■ Tolerant
■ Energetic	■ Predictable	■ Trustworthy
■ Enthusiastic	■ Prompt	■ Warm

What employers don't want are employees who lack initiative and who are undependable, untrustworthy, unpredictable, and make excuses for irresponsible behaviors as expressed in these attitudes:

1. No one told me.
2. I did what you said.
3. Your directions were bad.

4. It's not my fault.
5. She did it.
6. It just seemed to happen.

7. It happens a lot.
8. What did he say?
9. I had a headache.
10. I don't understand why.
11. I don't know how to do it.
12. That's your problem.
13. It wasn't very good.
14. Maybe you did it.
15. I thought I wrote it down.
16. That's not my style.
17. He told me to do it that way.
18. I've got to go now.
19. Where do you think it went?
20. We can talk about it later.
21. My computer crashed.
22. The Internet went down.
23. I think someone gave me a computer virus.
24. I didn't get your email. Where did you send it?
25. I don't text.
26. My prayers weren't answered.

Above all, employers who hire ex-offenders want **evidence of rehabilitation and proof of performance** – that you have the right skills, including attitudes and interpersonal behaviors, to get the job done. Rather than rely solely on impressive but self-serving commentary about yourself during a job interview (*"I'm very dependable and can be trusted"*), prospective employers want to look at your most recent job performance record. In other words, when faced with the possibility of hiring an ex-offender, employers say to themselves the following cautionary words:

> *"Don't just tell me about yourself – show me the evidence that backs up your claims of performance and rehabilitation. Do you have some type of certification that will convince me that I'm making a wise hiring decision, or is this a lot of persuasive talk to con me into hiring you despite my reservations to the contrary? If I look at your past pattern of behavior, I can't think of any good reason to hire you. I've been disappointed before. Despite your seeming good intentions, you'll probably disappoint me again."*

If you have no such evidence, then you become a very risky hire. An employer will have to hire you on the basis of **faith** – a gut feeling that you might over time become a good employee.

The evidence that you offer employers can come in several forms. You might, for example, assemble a **character and performance portfolio**, which includes letters of recommendation from people who you've worked with and know you well. While these letters are obviously self-serving and very selective, nonetheless, they provide some evidence about your skills and character. If you do graphic, artistic, or other types of show-and-tell work, your portfolio might also include samples of your work.

Assuming that you will be assembling a character and performance portfolio to present to employers, complete the following exercise:

What evidence can you give to employers as proof of rehabilitation and job performance?

1. My proof of rehabilitation: _____

_____

_____

_____

_____

_____

2. My proof of job performance: _____

_____

_____

_____

_____

_____

_____

_____

If you have difficulty completing this exercise, chances are you lack sufficient experience to provide such evidence and proof. So what are you planning to do to fill in this important gap in your life? What action can you take now to ensure that you'll be able to present evidence of your rehabilitation and proof of your work-related performance?

Importance of Transitional Work Experiences

Employers who hire ex-offenders report the importance of recent transitional work experiences in their hiring decision. While they can routinely scrutinize an application and resume, listen to a candidate's answers to interview questions, and check out references in the process of making judgments about the suitability or "fit" of a candidate, what really impresses them the most is the evidence provided in recent transition work experiences. Such experiences are the closest ex-offenders can get to being **certified** as trustworthy and competent. Pre-incarceration work experiences have less credibility than incarceration and halfway house experiences simply because these latter factor in prison and post-prison experiences – extremely important and presumably life-changing experiences that are a much sounder basis for making hiring decisions than pre-incarceration experiences.

Creating Your New Record

Depending on where you serve time, many prisons, jails, and detention centers offer important transitional work experiences in the form of halfway houses, job readiness training, and transitional jobs programs, which are often contracted out to a variety of community-based nonprofit organizations. As part of their transition to communities, many ex-offenders are offered subsidized job training and wage-paid temporary work with wraparound supports and services. These work experiences may be with government agencies, nonprofit organizations, or local businesses, especially in the construction, manufacturing, food preparation, hospitality, printing, transportation, warehousing, and distribution industries. Some jobs may be more seasonal and unpredictable, such as landscaping, construction, and transportation/ moving. Many ex-offenders may find work with local governments as uniformed street sweepers and trash haulers.

Your prison, jail, or detention center may partner with community groups that offer transitional job programs for youth, the homeless, welfare recipients, and ex-offenders. In addition to halfway houses, one of the major groups offering transitional job programs is Goodwill Industries. Ex-offenders participating in such programs as part of their probation may receive two weeks of job readiness training followed by 10 weeks of paid work experience. Once they complete the program, they are ostensibly ready to enter the world of unsubsidized employment. Most important of all, they will have created a recent employment training and work **record** that employers may view as a form of certification relating to rehabilitation and workplace behavior. They should be able to consult with program managers who can give them feedback on the candidate's suitability for a new workplace.

It would be unfair to imply that all is well with transitional employment programs. They have their own set of issues that is often troubling for everyone involved. Many programs, for example, encounter difficulties with employers who may take advantage of tax credits by only offering temporary employment as well as failing to offer decent wages and benefits. Many transitional jobs are low-paying entry-level jobs that may not have much of a future beyond the temporary halfway house experience. Nonetheless, one should view these jobs as a new starting point – a place to get some direct work experience however limiting it may be.

> *You want to communicate to employers a recent **work record** – not your prison record or rap sheet.*

Other programs may lack strong support services for helping ex-offenders transition to full-time unsubsidized employment. Many ex-offenders are not mentally ready for the ups and downs that accompany the job-search experience, encountering rejections, and ending up unemployed or underemployed. In some communities ex-offenders may be competing with illegal immigrants who will work for very low wages and no benefits and with no complaints. And there are always the issues of housing, transportation, and clothing that can complicate the employability of ex-offenders. Indeed, keeping that job can be difficult!

It's this **transitional employment record** you want to create and communicate to employers – not your other record or rap sheet. Your **new record** will go a long way to offsetting the many red flags that may scream from your criminal record.

Whatever you do, try to get transitional employment experience prior to going out into the free world with your criminal record. Trust me on this one – this new record may well become your ticket to re-entry success, especially if you take the transitional work experience very seriously, treating it as a major stepping stone to a brighter future!

Best Employer-Centered Approaches for Ex-Offenders

Counselors and program managers who work in transitional employment programs will tell you the inside secrets of what separates the best participants from all the others. **First**, they look at the employers and will tell you what they really hate – high **turnover** of personnel. It's one of their biggest headaches, and ex-offenders often contribute to the problem. Employee turnover is very costly to employers who must recruit and train new employees. They want to hire people who are relatively talented and who know what they want to do – not just anyone who needs a job for wages and benefits. They are not looking for beggars – only bright-eyed, enthusiastic, and loyal workers who can do the job well and plan to stay around for awhile.

Second, ex-offenders who work the best with employers **know their interests and skills** and communicate them through **enthusiasm and drive**. They let employers know that they have **goals** and say so by indicating what they really want to do today, tomorrow, next week, next month, next year, or five years from now. If, for example, an individual is being interviewed for a warehouse position, he might indicate to the interviewer that what he eventually wants to do – maybe next year – is to drive the big yellow forklift that's parked near the bay door. This type of conversation indicates the prospective employee probably plans to stay around for a while, especially since he wants to move up in the company to become a forklift driver.

The problem is this: If you don't know where you want to go, you'll probably end up somewhere after learning where you don't want to go! As noted motivation guru Earl Nightingale observes,

"People with goals succeed because they know where they are going. It's as simple as that."

This simple notion of **goal-driven success** is perhaps best stated in reverse logic:

If you don't know where you're going, you're impulsive, and you're not in control, chances are you'll end up somewhere unintended, such as where you are today! That's not good.

Not surprisingly, goal-oriented people also make good impressions on potential employers.

Third, the most successful ex-offenders break out of the temporary job mode and focus on permanent jobs with a promising future. They have immediate income needs, but they understand their future depends on the smart decisions they make today and tomorrow.

Employee turnover is one of the biggest headaches, and ex-offenders often contribute to the problem.

Fourth, the best employees have the **right attitude and motivation** to succeed in the workplace. They communicate in complete sentences and use proper grammar – not low-class street language that marks them as unreformed ex-offenders who still hang around with the wrong crowd. The best employees incorporate many of the positive workplace characteristics we discussed on page 16. Above all, they communicate well with others.

Fifth, the best employees have a **new mindset** that focuses on the value of hard work and performance. It's not about them – it's about fellow workers, the employer, customers, and clients. They become other-directed by constantly asking themselves what they can do to be more helpful to others rather than be self-centered and concerned with how to cut corners and take advantage of others and the workplace for their own personal satisfaction. Whatever you do, learn the value and power of this new mindset. It will serve you well throughout what is hopefully a very long, purposeful, productive, and happy life in the free work world!

3

Job Restrictions Affecting Ex-Offenders

"Don't ever think you're just a poor victim of a so-called 'system' that discriminates against ex-offenders who served their time and should now be on an even playing field. That's simply delusional. It's not how the world works. In many respects, being incarcerated is a life sentence. Barriers to your employment come from both within you and outside you. You need to understand how both may work against you, and what you need to do to tackle those barriers that are within your power to overcome."

FOR PURPOSES OF DISCUSSION, let's assume that most ex-offenders want to get out and stay out for good. Despite their past mistakes, bad luck, and all the craziness that goes on in prisons and jails, they still want to change their lives for the better. Above all, they want to forget the past and live a new life complete with a decent job, good housing, a terrific family, supportive friends, and lots of nice "stuff" that's associated with living the American Dream.

Perhaps this is not a realistic assumption, especially when you look around at all the weird body art that someday will be staring at potential employers who will say *"Tell me about yourself"* and then ask *"Why should I hire you?"* Nonetheless, this is a good working assumption, because it gives us all hope for a brighter future. And **hope** is what motivates many ex-offenders to keep on moving toward a better place in life.

I've Fallen Down and . . .

Except for the sociopaths, most ex-offenders really don't want to talk, much less tell the whole ugly truth, about the red flags in their background. They know about the importance of **disclosure**, but they know telling the truth is often a set-up for **rejection**. When asked by a potential employer if they have ever been convicted of a crime, they may hesitate, trying to decide whether to tell the whole truth, parse the truth, or just lie-and-pray their rap sheet away, hoping it won't come back to bite them in the rear end. They want to start fresh without that "Big Brother" computerized record following them everywhere they go. It's tough knowing what best to do when employers pop that killer question.

Not surprisingly, there's no place to hide these days. "Big Brother" does a real good job keeping an eye on your record for employers, landlords, and others who bother to do a little checking on your background. And it keeps getting better at doing that job. Therefore, since you're unlikely to beat the system, it's best to tell the **truth**, especially sharing a compelling story about your **rehabilitation**. If you're a reservoir for lots of scary body art and decorative body piercings, it's probably a good idea to consider some painful removals. Done at one time as an expression of selfish freedom or an impulsive act of self-destruction, your body art and re-alignments probably only look good to you and a few weird buddies and questionable partners. They really don't impress employers who are trying to decide which stranger to hire and trust to make good decisions for them – *"He did what to himself?"*

Asking for a second chance at freedom is a lot to ask for, but it's something many ex-offenders manage to do and with positive results. Indeed, this revised take on the old adage about falling down and getting up is very appropriate for ex-offenders:

> *It's not how far, hard, or often you've fallen that's important. What's really important is how well you get up, dust yourself off, and move on toward achieving dreams that relate to your purpose and legacy in life. If you're unwilling to get up and try your best to move ahead toward a meaningful goal, you'll probably be in serious trouble for the rest of your life! Some day you simply won't be able to get up. Worst of all, no one will want to extend you another helping hand.*

Perhaps you've fallen many times. Now it's time to get up, dust yourself off, and start moving in the right direction for good. If others can do it, why can't you? Each day take a good look at yourself. Tell that person exactly what he or she needs to do to stay up and keep moving ahead. If you have a copy of my companion book, ***The Ex-Offender's Re-Entry Success Guide***, complete its many exercises that will help propel you to re-entry success.

Barriers to Employment From Within Yourself

Let's look at the challenging "loser" profile ex-offenders present as a statistical group, which many employers know all too well and causes them to hesitate in hiring ex-offenders:

- 70% are high school dropouts
- 50% are functionally illiterate
- 2-3% have AIDS or are HIV positive
- 18% have hepatitis C
- 15-18% have some type of emotional disorder
- nearly 70% have substance abuse issues
- nearly 70% return to jail or prison within three years of release

For employers, this means that ex-offenders as a whole are **risky business**, because they come to the workplace with these potential work-related problems:

Facts/Realities	Potential Problems
■ Limited education and cognitive skills	Difficult to train and makes mistakes
■ Little work experience	Requires lots of training and workplace adjustments
■ Unstable work history	Potential job-hopper and disloyal
■ Limited workplace skills	May not show up on time and undependable
■ Few on-the-job skills	Problems operating equipment and communicating
■ Many physical and mental health issues	Frequent absences and endangers others
■ Substance abuse and addictive behaviors	Negatively affects work output
■ Anger and rage issues	Threatens boss, fellow workers, and customers
■ A lengthy rap sheet	Predictable negative pattern of behavior

While some of these problems are created by several undiagnosed and untreated mental health issues, such as ADD (Attention Deficit Disorder), ADHD (Attention Deficit and Hyperactivity Disorder), bipolarism, depression, and borderline personality disorders, others are simply problems related to individual **choice and judgment**. In fact, the act of dropping out of high school – an extremely common first step toward entering the criminal justice system – is often related to reading, learning, and bullying problems precipitated by undiagnosed ADD or ADHD. As adults with ADHD, they have difficulty concentrating, listening, following instructions, and getting and staying organized, focused, and task-oriented. Ex-offenders with ADHD make poor initial impressions on employers who are looking for people who listen, appear interested in the job, and maintain eye contact – all nonverbal clues adults with ADHD have difficulty managing for very long.

Studies show that employers would much prefer hiring a poor and relatively unskilled welfare recipient than an ostensibly risky ex-offender who is likely to become another recidivism statistic. Frankly, many employers view ex-offenders as losers or the dregs of society. They are often seen as human trash that gets recycled every three years when they predictably re-offend and get locked up again. While forgiveness and mercy are fine, and giving someone a second change is commendable, who wants to take such risks in the face of these disappointing recidivism statistics?

Most employers are businesses – not social experiments. They have employees and a bottom line to protect. You must first understand where they are coming from.

Most employers are businesses – not social experiments or empathetic nonprofits engaged in second-chance experiments. They have employees and a bottom line to protect. You must **understand** – not be embittered by – the choices facing employers who may want to give you a second chance but still can't bring themselves to take the risks. In fact, while Title VII of the Civil Rights Act prohibits discriminating in employment decisions (hiring, firing, promoting) based solely on one's conviction record, at the same time, it's legal for employers to refuse to hire an ex-offender if it can be shown there is a "business necessity" in not hiring someone with a conviction record.

Regardless of attempts by state and local governments to "ban the box" on application forms and **incentivize** the hiring of ex-offenders with special tax credits and bonding arrangements, most employers are still reluctant to take on what they see as the unnecessary **liability** that may come with hiring ex-offenders. In fact, studies show that when employers are sued by employees for endangering the workplace by employing an ex-offender who injured fellow workers, the employees usually win. The average judgment against the employer has been $1.6 million – a cost most employers are unwilling to bear through a risky hire. Indeed, it's not wise to hire an ex-offender unless that ex-offender could be certified by the state as being rehabilitated – something many states have talked about doing but thus far have been unwilling to do. In the meantime, employers aren't dumb – hiring an ex-offender is a risky crapshoot. Employers tend to be very conservative gamblers who know the costs of making poor hiring decisions – they want to play with very good odds. They may empathize with your situation, but they don't have to hire you. Getting hired is your problem – not the employer's.

Take another look at the above list of "facts" about ex-offenders as a whole. Most of these facts are barriers to employment, which are largely the **responsibility** of the ex-offender. In other words, these are **self-inflicted actions** – not things that just happened to them or were the responsibility of others, such as the judge who put you in a cage and the correctional officers who supervised your cage behavior. Ex-offenders did these things to themselves through their many short-sighted **choices**. For example, they chose to drop out of high school. They chose to get involved with alcohol and drugs. The chose a troubled crowd to hang around with. They chose to commit a crime. These are all things they can **change**, but only if they are sufficiently **motivated** to make the changes and seek help. For example, they can get a GED, stop substance abuse, control their anger, acquire job skills, get more work experience, and hang around better quality people. They can reduce these barriers significantly by taking the right actions to improve themselves. In other words, they have to **take responsibility and ownership** for their own future by finding a job that's right for them. No one else can or will do this for them.

External Barriers to Employment

On the other hand, many employment barriers are beyond the control of ex-offenders. Most are in the hands of the legal system that mandates what an ex-offender can and can't do after leaving prison or jail. Some are laws passed by federal, state, and local representatives while others are bureaucratic and/or policy interpretations made by federal, state, and local agencies. The overall effect of such actions is to create a special class of restrictive employment for ex-offenders.

Federal Restrictions

The first thing you need to know about such external barriers to employment are the differences in federal, state, and local laws affecting the employability of ex-offenders. While Title VII of the Civil Rights Act prohibits discrimination based on criminal history, nonetheless, several federal laws also restrict ex-offenders from entering certain types of occupations:

- **Banking/commodities/securities:** Anyone convicted of dishonesty, breach of trust, or money laundering is disqualified from working for banking and related institutions insured by the Federal Deposit Insurance Corporation (FDIC). However, there are exceptions to this blanket prohibition. The FDIC, for example, can grant waivers for certain types of convictions. Unknown to some financial institutions, they can submit a waiver request to the FDIC on behalf of the job applicant. For more information on this prohibition, visit this relevant website: http://www.fdic.gov/regulations/laws/rules/5000-1300.html.

- **Insurance:** Certain classes of felons are prohibited from working in the insurance industry, unless they receive permission from insurance regulatory officials.

- **Unions:** Certain classes of felons (robbery, bribery, drug violations, murder) are prohibited for at least 13 years from holding positions in unions or other organizations that manage employee benefit plans. This restriction also applies to serving as a union officer or director of a union governing board.

- **Health care:** Any health care service receiving Medicare payments is prohibited from hiring ex-offenders convicted for certain crimes. Many ex-offenders also are prohibited from working in the generic drug industry.

- **Child care:** Federal law requires criminal background checks for anyone working in the child care field. To facilitate criminal background checks, the Federal Child Protection Act authorizes states to do mandatory or voluntary fingerprinting of individuals intending to work in this field.

- **Transportation of prisoners:** Federal regulations prohibit individuals with a felony conviction or domestic violence conviction from being employed with a company providing prisoner transportation. Such employees are required to undergo criminal background checks and pre-employment drug testing.

- **Defense contractors and subcontractors:** Five-year prohibition for those with fraud or felony conviction.

- **Aviation:** FAA regulations restrict ex-offenders from working in many airport jobs that give them access to airplanes and affect airline security.

- **Military, Job Corps, or AmeriCorps:** Felons are prohibited from becoming members of these groups. However, in the recent past the military (especially the Army) had been generous in issuing "moral waivers," which allowed them to recruit ex-offenders, including felons, in order to meet mission requirements for the wars in Iraq and Afghanistan. These controversial exceptions allowed the military to reach its recruitment goals during tough recruitment times (over 100,000 moral waivers issued between 2003 and 2006). In 2007 alone, for example, nearly 12 percent of all Army recruits received moral waivers. However, in 2012, the military suspended its moral waivers policy, because it more than met its annual recruitment goals through its normal restrictive recruitment process. It no longer accepts new recruits who have a history of drug or alcohol abuse of any kind of misconduct conviction. However, this situation can change, depending on recruitment needs.

Certain occupations requiring federal licenses may be closed to ex-offenders: custom broker's license, export license, locomotive engineer's license, and merchant marine license.

State and Local Restrictions

But most employment restrictions on ex-offenders are found at the state and local levels. Indeed, employment prohibitions vary from state to state. Depending on the state to which you are paroled, you will be restricted from working in particular jobs. In fact, the restrictions tend to relate to:

- particular occupations
- particular places of work

For example, in many states you may be prohibited from working as a barber (an occupation) – a vocational skill taught in many prisons – or in a position that serves alcohol, such as a bartender (an occupation). At the same time, you may be barred from working in a daycare center (a place).

Most states also prohibit ex-offenders from acquiring certain professional licenses and vocational certifications. You need to inquire about any such restrictions **before** looking for a job or acquiring training and certification, but do so through the state licensing agency rather than through educational institutions that have a vested interest in selling you programs that are not directly linked to future jobs. For example, some ex-offenders who have completed nursing programs are terribly disappointed when they first learn they cannot work in various nursing areas because of a prior drug conviction – a shocking revelation after having spent the time and money getting such training and having been initially told by representatives of the educational institution that getting a nursing job is "no problem" for ex-offenders with nursing credentials. Many government agencies also have unwritten rules not to hire ex-offenders, even though they are not supposed to discriminate.

Before deciding on what job you wish to pursue and where, you need to understand the laws, rules, and regulations restricting and governing your employment in the particular state or locality you may wish to live in after release. At the same time, you need to understand any exceptions to the rules. Restrictions tend to relate to certain types or classes of convictions, such as felonies, violent crimes, or robbery. In some cases "waivers" can be issued if someone appears to be rehabilitated or the nature of the crime or the time that has passed was such that the person longer appears to pose a potential public safety issue. Therefore, it is incumbent upon **you** to acquire such information on job restrictions. Again, it's your problem – not someone else's.

Take, for example, working in correctional settings. Most states permit ex-offenders who have been convicted of nonviolent crimes to apply for certain jobs in prisons and jails. A study of state department of corrections (DOCs) in 2002 conducted by the National Institute of Corrections found that 81% of DOCs had formal policies on hiring ex-offenders. Thirty-six

DOCs permanently barred people convicted of certain crimes from correctional employment. Thirty-one DOCs prohibited employment to anyone convicted of any felony. Fourteen DOCs specified bans on correctional officer and security positions or any position requiring the possession of firearms. Some DOCs prohibited hiring in cases of domestic violence convictions; misdemeanor drug offenses; class A misdemeanors; misdemeanors involving personal injury, perjury, or moral turpitude; and misdemeanors involving jail time. Many DOCs also put time-limited restrictions on hiring people with criminal convictions, which could range from 1 to 15 years. Here are some examples of these time limits in reference to the type of offense committed:

Time Required	Offense Type
1 year from:	▪ Misdemeanor conviction, for peace officer positions (California)
	▪ Driving offenses (Ohio, Vermont)
	▪ Sentence served in facility in which employment sought (Tennessee)
	▪ Marijuana use/experimentation (Alaska, Arizona)
2 years from:	▪ Disposition of single misdemeanor offense (Connecticut)
	▪ DUI conviction, or marijuana misdemeanor, i.e., use (Utah)
3 years from:	▪ Felony conviction for non-custody position (Missouri)
	▪ Three or more Class A misdemeanors (i.e., maximum of two misdemeanors within 3 years)
	▪ Misdemeanor convictions (Nebraska, North Carolina)
	▪ Conviction of any kind (Rhode Island)
	▪ Misdemeanor involving property (Vermont)
	▪ Misdemeanor involving vehicular negligence (Vermont)
4 years from:	▪ Non-substance-abuse related misdemeanor conviction (Utah)
5 years from:	▪ Hard drug use conviction (Utah)
	▪ Felony conviction involving property, felony vehicular negligence, or misdemeanor conviction involving violence against a person (Vermont)
	▪ Completion of felony sentence, including any form of supervision (Wyoming, Nebraska, Oregon)
	▪ Conviction, if pardon granted (Canada)
	▪ Class A or B misdemeanor conviction (Texas)
	▪ Drug offenses other than marijuana (Arizona)
7 years from:	▪ Any conviction (Guam)
	▪ Experimentation with drugs other than marijuana (Arizona)
	▪ Completion of sentence for multiple misdemeanor incarcerations (Connecticut)
10 years from:	▪ Felony conviction (North Carolina, South Carolina)
	▪ Possession or use of drugs other than marijuana (Alaska)
15 years from:	▪ Felony conviction, for specified positions (Texas)

The following employment restrictions affect ex-offenders in many states where they cannot become:

- Teachers – if convicted of violent crimes or crimes against children
- Police or correctional officers – if convicted of a felony
- Public office holder – if convicted of a felony
- Private investigator and/or detective
- Security guard
- Security alarm installer
- Caregivers (depends on offense/conviction)

For a state-by-state survey of legal barriers to ex-offender re-entry, be sure to visit the "After Prison: Roadblocks to Reentry" section of the HireNetwork website:

- www.hirenetworkorg/content/updates-landmark-study-many-obstacles-re-entry (interactive map)
- lac.org/roadblocks-to-re entry (full report)

What You Need to Do

In preparation for finding a job appropriate for your background, you need to do two things as soon as possible:

1. **Review your RAP Sheet.** This is your Record of Arrest and Prosecution (RAP). It's your history of arrests based upon your fingerprints. Here's how it works. Every time you are fingerprinted by a law enforcement agency, a record of your arrest, along with its final disposition, goes to a central repository in that state. If you've committed crimes in more than one state, your current state rap sheet may indicate that a record also is on file with the Interstate Identification Index, a repository maintained by the Federal Bureau of Investigation (FBI).

   It's very important that you examine your rap sheets at both the federal and state levels in order to (1) understand what employers are likely to access when they do a background check (you need to deal with the whole truth that's represented on your rap sheets!), (2) understand whether or not any of your arrests and convictions will bar you from certain federal, state, and local jobs, and (3) check on the accuracy of your rap sheet (sometimes there are mistakes that need to be corrected).

   For information on how to get a copy of your state rap sheet, check out the relevant state requirements at www.hirenetwork.org (look for a subsection called "Criminal Record Repository"). You can get a copy of your FBI rap sheet by contacting the FBI's Criminal Justice Information Services (CJIS) division: FBI CJIS Division, Record Request, 1000 Custer Hollow Road, Clarksburg, WV 26306. For more information on how this process works with the FBI, visit their relevant website: www.fbi.gov/about-us/cjis/identify-history-summary -checks. The FBI takes 12-14 weeks plus mail delivery time to process such requests.

2. **Explore useful state resources:** You should also explore the many state-by-state resources available through the National H.I.R.E. Network – www.hirenetwork.org/clearing house. This organization closely monitors developments at the state level for ex-offenders. Take, for example, this entry for the state of Alabama:

ALABAMA

I. Alabama Department of Labor

CONTACT:
P.O. Box 303500
Montgomery, AL 36130
334-242-3460, 334-240-3417 fax

Information about State Department of Labor resources may be of interest to:

- potential employers looking for incentives to hire individuals with criminal histories;
- service providers and individuals with criminal histories who are looking for assistance in finding employment; and
- researchers and policy makers looking at current programs to ascertain what programs are effective and serve their intended purpose.

A. Federal Bonding Program

The Federal Bonding Program provides fidelity bonding insurance coverage to individuals with criminal histories and other high-risk job applicants who are qualified, but fail to get jobs because regular commercial bonding is denied due to their backgrounds.

CONTACT:
Federal Bonding Program
Employment Service Division
Alabama Department of Labor Building
649 Monroe Street, Room 2813
Montgomery, AL 36131
334-242-8039
334-242-8012 fax

B. Tax Credits

The Work Opportunity Tax Credit (WOTC) is a federal tax credit to reduce the federal tax liability of private for-profit employers to be used as an incentive for employers to hire individuals from eight different targeted groups: TANF recipients, veterans, ex-felons, high-risk youth, summer youth, Food Stamp recipients, SSI recipients, and vocational rehabilitation referrals.

CONTACT:
WOTC
Employment Service Division
Alabama Department of Labor Building
Finance Department
649 Monroe Street , Room 2813
Montgomery, AL 36131
334-242-8303
334-242-9064 fax
E-mail: WOTC.ALCC@alcc.alabama.gov
Website: http://wotc.alabama.gov

C. Unemployment Insurance Office

Unemployment compensation is a social insurance program designed to provide benefits to most individuals out of work, generally through no fault of their own, for periods between jobs. In order to be eligible for benefits, jobless workers must demonstrate that they have worked, usually measured by amount of wages and/or weeks of work, and must be able and available for work.

The unemployment compensation program is based upon federal law, but administered by states under state law.

CONTACT:
Alabama Department of Industrial Relations
649 Monroe Street
Montgomery, AL 36131
334-242-8025
334-242-8021 fax
E-mail: uc@dir.alabama.gov
Website: www.dir.alabama.gov/uc

II. Criminal Record Repository

This is the agency individuals may contact to obtain a copy of their state rap. The criminal record repository can also tell the individual who else is legally entitled to have access to his or her record.

An individual or employer must call or write the Bureau of Investigations to request a release form. The release form must be signed by the individual whose record is being requested along with a $25 fee. Searches for a criminal record can be done based on a name or a set of fingerprints. Each procedure costs $25.

CONTACT:
Alabama Department of Public Safety

Bureau of Investigations
301 South Ripley Street
P.O. Box 1511
Montgomery, AL 36104
334-353-1100

III. State Attorney General

Employers and service providers may obtain information from the state attorney general regarding occupational bars, the licensing of individuals with criminal records in certain jobs, and whether the state has laws that limit what employers may ask job applicants or protections against employment discrimination based on a criminal record.

CONTACT:
Office of the Attorney General
501 Washington Avenue
Montgomery, AL 36130
334-242-7300
Website: www.ago.state.al.us

IV. State Department of Corrections

CONTACT:
Alabama Department of Corrections
301 South Ripley Street
Montgomery, AL 36130-1501
334-353-3883
E-mail: pio@doc.state.al.us
Website: www.doc.state.al.us

V. State Department of Parole/Probation

The Alabama Board of Pardons and Paroles provides adult probation and parole services in Alabama.
CONTACT:
Alabama Board of Pardons and Paroles
301 South Ripley Street
Montgomery, AL 36130-2405
334-242-8700
E-mail: questions4pardonsandparoles@alabpp.gov
Website: www.paroles.state.al.us

VI. Legal Assistance

Free or low-cost legal resources, both in civil and criminal law, are helpful to individuals with criminal histories in learning about relevant state laws governing the expungement or sealing of criminal histories or addressing other legal issues resulting from having a criminal history.

A. State Public Defender

There is no state Public Defender office in Alabama. Defense attorneys are appointed by judges when necessary to provide legal counsel for indigent clients.

B. Legal Services

Alabama's legal services programs are independent, non-profit organizations that provide qualifying low-income families with legal assistance in civil matters.

CONTACT:
Legal Services Corporation of Alabama, Inc.
207 Montgomery Street, Suite 1100
Montgomery, AL 36104
334-832-4570
334-241-8683 fax
Website: www.alabamalegalservices.org

C. State Bar Association

CONTACT:
Alabama State Bar
415 Dexter Avenue
Montgomery, AL 36104
334-269-1515
334-261-6310 fax
Website: www.alabar.org

VII. Local Service Providers

Community agencies are available to assist individuals with criminal records find employment. This information will inform individuals with criminal records about government agencies and community-based organizations that assist with employment, education or vocational training. Researchers and policymakers may find this information useful in identifying agencies and service providers in order to evaluate the effectiveness of these programs.

A. One-Stop Center

The One-Stop Center is also known as the Alabama Department of Industrial Relations local office.

CONTACT:
Employment Services Division
Alabama Department of Industrial Relations
649 Monroe Street
Montgomery, AL 36131
Website: www.dir.alabama.gov

B. Aid to Inmate Mothers (AIM)

Aid to Inmate Mothers provides services to promote the successful reintegration of women with criminal records by helping them become gainfully employed, obtain clothing, and secure housing.

CONTACT:
Aid to Inmate Mothers
P.O. Box 986
Montgomery, AL 36101
800-679-0246
334-262-2296 (fax)
Website: www.inmatemoms.org

C. The Ordinary People Society (T.O.P.S.)

T.O.P.S. is a nonprofit, faith-based organization that offers hope, without regard to race, sex, creed, color or social status, to individuals and their fam-

ilies who suffer the effects of drug addiction, incarceration, homelessness, unemployment, hunger and illness, through comprehensive faith-based programs that provide a continuum of unconditional acceptance and care. Programs include: Criminal Rehabilitation and Reintegration; Early Intervention and Mentoring; Drug Prevention and Addiction Assistance; Adult Literacy; Hunger and homelessness Prevention; and other important services that help individuals achieve their goals.

CONTACT:
The Ordinary People Society (T.O.P.S.)
403 West Powell Street
Dothan, AL 36303
334-671-2882
Website: theordinarypeoplesociety.com

D. Re-Entry Ministries, Inc.

Re-Entry Ministries, Inc. works with persons with criminal records and offers limited services to prisoners. Programs include support groups for people with criminal records and families of prisoners, church services, job assistance, and Alcoholics Anonymous meetings.

CONTACT:
Re-Entry Ministries, Inc.
2224 3rd Avenue North
Birmingham, AL 35210
205-320-2101

E. Renascence, Inc.

Renascence, Inc. assists in the transition of non-violent, male ex-offenders from prison to steady employment and responsible living. Renascence provides housing, appropriate monitoring, interpersonal and life skills programs, recovery support groups, as well as access to employment, health, and educational services/opportunities.

CONTACT:
Renascence, Inc.
215 Clayton Street
Montgomery, AL 36104
334-832-1402
E-mail: renascence@bellsouth.net

Explore the many state-by-state resources available through the National H.I.R.E. Network – www. hirenetwork. org/clearinghouse. This organization closely monitors developments at the state level for ex-offenders.

What Employers Know About Your Record

It's true – there's no place in America to hide these days. If you can move abroad to some Third World country, perhaps you can start all over again. But, then, you'll probably have difficulty getting a passport and visas (felons have international travel restrictions, and few countries issue visas to such ex-offenders). And escaping to another country may not be such a great idea after all, especially after encountering cultural shock and discovering there's not much you can do there to make a decent living. Finding an "offshore" job to start a new life is often a fantasy, not a reality. Even if you manage to get into another country, the authorities may quickly discover your record and deport you as an undesirable. Nonetheless, www.escapeartist.com may give you some useful ideas.

If you think you can make your record go away by lying or parsing the truth, think again. In today's high-tech society, employers have a high probability of uncovering the **truth about you**. However, small companies (under 50 employees) that lack their own human resources departments may not do a very good job of screening candidates with criminal backgrounds. As a result, many ex-offenders seek out such "few questions asked" companies because they know these places may allow them to get in under the radar.

Employers have three sources of information for uncovering your criminal record:

1. **Information you provide employers on applications and in interviews:** Most states permit employers to ask applicants about their criminal history. As of 2015, 16 states (California, Colorado, Connecticut, Delaware, Georgia, Hawaii, Illinois, Maryland, Massachusetts, Minnesota, Nebraska, New Jersey, New Mexico, Rhode Island, Vermont, and Virginia) "banned the box" on job applications – they cannot ask about prior convictions. However, all states permit employers to ask this question during interviews and through background checks. If asked about your criminal record, it's best to tell the truth since the truth will most likely come out from other information sources available to the employer.

2. **Information employers gather from background checks:** Most employers can inexpensively conduct background checks on applicants. For less than $50.00, they can quickly access through several private firms – many operating via the Internet – information on your criminal, employment, and credit history.

3. **Information employers gather from your references:** Most employers check references. However, references often provide little useful information other than verify employment dates. But some are very forthcoming when faced with these two frequently asked reference questions:

   "Is there anything in this candidate's background that might disqualify him or her for this position?"

   "Knowing what you do about this person, would you hire him or her again?"

Again, before setting your sights on particular jobs or careers you might love to pursue, be sure you fully understand the **limitations** you may face given federal, state, and local laws prohibiting or restricting ex-offenders from working in particular jobs. If you face restrictions, you need to know whether you are eligible for **waivers**. And above all, tell the truth about **you**. Develop a compelling story about your rehabilitation **and** performance!

4

Construction Trades and Related Jobs

"The construction trades are relatively open to ex-offenders. While many day laborer jobs attract ex-offenders, these are primarily stop-gap jobs without a promising future. Some of the best construction jobs involve on-the-job training, apprenticeships, and advancement to positions of responsibility, including starting a construction trade business."

THE CONSTRUCTION TRADES offer numerous job opportunities for people re-entering the workforce, changing careers, or jump-starting their lives. Indeed, ex-offenders disproportionately seek many entry-level, high-turnover construction positions, especially construction laborer jobs where background checks tend to be lax. These jobs especially appeal to people with challenging backgrounds – those with or without a high school diploma or a four-year degree, those with unstable work histories, people with mental health issues (bipolarism, depression, personality, addiction, anger), ADD and ADHD, learning disabilities (dyslexia, dyscalculia, dysgraphia), small-time owner/operators, people with tax (IRS) issues, and those seeking temporary or part-time work. Since many of these jobs require basic education skills, on-the-job training, and/or apprenticeships, these jobs can become important stepping stones to more stable and professional jobs as well as to owning one's own construction trade business. Just getting one of these jobs with an eye toward enhancing your skills can be a great way to jump-start your life on the outside. Let's look at some important options for doing so.

Promising Opportunities, Unstable Future

Ex-offenders re-entering growing communities often quickly find jobs in the construction trades. Many start at the very bottom in minimum-wage and relatively unskilled positions where they must demonstrate their ability to show up on time, be dependable, follow orders, and avoid making costly mistakes. Not surprisingly, such laborers also discover they are working next to individuals with similar interests, skills, and backgrounds – people with spotted pasts – as well as those who work in the underground economy, especially undocumented immigrants.

However, there is a certain boom/bust quality to many construction and related jobs that is not as prevalent elsewhere in the job market. When the economy is hot and new commercial and residential construction is booming, many construction jobs will be in high demand. These jobs disproportionately attract young people with a high school education or less, undocumented immigrants, job-hoppers, day laborers, and ex-offenders. When the economy softens, which it dramatically did for the construction trades in 2007-2015, many high-demand construction jobs disappear and companies may go out of business. Unemployment will be high among relatively unskilled construction workers who don't know what else to do with their lives given their limited interests, skills, and once comfortable incomes.

Wages, benefits, and work hours for construction jobs can vary greatly depending on the projects, weather conditions, and labor-management relationships. In general, most people working in construction only get paid when they work. If, for example, you expect to get wages for a 40-hour week (at $20.00 an hour, that would come to $800.00 for the week) but weather conditions knock out 20 hours for the week, you'll only get paid for the actual 20 hours you work ($400.00). You'll also need to factor in the costs of transportation (getting to and from work sites) and benefits, such as health insurance, that may be limited with many construction jobs. In this sense, construction jobs often become temporary or part-time jobs. Benefits may be severely limited as employers try to get by with paying only basic hourly wages.

Turnover Occupations

The construction trades have always been cyclical occupational fields. When economic times are good, individuals in these fields have plenty of work, and their skills command top dollar. However, during recessions many of these workers have difficulty finding full-time employment, and some leave their trade for other types of employment. In fact, it may be a good idea to view many construction jobs as temporary stop-gap positions that hopefully will lead to other more stable and rewarding employment in the future. Many people have a tough time developing a stable career in construction given the volatility of the work, which is tied to the state of local economies.

Working in the construction trades often involves hard work, uncomfortable working conditions, stressful projects, and unpredictable employment. Many people drop out of these trades because of unhappy experiences. As workers age in many "hard labor" jobs, they seek less physically demanding jobs in other occupations. Given the constant turnover of construction workers, opportunities regularly open for skilled, enterprising, and relatively young and physically active workers.

Recession-Proof Trades

But if you are very skilled and enjoy this type of work, you'll find excellent opportunities in the construction and related trades. Indeed, you may be pleasantly surprised how well you can do in these jobs, especially ones that require specialty skills and are relatively recession-proof. After all, construction, repairing, and remodeling continue even during bad economic times.

You may want to focus on trades that are relatively recession-proof, especially ones that lead to long-term and stable careers.

The skills of electricians, plumbers, and heating and air-conditioning specialists – three very well paid trades (some make six-figure incomes) – are always in demand, more so than carpenters and heavy machine operators. In fact, electricity, plumbing, heating, and air conditioning are constants in everyone's life. These are critical residential and commercial systems that must be maintained and repaired. In fact, when you consider jobs and careers in the construction trades, you may want to focus on those that are relatively recession-proof. Such trades can lead to very rewarding long-term careers, including owning your own electrical, plumbing, or HVAC business.

Many people without a four-year degree enter these trades because doing so is based more on interests, skills, and on-the-job training than on education requirements. Many individuals with or without a high school diploma initially break into the building and construction trades through **apprenticeship programs**, where they acquire the necessary skills and experience to advance into their respective trades. Many apprenticeships are sponsored by unions, which are often ex-offender-friendly. In fact, many unions with apprenticeship programs in large cities regularly hire ex-offenders at attractive wage levels. These programs are excellent ways to break into and advance within the construction job market.

Useful Online Resources

Individuals interested in job and career opportunities in the construction and related trades should explore the major online employment websites (www.monster.com, www.careerbuilder com, and www.indeed.com) as well as the following specialty websites:

■ **Construction Jobs**	www.constructionjobs.com
■ **Construction Job Store**	www.constructionjobstore.com
■ **Architect Jobs**	www.architectjobs.com
■ **Carpenter Jobs**	www.carpenterjobs.com
■ **Construction Manager Jobs**	www.constructionmanagerjob.com
■ **Electrician Jobs**	www.electricianjobs.com
■ **Engineer Jobs**	www.engineerjobs.com
■ **Estimator Jobs**	www.estimatorjobs.com
■ **iHireConstruction**	www.ihireconstruction.com
■ **PlumberJobs**	www.plumberjobs.com
■ **Project Manager Jobs**	www.projectmanagerjobs.com
■ **Trade Jobs Online**	www.tradejobsonline.com

Brickmasons, Blockmasons, and Stonemasons

- ■ **Annual Earnings:** $43,950 ($21.61 per hour)
- ■ **Education/Training:** High school diploma or equivalent; apprenticeship
- ■ **Outlook:** Very good – 34% growth from 2012 to 2022 (from 85,100 to 114,400 jobs)

Employment Outlook: Employment opportunities for brickmasons, blockmasons, and stonemasons are expected to be very good in the decade ahead. Many openings will result from the need to replace workers who retire, transfer to other occupations, or leave these trades for other reasons. There may be fewer applicants than needed because many potential workers prefer to work under less strenuous, more comfortable conditions. Employment in these trades is expected to increase faster than average for all occupations as population and business growth create a need for new houses, industrial facilities, schools, hospitals, offices, and other structures. Employment of brickmasons, blockmasons, and stonemasons, like that of many other construction workers, is sensi-

tive to changes in the economy. When the level of construction activity falls, workers in these trades can experience periods of unemployment.

Nature of Work: Brickmasons, blockmasons, and stonemasons work in closely related trades creating attractive, durable surfaces, and structures. The work varies in complexity, from laying a simple masonry walkway to installing an ornate exterior on a high-rise building. Brickmasons and blockmasons – who often are called simply **bricklayers** – build and repair walls, floors, partitions, fireplaces, chimneys, and other structures with bricks, precast masonry panels, concrete block, and other masonry materials. Some brickmasons specialize in installing firebrick linings in industrial furnaces. Stonemasons build stone walls, as well as set stone exteriors and floors. They work with two types of stone – natural cut stone, such as marble, granite, and limestone, and artificial stone made from concrete, marble chips, or other masonry materials. Stonemasons usually work on nonresidential structures, such as houses of worship, hotels, and office buildings.

Working Conditions: Brickmasons, blockmasons, and stonemasons usually work outdoors and are exposed to the elements. They stand, kneel, and bend for long periods and often have to lift heavy materials. Common hazards include injuries from tools and falls from scaffolds, but these can often be avoided when proper safety equipment is used and safety practices are followed.

Education, Training, & Qualifications: Most brickmasons, blockmasons, and stonemasons pick up their skills informally, observing and learning from experienced workers. Many others receive training in vocational education schools or from industry-based programs that are common throughout the country. Another way to learn these skills is through an apprenticeship program, which generally provides the most thorough training. Individuals who learn the trade on the job usually start as helpers, laborers, or mason tenders. These workers carry materials, move scaffolds, and mix mortar.

Earnings: Median hourly earnings of brickmasons and blockmasons in 2012 was $46,440; the median annual wage for stonemasons was $37,350. The starting pay for apprentices is usually about 50% of fully trained workers. About 20% of masons are self-employed. Earnings for workers in these trades can be reduced on occasion because poor weather and downturns in construction activity limit the time they can work.

Key Contacts: For information about training for brickmasons, blockmasons, or stonemasons, as well as these three career fields in general, contact:

- **International Masonry Institute National Training Center:** 17101 Science Drive, Bowie, MD 20715. Website: www.imiweb.org.
- **International Union of Bricklayers and Allied Craftworkers, International Masonry Institute National Training Center:** 620 F Street, NW, Washington, DC 20004. Website: http://bacweb.org.
- **Mason Contractors Association of America:** 1481 Merchant Drive, Algonquin, IL 60102. Website: www.masoncontractors.org.
- **Brick Industry Association:** 1850 Centennial Park Dr., Suite 301, Reston, VA 20191. Website: www.gobrick.com.
- **National Association of Home Builders:** 1201 15th Street NW, Washington, DC 20005. Website: www.nahb.org.

- **National Concrete Masonry Association:** 13750 Sunrise Valley Drive, Herndon, VA 20171-4662. Website: https://ncma.org.

Carpenters

- **Annual Earnings:** $39,940 ($19.20 per hour)
- **Education/Training:** High school diploma or equivalent; apprenticeship
- **Outlook:** Faster than average – 24% growth from 2012 to 2022 (from 901,200 to 1,119,400 jobs)
- **Self-employed:** 36% (largest percent in construction trade)

Employment Outlook: Job opportunities for carpenters are expected to be faster than average for occupations as a whole given above average job growth along with replacement needs. Because there are no strict training requirements for entry, many people with limited skills take jobs as carpenters but eventually leave the occupation because they dislike the work or cannot find steady employment. Construction activity should increase in response to new housing and commercial and industrial plants and the need to renovate and modernize existing structures. A strong home remodeling market will create increased demands for carpenters. Construction of roads and bridges as well as restaurants, hotels, and other businesses will increase the demand for carpenters in the coming decade. Carpenters can experience periods of unemployment because of the short-term nature of many construction projects and the cyclical nature of the construction industry.

Nature of Work: Carpenters are involved in many different kinds of construction activity. They cut, fit, and assemble wood and other materials for the construction of buildings, highways, bridges, docks, industrial plants, boats, and many other structures. Carpenters' duties vary by type of employer. Builders increasingly are using specialty trade contractors who, in turn, hire carpenters who specialize in just one or two activities. Such activities include setting forms for concrete construction, erecting scaffolding, or doing finishing work, such as interior and exterior trim. However, a carpenter directly employed by a general building contractor often must perform a variety of the tasks associated with new construction, such as framing walls and partitions, putting in doors and windows, building stairs, laying hardwood floors, and hanging kitchen cabinets. Carpenters employed outside the construction industry perform a variety of installation and maintenance work. They may replace panes of glass, ceiling tiles, and doors, as well as repair decks, cabinets, and other furniture.

Working Conditions: As is true of other building trades, carpentry work is sometimes strenuous. Prolonged standing, climbing, bending, and kneeling often are necessary. Carpenters risk injury working with sharp or rough materials, using sharp tools and power equipment, and working in situations where they might slip or fall. Many carpenters work outdoors. Some change employers each time they finish a construction job. Others alternate between working for a contractor and working as contractors themselves on small jobs.

Education, Training, & Qualifications: Carpenters learn their trade through on-the-job training, as well as formal training programs. Most pick up skills informally by working under the supervision of experienced workers. Many acquire skills through vocational education. Others participate in employer training programs or apprenticeships. Most employers recommend an apprenticeship as the best way to learn carpentry. Apprenticeship programs are administered by local point union-management committees of the United Brotherhood of Carpenters and Joiners of America, the Associated General Contractors of America, Inc., and the National Association of Home Builders.

Earnings: Median hourly earnings of carpenters were $19.20 ($39,940 in annual earnings). The top 10% earned more than $72,580 a year whereas the lowest 10% earned less than $24,880. Earnings can be reduced on occasion, because carpenters lose work time in bad weather and during recessions when jobs are unavailable. Some carpenters are members of the United Brotherhood of Carpenters and Joiners of America.

Key Contacts: For information on training opportunities and carpentry in general, contact:

- **Associated Builders and Contractors:** 440 1st Street, NW, Suite 200, Washington, DC 20001. Website: www.abc.org.
- **Associated General Contractors of America, Inc.:** 2300 Wilson Blvd., Suite 300, Arlington, VA 22201. Website: www.agc.org.

- **NCCER (National Center for Construction Education and Research):** 13614 Progress Boulevard, Alachua, FL 32615. Website: www.nccer.org/carpentry?pID=105
- **National Association of Home Builders, Home Builders Institute:** 1201 15th St., NW, Sixth Floor, Washington, DC 20005. Website: www.hbi.org.
- **United Brotherhood of Carpenters and Joiners of America, Carpenters Training Fund** (includes regional training centers): 40 Telfair Place, Savannah, GA 31415. Website: www.carpenters.org.

Carpet, Floor, & Tile Installers & Finishers

- **Annual Earnings:** $36,740 ($17.66 per hour)
- **Education/Training:** Less than high school. Combination of on-the-job training, apprenticeships, and classroom instruction
- **Outlook:** About average – 9-13%

Employment Outlook: Overall employment is expected to grow by 9-13% between 2012 and 2022, about average for all occupations. Tile and marble setters, the largest specialty, will experience faster than average job growth because population and business growth will result in more construction of shopping malls, hospitals, schools, restaurants, and other structures in which tile is used extensively. Carpet installers, the second largest specialty, will have average job growth as residential investors and homeowners continue to choose hardwood floors because of their durability, neutral colors, and low maintenance, and because owners feel these floors will add to the value of their homes. Workers who install other types of flooring, including laminate, cork, rubber, and vinyl, should experience declining employment because these materials are used less often and are often laid by other types of construction workers.

Nature of Work: Carpet, tile, and other types of floor coverings not only serve an important basic function in buildings, but their decorative qualities also contribute to the appeal of the buildings. Carpet, floor, and tile installers and finishers lay floor coverings in homes, offices, hospitals, stores, restaurants, and many other types of buildings. Tile also may be installed on walls and ceilings.

Carpet installers inspect surfaces to be covered to determine their condition and, if necessary, correct any imperfections that could show through the carpet or cause the carpet to wear unevenly. They install wall-to-wall carpet using a combination of padded cushion or underlay, tacks, and tackless strips. Using a power stretcher, they stretch the carpet, hooking it to the tackless strip to hold it in place. They finish the edges using a wall trimmer.

Floor installers and floor layers lay floor coverings such as laminate, linoleum, vinyl, cork, and rubber for decorative purposes, or to deaden sounds, absorb shocks, or create air-tight environments. When installing linoleum or vinyl, they may use an adhesive to cement the material directly to the floor. For laminate floor installation, workers may unroll and install a polyethylene film which acts as a moisture barrier, along with a thicker, padded underlayer which helps reduce noise.

Floor sanders and finishers complete the work done by floor installers by smoothing any imperfections in the wood and applying finish coats of varnish or polyurethane.

Tile installers, tilesetters, and marble setters apply hard tile and marble to floors, walls, ceilings, countertops, patios, and roof decks. Prior to installation, tilesetters use measuring devices and levels to ensure that the tile is placed in a consistent manner. Spacers are used to maintain exact distance between tiles.

Working Conditions: Carpet, floor, and tile installers and finishers usually work indoors and have regular daytime hours. However, when floor covering installers need to work in occupied stores or offices, they may work evenings and weekends to avoid disturbing customers or employees. Installing these materials is labor intensive; workers spend much of their time bending, kneeling, and reaching – activities that require endurance. The work can be very hard on workers' knees and back. Carpet installers frequently lift heavy rolls of carpet and may move heavy furniture, which requires strength and can be physically exhausting.

Education, Training, Qualifications: The vast majority of carpet, floor, and tile installers and finishers learn their trade informally on the job. A few, mostly tilesetters, learn through formal apprenticeship programs, which include classroom instruction and paid on-the-job training. Informal training for carpet installers often is sponsored

by individual contractors. Workers start as helpers, and begin with simple assignments, such as installing stripping and padding, or helping to stretch newly installed carpet. Tile and marble setters also learn their craft mostly through on-the-job training. Other floor layers also learn on the job and begin by learning how to use the tools of the trade. They next learn to prepare surfaces to receive flooring. As they progress, they learn to cut and install the various floor coverings.

Skills needed to become carpet, floor, and tile installers and finishers include manual dexterity, eye-hand coordination, physical fitness, and a good sense of balance and color. The ability to solve basic arithmetic problems quickly and accurately also is required. In addition, reliability and a good work history are viewed favorably by contractors.

Earnings: In 2012, the median annual earnings for carpet installers was $36,740 ($17.66 per hour).

Key Contacts: For general information about the work of carpet installers and floor layers, contact:

- **Floor Covering Contractors Association:** 7439 Milwood Drive, West Bloomfield, MI 48322. Website: www.fcica.com.

Additional information on training for carpet installers and floor layers is available from:

- **Finishing Trades Institute, International Union of Painters and Allied Trades:** 7230 Parkway Drive, Hanover, MD 21076. Website: www.finishingtradesinstitute.org.

For general information about the work of tile installers and finishers, contact:

- **International Masonry Institute:** 17101 Science Drive, Bowie, MD 20715. Website: www. imiweb.org.

For general information about tile setting and tile training, contact:

- **National Tile Contractors Association:** P.O. Box 13629, Jackson, MS 39236. Website: www.tile-assn.com.

For information concerning training of carpet, floor, and tile installers and finishers, contact:

- **United Brotherhood of Carpenters and Joiners of America:** 40 Telfair Place, Savannah, GA 31415. Website: www.carpenters.org.

Construction and Building Inspectors

- **Annual Earnings:** $53,450 ($25.70 per hour)
- **Education/Training:** High school diploma or equivalent
- **Outlook:** As fast as average – 12% growth from 2012 to 2022 (from 102,300 to 112,800 jobs)

Employment Outlook: Employment of construction and building inspectors is expected to grow about as fast as the average for all occupations in the coming decade. Growing concern for public safety and improvements in the quality of construction should continue to stimulate demand for construction and building inspectors. In addition to the expected employment growth, some job openings will arise from the need to replace inspectors who transfer to other occupations or leave the labor force. Inspectors are involved in all phases of construction, including maintenance and repair work, and are therefore less likely to lose jobs when new construction slows during recessions. As the population grows and the volume of real estate transactions increases, greater emphasis on home inspections should result in strong demand for home inspectors. In 2012 construction and building inspectors held 102,300 jobs. Local governments – primarily municipal or county building departments – employed 41%. Approximately 26% of construction and building inspectors work for architectural and engineering services firms.

Nature of Work: There are many types of specialized inspectors related to the construction and repair processes: building, plan, electrical, elevator, mechanical, plumbing, public works, specification, and home inspectors. Construction and building inspectors examine the construction, alteration, or repair of buildings, highways and streets, sewer and water systems, dams, bridges, and other structures to ensure compliance with building codes and ordinances, zoning regulations, and contract specifications. Building codes and standards are the primary means by which building construction is regulated in the United States for health and safety of the general public. Building inspectors inspect the structural quality and general safety of buildings. Some specialize in such areas as structural steel or reinforced concrete structures. Home inspectors conduct inspections of newly built or previously owned homes. Home inspection has become a standard practice in the home purchasing process. Although inspections are primarily visual, inspectors may use tape measures, survey instruments, metering devices, and test equipment such as concrete strength measurers. They keep a log of their work, take photographs, file reports, and, if necessary, act on their findings. Many inspectors also investigate construction or alterations being done without proper permits.

Working Conditions: Construction and building inspectors usually work alone. However, several may be assigned to large, complex projects, particularly because inspectors tend to specialize in different areas of construction. Although they spend considerable time inspecting construction worksites, inspectors also spend time in a field office reviewing blueprints, answering letters or telephone calls, writing reports, and scheduling inspections. Inspection sites are dirty and may be cluttered with tools, materials, or debris. Inspectors may have to climb ladders or many flights of stairs, or crawl around in tight spaces. Although their work generally is not considered hazardous, inspectors, like other construction workers, wear hard hats and adhere to other safety requirements while at a construction site. Inspectors normally work regular hours. However, they may work additional hours during periods when a lot of construction is taking place.

Education, Training, & Qualifications: Although requirements vary considerably depending upon where one is employed, construction and building inspectors should have a thorough knowledge of construction materials and practices in either a general area, such as structural or heavy construction, or in a specialized area, such as electrical or plumbing systems, reinforced concrete, or structural steel. Applicants for construction or building inspection jobs need several years of experience as a construction manager, supervisor, or craftworker. Many inspectors previously worked as carpenters, electricians, plumbers, or pipefitters. Because inspectors must possess the right mix of technical knowledge, experience, and education, employers prefer applicants who have formal training as well as experience. Most employers require at least a high school diploma or equivalent, even for workers with considerable experience. Construction and building inspectors usually receive much of their training on the job, although they must learn building codes and standards on their own. Most states and cities require some type of certification for employment. To become certified, inspectors with substantial experience and education must pass stringent examinations on code requirements, construction techniques, and materials.

Earnings: Median annual earnings for construction and building inspectors were $53,450 in 2012. The top 10% earned more than $83,700 a year whereas the bottom 10% earned less than $32,050 a year. Generally, building inspectors, including plan examiners, earn the highest salaries. Salaries in large metropolitan areas are substantially higher than those in small jurisdictions.

Key Contacts: For information on careers and certification, contact the following organizations:

- **International Code Council:** 500 New Jersey Ave., NW, 6th Floor, Washington, DC 20001-2070. Website: www.iccsafe.org.
- **Association of Construction Inspectors:** P.O. Box 879, Palm Springs, CA 92263. Website: www.aci-assoc.org.
- **International Association of Electrical Inspectors:** 901 Waterfall Way, Suite 602, Richardson, TX 75080-7702. Website: www.iaei.org.
- **American Society of Home Inspectors:** 932 Lee Street, Suite 101, Des Plaines, IL 60016. Website: www.ashi.org.
- **National Association of Home Inspectors:** 4426 5th Street West, Bradenton, FL 34207. Website: www.nahi.org.

Construction Equipment Operators

- **Annual Earnings:** $40,980 ($19.70 per hour)
- **Education/Training:** High school diploma or equivalent; on-the-job training and apprenticeships
- **Outlook:** Faster than average growth – 19% increase from 2012 to 2022 (from 409,700 to 487,900 jobs)

Employment Outlook: Above average job growth, reflecting increased demand for their services, and the need to replace workers who leave the occupation should result in very good job opportunities for construction equipment operators. Employment of construction equipment opportunities is expected to increase 19% between 2012 and 2022, which is faster than average for all occupations.

In 2012 construction equipment operators held 409,700 jobs. They were found in every section of the country and were distributed among various types of operators as follows:

- Operating engineers and other construction equipment operators   351,200
- Paving, surfacing, and tamping equipment operators   54,700
- Pile-driver operators   3,800

Nature of Work: Construction equipment operators use machinery to move construction materials, earth, and other heavy materials at construction sites and mines. They operate equipment that clears and grades land to prepare it for construction of roads, buildings, and bridges. They use machines to dig trenches to lay or repair sewer and other pipelines and hoist heavy construction materials. They may even work off-shore constructing oil rigs. Construction equipment operators also operate machinery that spreads asphalt and concrete on roads and other structures.

These workers also set up and inspect the equipment, make adjustments, and perform some maintenance and minor repairs. Construction equipment operators control equipment by moving levers, foot pedals, operating switches, or joysticks. Included in the construction equipment operator occupation are paving, surfacing, and tamping equipment operators; pile-driver operators; and operating engineers. All use specialized equipment.

Working Conditions: Construction equipment operators work outdoors, in nearly every type of climate and weather condition, although in many areas of the country, some types of construction operations much be suspended in winters. Bulldozers, scrapers, and especially tampers and pile-drivers are noisy and shake or jolt the operators. Operating heavy construction equipment can be dangerous.

Operators may have irregular hours because work on some construction projects continues around the clock or must be performed late at night or early in the morning.

Education, Training, Qualifications, & Licenses: Construction equipment operators usually learn their skills on the job, but formal apprenticeship programs provide more comprehensive training. Employers of construction equipment operators generally prefer to hire high school graduates, although some employers may train non-graduates to operate some types of equipment. On the job, workers may start by operating light equipment under the guidance of an experienced operator. Later, they may operate heavier equipment, such as bulldozers and cranes. Technologically advanced construction equipment with computerized controls and improved hydraulics and electronics requires more skill to operate. Operators of such equipment may need more training and some understanding of electronics. They often need a commercial driver's license to haul their equipment to various jobsites. A few states have special operator's licenses for operators of backhoes, loaders, and bulldozers. As of 2015, 18 states require pile-driver operators to have a crane license because these states classify pile-drivers as cranes.

Earnings: Earnings for construction equipment operators vary. In 2012, median annual wages averaged $40,980 ($19.70 per hour). Medium annual earnings in the industries employing the largest numbers of construction equipment operators were:

- Pile-driver operators $48,480
- Operating engineers and other construction equipment operators $41,870
- Construction trades workers $38,970
- Paving, surfacing, and tamping equipment operators $35,840

Union Membership: Compared to workers in other occupations, a much larger percentage of construction equipment operators belong to unions. The largest organizer of these workers is the International Union of Operating Engineers.

Key Contacts: For general information about the work of construction equipment operators, including training requirements and opportunities, contact:

- **Associated General Contractors of America:** 2300 Wilson Blvd., Suite 300, Arlington, VA 22201. Website: www.agc.org.
- **International Union of Operating Engineers:** 1125 17th Street, NW, Washington, DC 20036. Website: www.iuoe.org.
- **National Center for Construction Education and Research:** 13614 Progress Blvd., Alachua, FL 32615. Website: www.nccer.org.

- **National Commission for the Certification of Crane Operators:** 2750 Prosperity Avenue, Suite 505, Fairfax, VA 22031. Website: www.nccco.org.
- **Pile Driving Contractors Association:** 33 Knight Boxx Road, Suite 1, Orange Park, FL 32065. Website: www.piledrivers.org.

Construction Laborers

- **Annual Earnings:** $29,160 ($14.02 per hour)
- **Education/Training:** On-the-job training and apprenticeships
- **Outlook:** Faster than average – 25% increase from 2012 to 2022 (from 1,284,600 to 1,609,800 jobs)

Employment Outlook: Employment is expected to grow faster than average – about 25% between 2012 and 2022. In many areas, there will be competition for jobs, especially for those requiring limited skills. Laborers who have specialized skills or who can relocate near new construction projects should have the best opportunities. Construction laborer jobs will be adversely affected by automation as some jobs are replaced by new machinery and equipment that improve productivity and quality. Also, laborers will be increasingly employed by staffing agencies that will contract out laborers to employers on a temporary basis, and in many areas employers will continue to rely on day laborers instead of full-time laborers on staff. Employment of construction laborers, like that of many other construction workers, is sensitive to the fluctuations of the economy.

Nature of Work: Construction laborers can be found on almost all construction sites performing a wide range of tasks from the very easy to the potentially hazardous. They can be found at building, highway, and heavy construction sites; residential and commercial sites; tunnel and shaft excavations; and demolition sites. Many of the jobs they perform require physical strength, training, and experience. Other jobs require little skill and can be learned in a short amount of time. While most construction laborers specialize in a type of construction, such as highway or tunnel construction, some are generalists who perform many different tasks during all stages of construction.

Construction laborers clean and prepare construction sites. They remove trees and debris, tend pumps, compressors and generators, and build forms for pouring concrete. They erect and disassemble scaffolding and other temporary structures. They load, unload, identify, and distribute building materials to the appropriate location according to project plans and specifications. Laborers also tend machines – mix concrete using a portable mixer or tend a machine that pumps concrete, grout, cement, sand, plaster, or stucco through a spray gun for application to ceilings and walls. They often help other craftworkers, including carpenters, plasterers, operating engineers, and masons.

Working Conditions: Most laborers do physically demanding work. They may lift and carry heavy objects, and stoop, kneel, crouch, or crawl in awkward positions. Some work at great heights, or outdoors in all weather conditions. Some jobs expose workers to harmful materials or chemicals, fumes, odors, loud noise, or dangerous machinery.

Construction laborers generally work eight-hour shifts, although longer shifts are common. Overnight work may be required with working on highways. In some parts of the country, construction laborers may work only during certain seasons.

Education, Training, & Qualifications: Many construction laborer jobs require a variety of basic skills, but others require specialized training and experience. Most construction laborers learn on the job, but formal apprenticeship programs provide the most thorough preparation.

While some construction laborer jobs have no specific educational qualifications or entry-level training, apprenticeships for laborers require a high school diploma or equivalent. High school classes in English, mathematics, physics, mechanical drawing, blueprint reading, welding, and general shop can be helpful.

Most workers start by getting a job with a contractor who provides on-the-job training. Increasingly, construction laborers find work through temporary help agencies that send laborers to construction sites for short-term work.

Laborers need manual dexterity, eye-hand coordination, good physical fitness, a good sense of balance, and an ability to work as a member of a team. Military service or a good work history is viewed favorably by contractors.

Earnings: Median hourly earnings of wage and salary construction laborers in 2012 were $14.02

($29,160 on an annual basis if working a steady 40-hour week, 52 weeks a year). The top 10% earned more than $55,750 per year; the bottom 10% earned less than $18,840. Median annual earnings in 2012 for construction laborers and helpers were as follows:

- Construction laborers $29,990
- Brickmason, blockmason, stonemason,
  and tile and marble setter helpers $28,220
- Electrician helpers $27,670
- Pipelayer, plumber, pipefitter,
  and steamfitter helpers $26,670
- Carpenter helpers $25,550
- Painter, paperhanger, plasterer,
  and stucco mason helpers $24,290
- Roofer helpers $23,300
- All other construction helpers $25,610

Key Contacts: For information about jobs as a construction laborer, contact local building or construction contractors, local joint labor-management apprenticeship committees, apprenticeship agencies, or the local office of your state employment service. For information on education programs for laborers, contact:

- **LIUNA (Laborers International Union of North America):** 37 Deerfield Road, P.O. Box 37, Pomfret Center, CT 06259. Website: www. liunatraining.org.
- **NCCER (National Center for Construction Education and Research):** 13614 Progress Boulevard, Alachua, FL 32615. Website: www.nccer.org/carpentry?pID=105.

Drywall Installers, Ceiling Tile Installers, and Tapers

- **Annual Earnings:** $37,920 ($18.23 per hour)
- **Education/Training:** Less than high school, experience, and apprenticeships
- **Outlook:** Faster than average – 16% increase from 2012 to 2022 (from 114,100 to 132,000 jobs)

Employment Outlook: Job opportunities for drywall installers, ceiling tile installers, and tapers are expected to be good in the decade ahead – to grow faster than average for all occupations, reflecting increases in new construction and remodeling projects. Employment is expected to grow by 16% between 2012 and 2022. In addition to jobs involving traditional interior work, drywall workers will find employment opportunities in the installation of insulated exterior wall systems, which are becoming increasingly popular. Many jobs will open up each year because of the need to replace workers who transfer to other occupations or leave the labor force. Some drywall installers, ceiling tile installers, and tapers with limited skills leave the occupation when they find that they dislike the work or fail to attain steady employment. Since most of their work is done indoors, these workers lose less work time because of inclement weather than do some other construction workers. Nevertheless, they may be unemployed between construction projects and during downturns in construction activity.

Nature of Work: There are two kinds of drywall workers – installers and tapers – although many workers do both types of work. Installers, also called applicators or hangers, fasten drywall panels to the inside framework of residential houses and other buildings. Tapers, or finishers, prepare these panels for painting by taping and finishing joints and imperfections. Ceiling tile installers, or acoustical carpenters, apply or mount acoustical tiles or blocks, strips, or sheets of shock-absorbing materials to ceilings and walls of buildings to reduce reflection of sound or to decorate rooms. Lathers fasten metal or rockboard lath to walls, ceilings, and partitions of buildings.

Working Conditions: As in many other construction trades, the work sometimes is strenuous. Drywall installers, ceiling tile installers, and tapers spend most of the day on their feet, either standing, bending, or kneeling. Some tapers use stilts to tape and finish ceiling and angle joints. Installers have to lift and maneuver heavy panels. Hazards include falls from ladders and scaffolds and injuries from power tools and from working with sharp materials. Because sanding a joint compound to a smooth finish creates a great deal of dust, some finishers wear masks for protection.

Education, Training, & Qualifications: Most drywall installers, ceiling tile installers, and tapers start as helpers and learn their skills on the job. Installer helpers start by carrying materials, lifting and holding panels, and cleaning up debris. Within a few weeks they learn to measure, cut, and install materials. Eventually they become fully experienced workers. Some drywall installers, ceiling tile installers, and tapers learn their trade in an apprenticeship program. The United Brotherhood of Carpenters and Joiners of America, in cooperation with local contractors, administers an apprenticeship program both in drywall installation and finishing and in acoustical carpentry. Apprenticeship programs consist of at least three years, or 6,000 hours, of on-the-job training and 144 hours a year of related classroom instruction. In addition, local affiliates of the Associated Builders and Contractors and the National Association of Home Builders conduct training programs for nonunion workers. The International Union of Painters and Allied Trades conducts an apprenticeship program in drywall finishing that lasts two to three years. Employers prefer high school graduates who are in good physical condition, but they frequently hire applicants with less education. High school or vocational school courses in carpentry provide a helpful background for drywall work. Drywall installers, ceiling tile installers, and tapers with a few years of experience and with leadership ability may become supervisors. Some workers start their own contracting businesses.

Earnings: In 2012, the median annual earnings of drywall and ceiling tile installers were $37,920. The top 10% earned more than $72,500 a year; the bottom 10% earned less than $24,720 a year. The medium annual wage for tapers was $45,290. The top 10% earned more than $83,700 a year; the bottom 10% earned less than $27,340 a year. Trainees usually started at about half the rate paid to experienced workers and received wage increases as they became more highly skilled.

Key Contacts: For information about work opportunities in drywall application and finishing and ceiling tile installation, contact local drywall installation and ceiling tile installation contractors, a local of the building unions, a local joint union-management apprenticeship committee, a state or local chapter of the Associated Builders and Contractors, or the nearest office of the state employment service or apprenticeship agency.

For details about job qualifications and training programs in drywall application and finishing and ceiling tile installation, contact:

- **Associated Builders and Contractors:** 440 1st Street, NW, Suite 200, Washington, DC 20001. Website: www.abc.org.

- **National Association of Home Builders, Home Builders Institute:** 1201 15ᵗʰ St., NW, Sixth Floor, Washington, DC 20005. Website: www.hbi.org.
- **International Union of Painters and Allied Trades:** 7234 Parkway Drive, Hanover, MD 21076. Website: www.iupat.org.
- **United Brotherhood of Carpenters and Joiners of America:** 40 Telfair Place, Savannah, GA 31415. Website: www.carpenters.org.

Electricians

- **Annual Earnings:** $49,840 ($23.96 per hour)
- **Education/Training:** High school diploma or equivalent; apprenticeship program (3-5 years)
- **Outlook:** Faster than average – 20% increase from 2012 to 2022 (from 583,500 to 698,200 jobs)

Employment Outlook: Job opportunities for electricians are expected to be very good. Numerous openings will arise each year as experienced electricians leave the occupation. In addition, many potential workers may choose not to enter training programs because they prefer work that is less strenuous and has more comfortable working conditions. Employment of electricians is expected to grow faster than the average for all occupations in the coming decade. As the population and economy grow, more electricians will be needed to install and maintain electrical devices and wiring in homes, factories, offices, and other structures. New technologies also are expected to continue to stimulate the demand for these workers.

Nature of Work: Electricians install, connect, test, and maintain electrical systems for a variety of purposes, including climate control, security, and communications. They also may install and maintain the electronic controls for machines in business and industry. Although most electricians specialize in construction or maintenance, a growing number do both. Electricians work with blueprints when they install electrical systems in factories, office buildings, homes, and other structures. Blueprints indicate the locations of circuits, outlets, load centers, panel boards, and other equipment. Electricians must follow the National Electric Code as well as comply with the building codes of states and localities when they install these systems. Maintenance work varies greatly, depending on where the electrician is employed. Maintenance electricians spend much of their time doing preventive maintenance. They periodically inspect equipment, and locate and correct problems before breakdowns occur. Electricians use hand tools such as screwdrivers, pliers, knives, hacksaws, and wire strippers. They also use a variety of power tools as well as testing equipment such as oscilloscopes, ammeters, and test lamps.

Working Conditions: Electricians' work is sometimes strenuous. They bend conduits, stand for long periods, and frequently work on ladders and scaffolds. Their working environment varies, depending on the type of job. Some may work in dusty, dirty, hot, or wet conditions, or in confined areas, ditches, or other uncomfortable places. Electricians risk injury from electrical shock, falls, and cuts. Most electricians work a standard 40-hour week, although overtime may be required. Those in maintenance work may work nights or weekends, and be on call.

Electricians held about 583,500 jobs in 2012. More than one-quarter of wage and salary workers were employed in the construction industry. The remainder worked as maintenance electricians outside the construction industry. About one in 10 electricians was self-employed.

Education, Training, & Qualifications: Most people learn the electrical trade by completing an apprenticeship program lasting three to five years. Apprenticeship gives trainees a thorough knowledge of all aspects of the trade and generally improves their ability to find a job. Although electricians are more likely to be trained through apprenticeship than are workers in other construction trades, some still learn their skills informally on the job. Others train to be residential electricians in a three-year program. Apprenticeship programs may be sponsored by joint training committees made up of local unions of the International Brotherhood of Electrical Workers and local chapters of the National Electrical Contractors Association; company management committees of individual electrical contracting companies; or local chapters of the Associated Builders and Contractors and the Independent Electrical Contractors Association. The typical large apprenticeship program provides at least 144 hours of classroom instruction and 2,000 hours of on-the-job-training each year. Those who do not enter a formal apprenticeship program can begin to learn the trade informally by working as helpers for experienced electricians.

Earnings: In 2012, median annual earnings of electricians were $49,840 ($23.96 per hour). The top 10% earned over $82,930 a year; the bottom 10% made less than $30,420 a year.

Key Contacts: For details about apprenticeships or other work opportunities in this trade, contact the offices of the state employment service, the state apprenticeship agency, local electrical contractors or firms that employ maintenance electricians, or local union-management electrician apprenticeship committees. For information about union apprenticeship programs, contact:

- **National Joint Apprenticeship Training Committee:** 301 Prince George's Blvd., Upper Marlboro, MD 20774. Website: www. njatc.org.
- **National Electrical Contractors Association:** 3 Bethesda Metro Center, Suite 1100, Bethesda, MD 20814. Website: www.necanet. org.
- **International Brotherhood of Electrical Workers:** 900 Seventh St., NW, Washington, DC 20001. Website: www.ibew.org.
- **Independent Electrical Contractors, Inc.:** 4401 Ford Avenue, Suite 1100, Alexandria, VA 22302. Website: www.ieci.org.

For information about independent apprenticeship programs, contact:

- **Associated Builders and Contractors:** Workforce Development Department, 4250 North Fairfax Drive, 9th Floor, Arlington, VA 22203. Website: www.abc.org.
- **Independent Electrical Contractors, Inc.:** 4401 Ford Avenue, Suite 1100, Alexandria, VA 22302. Website: www.ieci.org.
- **National Association of Home Builders, Home Builders Institute:** 1201 15th St., NW, Sixth Floor, Washington, DC 20005. Website: www.hbi.org.
- **Home Builders Institute:** 1201 15th Street, NW, 6th Floor, Washington, DC 20005. Website: www.hbi.org.

Elevator Installers and Repairers

- **Annual Earnings:** $76,650 ($36.85 per hour)
- **Education/Training:** High school diploma or equivalent; apprenticeships
- **Outlook:** Faster than average – 25% increase from 2012 to 2022 (increase from 18,700 to 24,500 jobs)

Employment Outlook: Employment of elevator installers and repairers is expected to increase 25% during the 2012-2022 decade, which is much faster than average for all occupations. Demand for additional elevator installers depends greatly on growth in nonresidential construction, such a commercial office buildings and stores that have elevators and escalators.

Nature of Work: Elevator installers and repairers – also called elevator constructors or elevator mechanics – assemble, install, and replace elevators, escalators, chairlifts, dumbwaiters, moving walkways, and similar equipment in new and old buildings. Once the equipment is in service, they maintain and repair it as well. They also are responsible for modernizing older equipment.

A service crew usually handles major repairs – for example, replacing cables, elevator doors, or machine bearings.

The most highly skilled elevator installers and repairers, called "adjusters," specialize in fine-tuning all the equipment after installation. Adjusters make sure that an elevator works according to specifications and stops correctly at each floor within a specified time. Adjusters need a thorough knowledge of electricity, electronics, and computers to ensure the newly installed elevators operate properly.

Working Conditions: Elevator installers lift and carry heavy equipment and parts, and they may work in cramped spaces or awkward positions. Potential hazards include falls, electrical shock, muscle strains, and other injuries related to handling heavy equipment. Most of their work is performed indoors in existing buildings or buildings under construction.

Education, Training, & Qualifications: Most elevator installers receive their education and training through an apprenticeship program. High school classes in mathematics, science, and shop may help applicants compete for apprenticeship openings. Most elevator installers and repairers learn their trade in an apprenticeship program administered by local joint educational committees representing the employers and the union – the International Union of Elevator Constructors. In nonunion shops, workers may complete training programs sponsored by independent contractors.

Earnings: Earnings of elevator installers and repairers are among the highest of all construction trades. Median annual earnings of elevator installers and repairers were $76,650 in 2012. The top 10% earned more than $106,450 a year; the lowest 10% earned less than $39,540 a year.

About three out of four elevator installers and repairers were members of unions or covered by a union contract, one of the highest proportions of all occupations. The largest numbers were members of the International Union of Elevator Constructors. In addition to free continuing education, elevator installers and repairers receive basic benefits enjoyed by other workers.

Key Contacts: For further information on opportunities as an elevator installer and repairer, contact:

- **International Union of Elevator Constructors:** 7154 Columbia Gateway Drive, Columbia, MD 21046. Website: www.iuec.org.
- **National Association of Elevator Contractors:** 1298 Wellbrook Circle, Conyers, GA 30012. Website: www.naec.org.

Glaziers

- **Annual Earnings:** $37,610 ($18.08 per hour)
- **Education/Training:** High school diploma or equivalent; experience and apprenticeship programs
- **Outlook:** Faster than average – 17% increase from 2012 to 2022 (increase from 46,700 to 54,700 jobs)

Employment Outlook: Job opportunities are expected to be good for glaziers, growing by 17 percent from 2012 to 2022, largely due to the numerous openings arising each year as experienced glaziers leave the occupation. In addition, many potential workers may choose not to enter this occupation because they prefer work that is less strenuous and has more comfortable working conditions. Employment of glaziers is expected

to grow faster than average for all occupations in the coming decade, as a result of growth in residential and commercial construction. Demand for glaziers will be spurred by the continuing need to modernize and repair existing structures and the popularity of glass in bathroom and kitchen design. The need to improve glass performance related to insulation, privacy, safety, condensation control, and noise reduction also is expected to contribute to the demand for glaziers in both residential and nonresidential remodeling. Glaziers held 46,700 jobs in 2012.

Nature of Work: Glaziers are responsible for selecting, cutting, installing, replacing, and removing glass. They generally work on one of several types of projects. Residential glazing involves work such as replacing glass in home windows; installing glass mirrors, shower doors, and bathtub enclosures; and fitting glass for tabletops and display cases. On commercial interior projects, glaziers install items such as heavy, often etched, decorative room dividers or security windows. Glazing projects also may involve replacement of street front windows for establishments such as supermarkets, auto dealerships, or banks. In the construction of large commercial buildings, glaziers build metal framework extrusions and install glass panels or curtain walls.

Working Conditions: Glaziers often work outdoors, sometimes in inclement weather. At times, they work on scaffolds at great heights. They do a considerable amount of bending, kneeling, lifting, and standing. Glaziers may be injured by broken glass or cutting tools, by falls from scaffolds, or by improperly lifting heavy glass panels.

Education, Training, & Qualifications: Many glaziers learn the trade informally on the job. They usually start as helpers, carrying glass and cleaning up debris in glass shops. They often practice cutting on discarded glass. After a while, they are given an opportunity to cut glass for a job. Eventually, helpers assist experienced workers on simple installation jobs. By working with experienced glaziers, they eventually acquire the skills of a fully qualified glazier. Employers recommend that glaziers learn the trade through a formal apprenticeship program that lasts three to four years. Apprenticeship programs, which are administered by the National Glass Apprenticeship and local union-management committees or local contractors' associations, consist of on-the-job training and a minimum of 144 hours of classroom instruction or home study each year. On the job, apprentices learn to use the tools and equipment of the trade; handle, measure, cut, and install glass and metal framing; cut and fit moldings; and install and balance glass doors.

Earnings: In 2012, median annual earnings of glaziers were $37,610 ($18.08 per hour). The top 10% earned more than $69,120 a year; the bottom 10% earned less than $24,170 a year.

Glaziers covered by union contracts generally earn more than their nonunion counterparts. Apprentice wage rates usually start at between 40 and 50% of the rate paid to experienced glaziers and increase as apprentices gain experience in the field.

Key Contacts: For more information about glazier apprenticeships or work opportunities, contact local glazing or general contractors, a local of the International Union of Painters and Allied Trades, a local joint union-management apprenticeship agency, or the nearest office of the state employment service or state apprenticeship agency. For information about the work and training of glaziers, contact:

- **International Union of Painters and Allied Trades:** 7234 Parkway Drive, Hanover, MD 21076. Website: www.iupat.org.
- **National Glass Association:** Education and Training Department, 1945 Old Gallows Road, Suite 750, Vienna, VA 22182. Website: www.glass.org.
- **Finishing Trades Institute:** 7230 Parkway Drive, Hanover, MD 21076. Website: www.finishingtradesinsti tute.org.

Hazardous Materials Removal Workers

- **Annual Earnings:** $37,590 ($18.07 per hour)
- **Education/Training:** High school diploma or equivalent; training
- **Outlook:** Good – 14% increase from 2012-2022 (increase from 37,500 to 42,800 jobs)

Employment Outlook: Job opportunities are expected to be good for hazardous materials removal workers. The occupation is characterized by a relatively high rate of turnover, resulting in a number of job openings each year. Many potential workers are not attracted to this occupation, because they prefer work that is less strenuous and under safer working conditions. Employment of hazardous materials removal workers is expected to grow about average for all occupations in the decade ahead, reflecting continuing concern for a safe and clean environment. Special-trade contractors will have strong demand for the largest segment of these workers, namely, asbestos abatement and lead abatement workers; lead abatement should offer particularly good opportunities. Mold remediation is an especially rapidly growing part of the occupation at the present time, but it is unclear whether its rapid growth will continue. Employment of decontamination technicians, radiation safety technicians, and decommissioning and decontamination workers is expected to grow in response to increased pressure for safer and cleaner nuclear and electric generator facilities.

Nature of Work: Hazardous materials workers identify, remove, package, transport, and dispose of various hazardous materials, including asbestos, lead, and radioactive and nuclear materials. The removal of hazardous materials, or "hazmats," from public places and the environment also is called abatement, remediation, and decontamination. Hazardous materials removal workers use a variety of tools and equipment, depending on the work at hand. Equipment ranges form brooms to personal protective suits that completely isolate workers from the hazardous materials. The equipment required varies with the threat of contamination and can include disposable or reusable coveralls, gloves, hard hats, shoe covers, safety glasses or goggles, chemical-resistant clothing, face shields, and devices to protect one's hearing. Most workers also are required to wear respirators while working, to protect them from airborne particles. Asbestos abatement workers and lead abatement workers remove asbestos, lead, and other materials from buildings scheduled to be renovated or demolished. Using a variety of hand and power tools, such as vacuums and scrapers, these workers remove the asbestos and lead from surfaces. Emergency and disaster response workers clean up hazardous materials after train derailments and trucking accidents. These workers also are needed when an immediate cleanup is required, as would be the case after an attack by biological or chemical weapons. Decommissioning and decontamination workers remove and treat radioactive materials generated by nuclear facilities and power plants. Treatment, storage, and disposal workers transport and prepare materials for treatment or disposal. Nearly 37,500 hazardous materials removal workers held jobs in 2012.

Working Conditions: Hazardous materials removal workers function in a highly structured environment, to minimize the danger they face. Each phase of an operation is planned in advance, and workers are trained to deal with safety breaches and hazardous situations. Crews and supervisors take every precaution to ensure that the worksite is safe. Whether they work in asbestos, mold, or lead abatement or in radioactive decontamination, hazardous materials removal workers must stand, stoop, and kneel for long periods. Some must wear fully enclosed personal protective suits for several hours at a time. These workers face different working conditions, depending on their area of expertise. Although many work a standard 40-hour week, overtime and shift work are common, especially in asbestos and lead abatement.

Education, Training, & Qualifications: No formal education beyond a high school diploma is required to work in this field. Federal regulations require an individual to have a license to work in the occupation, although, at present, there are few laws regulating mold removal. Most employers provide technical training on the job, but a formal 32- to 40-hour training program must be completed if one is to be licensed as an asbestos abatement and lead abatement worker or a treatment, storage, and disposal worker. For decommissioning and decontamination workers employed at nuclear facilities, training is more extensive. Workers in all fields are required to take refresher courses every year in order to maintain their license. Because much of the work is done in buildings, a background in construction is helpful.

Earnings: In 2012, median annual earnings of hazardous materials removal workers were $37,590 ($18.07 per hour). The top 10% earned more than $66,730 a year; the bottom 10% earned less than $25,000 a year. Treatment, storage, and disposal workers usually earn slightly more than asbestos abatement and lead abatement workers. Decontamination and decommissioning workers and radiation protection technicians, though constituting the smallest group, tend to earn the highest wages.

Key Contacts: For more information on hazardous materials removal workers, including information on training, contact:

- **LIUNA Training and Education Fund**: 37 Deerfield Road, Pomfret, CT 06259. Website: www.liunatraining. org.

For more information on working in the nuclear industry, visit:

- **Nuclear Energy Institute:** 1201 F St., NW, Suite 1100, Washington, DC 20004-1218 Website: www.nei.org.

Insulation Workers

- **Annual Earnings:** $35,940 ($17.28 per hour)
- **Education/Training:** Experience and apprenticeships
- **Outlook:** Much faster than average – 38% increase from 2012 to 2022 (from 52,100 to 71,700 jobs)

Employment Outlook: Job opportunities are expected to be excellent for insulation workers, growing by 38% from 2012 to 2022. Because there are no strict training requirements for entry, many people with limited skills work as insulation workers for a short time and then move on to other types of work, creating many job openings. Employment of insulation workers should grow as fast as average for all occupations in the coming decade, due to growth in residential and commercial construction. Demand for efficient use of energy to heat and cool buildings will create an increased demand for these workers in the construction of new residential, industrial, and commercial buildings. Insulation workers in the construction industry may experience periods of unemployment because of the short duration of many construction projects.

Nature of Work: Insulation workers cement, staple, wire, tape, or spray insulation. When covering a steam pipe, for example, insulation workers measure and cut sections of insulation to the proper length, stretch it open along a cut that runs the length of the material, and slip it over the pipe. They fasten the insulation with adhesive, staples, tape, or wire bands. When covering a wall or other flat surface, workers may use a hose to spray foam insulation onto a wire mesh that provides a rough surface to which the foam can cling and which adds strength to the finished surface. In attics or exterior walls of uninsulated buildings, workers blow in loose-fill insulation. In new construction or on major renovations, insulation workers staple fiberglass or rock-wool batts to exterior walls and ceilings before drywall, paneling, or plaster walls are put in place. Insulation workers use common hand tools – trowels, brushes, knives, scissors, saws, pliers, and stapling guns. They use power saws to cut insulating materials, welding machines to join sheet metal or secure clamps, and compressors to blow or spray insulation.

Insulation workers held about 52,100 jobs in 2012. The construction industry employed 91% of workers; 53% work for drywall and insulation contractors.

Working Conditions: Insulation workers usually work indoors. They spend most of the workday on their feet, either standing, bending, or kneeling. Sometimes they work from ladders or in tight spaces. The work requires more coordination than strength. Insulation work often is dusty and dirty, and the summer heat can make the insulation worker very uncomfortable. Minute particles from insulation materials, especially when blown, can irritate the eyes, skin, and respiratory system. Workers must follow strict safety guidelines to protect themselves from the dangers of insulating irritants. They keep work areas well ventilated; wear protective suits, masks, and respirators; and take decontamination showers if necessary.

Education, Training, & Qualifications: Most insulation workers learn their trade informally on the job, although some complete formal apprenticeship programs. For entry-level jobs, insulation contractors prefer high school graduates who are in good physical condition and licensed to drive. Applicants seeking apprenticeship positions should have a high school diploma or its equivalent and be at least 18 years old. Trainees who learn on the job receive instruction and supervision from experienced insulation workers. Trainees begin with simple tasks, such as carrying insulation or holding material while it is fastened in place. On-the-job training can take up to two years, depending on the nature of the work.

Earnings: In 2012, median annual earnings of insulation workers were $35,940 ($17.28 per hour). The top 10% earned over $75,390 a year; the bottom 10% earned less than $25,630 a year.

Key Contacts: For information on training programs or other work opportunities in this trade, contact a local insulation contractor, the nearest office of the state employment service or apprenticeship agency, or the following organizations:

- **National Insulation Association:** 12100 Sunset Hills Road, Suite 330, Reston, VA 20190. Website: www.insulation.org.
- **International Association of Heat and Frost Insulators and Allied Workers:** 9602 Martin Luther King Jr. Hwy., Lanham, MD 20706. Website: www.insulators.org.
- **Insulation Contractors Association of America:** 1321 Duke Street, Suite 303, Alexandria, VA 22314. Website: www.insulate.org.

Painters, Construction, and Maintenance

- **Annual Earnings:** $35,190 ($16.92 per hour)
- **Education/Training:** Experience and apprenticeships
- **Outlook:** Faster than average – 20% increase from 2012 to 2022 (from 316,200 to 378,800 jobs)

Employment Outlook: Job prospects should be very good – faster than average for all occupations (expected to grow by 20% between 2012 and 2022) – as thousands of construction, maintenance, and artisan painters transfer to other occupations or leave the labor force each year. Because there are no strict training requirements for entry, many people with limited skills work as painters for a short time and then move on to other work. Employment of painters and paperhangers is expected to grow about as fast as average for all occupations in the decade ahead, reflecting increases in the level of new construction and in the supply of buildings and others structures that require maintenance and renovation.

Nature of Work: Painters apply paint, stain, varnish, and other finishes to buildings and other structures. They choose the right paint or finish for the surface to be covered, taking into account durability, ease of handling, method of applications, and customers' wishes. Painters first prepare the surfaces to be covered. This may require removing the old coat of paint by stripping, sanding, wire brushing, burning, or water and abrasive blasting. Painters also wash walls and trim to remove dirt and grease, fill nail holes and cracks, sandpaper rough spots, and brush off dust. When working on tall buildings, painters erect scaffolding, including "swing stages," scaffolds suspended by ropes, or cables attached to the roof hood. Painters held 316,200 jobs in 2012.

Working Conditions: Most painters work 40 hours a week or less; about one-quarter have variable schedules or work part time. Painters must stand for long periods. Their jobs also require a considerable amount of climbing and bending. These workers must have stamina, because much of the work is done with their arms raised overhead. Painters often work outdoors but seldom in wet, cold, or inclement weather. These workers risk injury from slipping or falling off ladders and scaffolds. They sometimes may work with materials that can be hazardous if masks are not worn or if ventilation is poor. Some painting jobs can leave a worker covered with paint. In some cases, painters may work in a sealed self-contained suit to prevent inhalation of, or contact with, hazardous materials.

Education, Training, & Qualifications: Painting is learned through apprenticeships or informal, on-the-job instruction. Although training authorities recommend completion of an apprenticeship program as the best way to become a painter, most painters learn the trade informally on the job as a helper to an experienced painter. Apprenticeships for painters consist of two to four years of on-the-job training, in addition to 144 hours of related classroom instruction each year. Apprentices receive instruction in color harmony, use and care of tools and equipment, surface preparation, application techniques, paint mixing and matching, characteristics of different finishes, blueprint reading, wood finishing, and safety. Painters may advance to supervisory or estimating jobs with painting and decorating contractors. Many establish their own painting businesses.

Earnings: Median annual earnings of painters (construction and maintenance) were $35,190 ($16.92 per hour). The top 10% earned more than $60,240 a year; the bottom 10% earned less than $22,980 a year. Earnings for painters may be reduced on occasion because of bad weather and the short-term nature of many construction jobs. Hourly wage rates for apprentices usually start at 40 to 50% of the rate for experienced workers and increase periodically.

Key Contacts: For information about the work of painters, contact local painting contractors, a local of the International Union of Painters and Allied Trades, a local joint union-management apprenticeship committee, or an office of the state apprenticeship agency or employment services:

- **International Union of Painters and Allied Trades:** 7234 Parkway Drive, Hanover, MD 21076. Website: www.iupat.org.
- **Associated Builders and Contractors:** 440 1st Street, NW, Suite 200, Washington, DC 20001. Website: www.abc.org.
- **Painting and Decorating Contractors of America:** 2316 Millpark Drive, Maryland Heights, MO 63043. Website: www.pdca. org.

Plumbers, Pipefitters, and Steamfitters

- **Annual Earnings:** $49,140 ($23.62 per hour)
- **Education/Training:** High school diploma or equivalent; apprenticeship
- **Outlook:** Faster than average – 21% increase from 2012 to 2022 (from 386,900 to 469,200 jobs)

Employment Outlook: Job opportunities are expected to be very good, especially for workers with welding experience. Employment of plumbers, pipefitters, and steamfitters is expected to grow 10 percent between 2006 and 2016, about as fast as the average for all occupations. The demand for skilled plumbers, pipefitters, and steamfitters is expected to outpace the supply of workers trained in these crafts. Many potential workers may prefer work that is less strenuous and has more comfortable working conditions. Employment of individuals in these trades is expected to grow about as fast as the average for all occupations in the coming decade. Demand for plumbers will stem from building renovation, including the growing use of sprinkler systems; repair and maintenance of existing residential systems; and maintenance activities for places having extensive systems of pipes, such as power plants, water and wastewater treatment plants, pipelines, office buildings, and factories. Employment of plumbers, pipefitters, and steamfitters generally is less sensitive to changes in economic conditions than is employment of some other construction trades. Even when construction activity declines, maintenance, rehabilitation, and replacement of existing piping systems, as well as the increasing installation of fire sprinkler systems, provide many jobs for plumbers, pipefitters, and steamfitters.

Nature of Work: Although pipefitting, plumbing, and steamfitting sometimes are considered a single trade, workers generally specialize in one of the three areas. Plumbers install and repair the water, waste disposal, drainage, and gas systems in homes and commercial and industrial buildings. Plumbers also install plumbing fixtures – bathtubs, showers, sinks, and toilets – and appliances such as dishwashers and water heaters. Pipefitters install and repair both high- and low-pressure pipe systems used in manufacturing, in the generation of electricity, and in heating and cooling buildings. They also install automatic controls that are increasingly being used to regulate these systems. Some pipefitters specialize in only one type of system. Steamfitters, for example, install pipe systems that move liquids or gases under high pressure. Sprinkler fitters install automatic fire sprinkler systems in buildings.

Plumbers, pipefitters, and steamfitters constitute one of the largest construction occupations, holding about 386,000 jobs in 2012. About 55% worked for plumbing, heating, and air-conditioning contractors engaged in new construction, repair, modernization, or maintenance work.

Working Conditions: Because plumbers, pipefitters, and steamfitters must lift heavy pipes, stand for long periods, and sometimes work in uncomfortable or cramped positions, they need physical strength as well as stamina. They also may have to work outdoors in inclement weather. In addition, they are subject to possible falls from ladders, cuts from sharp tools, and burns from hot pipes or soldering equipment. Plumbers, pipefitters, and steamfitters engaged in construction generally work a standard 40-hour week. Those involved in maintenance services under contract may have to work evening or weekend shifts, as well as be on call. These maintenance workers may spend quite a bit of time traveling to and from work sites.

Education, Training, & Qualifications: Virtually all plumbers, pipefitters, and steamfitters undergo some type of apprenticeship training. Many apprenticeship programs are administered by local union-management committees made up of members of the United Association of Journeymen and Apprentices of the Plumbing and Pipefitting Industry of the United States and Canada, and local employers who are members of either the Mechanical Contractors Association of America, the National Association of Plumbing-Heating-Cooling Contractors, or the National Fire Sprinkler Association. Nonunion training and apprenticeship programs are administered by local chapters of the Associ-

ated Builders and Contractors, the National Association of Plumbing-Heating-Cooling Contractors, the American Fire Sprinkler Association, or the Home Builders Institute of the National Association of Home Builders. Apprenticeships – both union and nonunion – consist of four or five years of on-the-job training, in addition to at least 144 hours per year of related classroom instruction. As apprentices gain experience, they learn how to work with various types of pipe and how to install different piping systems and plumbing fixtures.

Earnings: Plumbers, pipefitters, and steamfitters are among the highest paid construction occupations. In 2012, median annual earnings for group were $49,140 ($23.62 per hour). The top 10% earned $84,440 a year; the bottom 10% earned $29,020 per year. Apprentices usually are paid about 50% of the wage rate paid to experienced pipelayers, plumbers, pipefitters, and steamfitters. About 30% of plumbers, pipefitters, and steamfitters belonged to a union.

Key Contacts: For information on apprenticeship opportunities for plumbers, pipefitters, and steamfitters, contact:

- **United Association of Journeymen and Apprentices of the Plumbing and Pipefitting Industry of the U.S. and Canada:** Three Park Place, Annapolis, MD 21401. Website: www.ua.org.

For more information about training programs for plumbers, pipefitters, and steamfitters, contact:

- **Associated Builders and Contractors:** 440 1st Street, NW, Suite 200, Washington, DC 20001. Website: www.abc.org.

- **National Association of Home Builders, Home Builders Institute:** 1201 15th St., NW, Sixth Floor, Washington, DC 20005. Website: www.hbi.org.

For general information about the work of pipelayers, plumbers, and pipefitters, contact:

- **Mechanical Contractors Association of America:** 1385 Piccard Drive, Rockville, MD 20850. Website: www.mcaa.org.

- **Plumbing-Heating-Cooling Contractors Association:** 180 S. Washington Street, Falls Church, VA 22046. Website: www.phccweb.org.

For general information about the work of sprinklerfitters, contact:

- **American Fire Sprinkler Association:** 12750 Merit Drive, Suite 350, Dallas, TX 75251. Website: www.firesprinkler.org.

- **National Fire Sprinkler Association:** 40 Jon Barrett Road, Patterson, NY 12563. Website: www.nfsa.org.

Roofers

- **Annual Earnings:** $35,290 ($16.97 per hour)
- **Education/Training:** Less than high school; on-the-job and apprenticeships
- **Outlook:** As fast as average – 11% increase from 2012 to 2022; increase from 132,700 to 147,900 jobs

Employment Outlook: Most job openings will arise from high turnover, because the work is hot, strenuous, and dirty, causing many people to switch to jobs in other construction trades. In fact, many workers treat roofing as a temporary job until they find other work, which partly explains why many ex-offenders initially gravitate toward this particular occupation.

Faster-than-average employment growth is expected – by 11% between 2012 and 2022. Roofs deteriorate faster than most other parts of buildings, and they need to be repaired or replaced more often.

Job opportunities for roofers will arise primarily because of the need to replace workers who leave the occupation. Indeed, the proportion of roofers who leave the occupation each year is higher than in most construction trades.

Nature of Work: A leaky roof can damage ceilings, walls, and furnishings. Roofers repair and install roofs made of tar or asphalt and gravel; rubber or thermoplastic; metal; or shingles to protect buildings and their contents from water damage. Repair and reroofing – replacing old roofs on existing buildings – makes up the majority of work for roofers.

Roofers held about 132,700 jobs in 2012. Almost all salaried roofers worked for roofing contractors. About 20% of roofers were self-employed. Many self-employed roofers specialized in residential work.

Working Conditions: Roofing work is strenuous. It involves heavy lifting, as well as climbing, bending, and kneeling. Roofers work outdoors in all types of weather, particularly when making repairs. Workers risk slips or falls from scaffolds, ladders, or roofs or burns from hot bitumen. Roofs can become extremely hot during summer, causing heat-related illnesses. The rate of injuries for roofing contractors in construction is almost twice that of workers overall.

Education, Training, & Qualifications: Most roofers learn their skills informally by working as helpers for experienced roofers and by taking classes, including safety training, offered by their employers; some complete three-year apprenticeships.

Earnings: In 2012, median annual earnings for roofers were $35,290 ($16.97 per hour). The top 10% earned $60,350; the bottom 10% earned $22,350.

Key Contacts: For information about the work of roofers, contact:

- **National Roofing Contractors Association:** 10255 W. Higgins Road, Suite 600, Rosemont, IL 60018-5607. Website: www.nrca.net.
- **United Union of Roofers, Waterproofers, and Allied Workers:** 1660 L Street, NW, Suite 800, Washington, DC 20036. Website: www.union roofers.com.

Sheet Metal Workers

- **Annual Earnings:** $43,290 ($20.81 per hour)
- **Education/Training:** High school diploma or equivalent; apprenticeship
- **Outlook:** Faster than average – 15% increase from 2012 to 2022 (from 142,300 to 164,300 jobs)

Employment Outlook: Employment opportunities are expected to be average – growing by 15% between 2012 and 2022 – for sheet metal workers in the construction industry and in construction-related sheet metal fabrication, reflecting both employment growth and openings arising each year as experienced sheet metal workers leave the occupation. In addition, many potential workers may prefer work that is less strenuous and that has more comfortable working conditions, thus limiting the number of applicants for sheet metal jobs. Opportunities should be particularly good for individuals who acquire apprenticeship training.

Employment of sheet metal workers in construction is expected to grow faster than average for all occupations in the decade ahead. This will be in response to growth in the demand for sheet metal installations as more industrial, commercial, and residential structures are built. The need to install energy-efficient air-conditioning, heating, and ventilation systems in the increasing numbers of old buildings and to perform other types of renovation and maintenance work also should boost employment.

Nature of Work: Sheet metal workers make, install, and maintain heating, ventilation, and air-conditioning duct systems, roofs, siding, rain gutters, downspouts, skylights, restaurant equipment, outdoor signs, railroad cars, tailgates, customized precision equipment, and many other products made from metal sheets. They also may work with fiberglass and plastic materials. Although some workers specialize in fabrication, installation, or maintenance, most do all three jobs. Sheet metal workers do both construction-related sheet metal work and mass production of sheet metal products in manufacturing. Sheet metal workers held about 142,300 jobs in 2012. Nearly two-thirds of all sheet metal workers were found in the construction industry. Of those employed in construction, almost half worked for plumbing, heating, and air-conditioning contractors; most of the rest worked for roofing and sheet metal contractors. About 21% of all sheet metal workers were in manufacturing industries, such as the fabricated metal products, machinery, and aerospace products and parts industries. Few sheet metal workers are self-employed.

Working Conditions: Sheet metal workers usually work a 40-hour week. Those who fabricate sheet metal products work in shops that are well-lighted and well-ventilated. However, they stand for long periods and lift heavy materials and finished pieces. Sheet metal workers must follow safety practices because working around high-speed machines can be dangerous. They also are subject to cuts from sharp metal, burns from soldering and welding, and falls from ladders and scaffolds. They usually wear safety glasses but must not wear jewelry or loose-fitting clothing that could easily be caught in a machine. Those performing installation work do considerable bending, lifting, standing, climbing, and squatting, sometimes in close quarters or in awkward positions.

Education, Training, & Qualifications: Apprenticeship generally is considered to be the best way to learn this trade. The apprenticeship program consists of four to five years of on-the-job training and an average of 200 hours per year of classroom instruction. Apprenticeship programs may be administered by local joint committees composed of the Sheet Metal Workers' International Association and local chapters of the Sheet Metal and Air-Conditioning Contractors National Association. On the job, apprentices learn the basics of pattern layout and how to cut, bend, fabricate, and install sheet metal. In the classroom, apprentices learn drafting, plan and specification reading, trigonometry and geometry applicable to layout work, the use of computerized equipment, welding, and the principles of heating, air-conditioning, and ventilating systems.

Some people pick up the trade informally, usually by working as helpers to experienced sheet metal workers. Most sheet metal workers in large-scale manufacturing receive on-the-job training, with additional classwork or in-house training when necessary.

Earnings: In May 2012, median annual earnings of sheet metal workers were $43,290 ($20.81 per hour). The top 10% averaged more than $74,740 per year; the bottom 10% averaged less than $25,310 per year.

Key Contacts: For more information on apprenticeships or other work opportunities, contact local sheet metal contractors or heating, refrigeration, and air-conditioning contractors; a local of the Sheet Metal Workers International Association; a local of the Sheet Metal and Air-Conditioning Contractors National Association; a local joint union-management apprenticeship committee; or the nearest office of your state employment service or apprenticeship agency.

For general and training information about sheet metal workers, contact:

- **Fabricators and Manufacturers Association, International:** 833 Featherstone Road, Rockford, IL 61107. Website: www.fmanet.org.

- **International Training Institute for the Sheet Metal and Air Conditioning Industry:** 8403 Arlington Blvd., Suite 100, Fairfax, VA 22031. Website: www.sheetmetal-iti.org.

- **Sheet Metal and Air Conditioning Contractors National Association:** 4201 Lafayette Center Drive, Chantilly, VA 20151-1209. Website: www.smacna.org.

- **Sheet Metal Workers International Association:** 1750 New York Avenue, NW, 6th Floor, Washington, DC 20006. Website: www.smwia.org.

Structural Iron and Steel Workers

- **Annual Earnings:** $46,140 ($22.18 per hour)
- **Education/Training:** High school diploma or equivalent; apprenticeships
- **Outlook:** Much faster than average – 22% increase from 2012 to 2022 (from 58,100 to 70,800 jobs)

Employment Outlook: Employment of structural and reinforcing iron and steel workers is expected to grow much faster than average for all occupations in the decade ahead – about 22% increase between 2012 and 2022 – largely on the basis of continued growth in industrial and commercial construction. The rehabilitation, maintenance, and replacement of a growing number of older buildings, factories, power plants, highways, and bridges is expected to create employment opportunities. The number of job openings fluctuates from year to year with economic conditions and the level of construction activity.

Nature of Work: Structural iron and steel workers place and install iron or steel girders, columns, and other construction materials to form buildings, bridges, and other structures. They also position and secure steel bars or mesh in concrete forms in order to reinforce the concrete used in highways, buildings, bridges, tunnels, and other structures. In addition, they repair and renovate older buildings and structures. Even though the primary metal involved in this work is steel, these workers often are known as ironworkers.

Working Conditions: Structural and reinforcing iron and metal workers usually work outside in all kinds of weather. However, those who work at great heights do not work during wet, icy, or extremely windy conditions. Because the danger of injuries due to falls is great, ironworkers use safety devices such as safety belts, scaffolding, and nets to reduce risk. Some ironworkers fabricate structural metal in fabricating shops, which usually are located away from the construction site. These workers usually work a 40-hour week. They held about 58,100 jobs in 2012.

Education, Training, & Qualifications: Most employers recommend a three- or four-year apprenticeship involving on-the-job training and evening classroom instruction as the best way to learn this trade. Apprenticeship programs usually are administered by committees made up of representatives of local unions of the International Association of Bridge, Structural, Ornamental and Reinforcing Iron Workers or the local chapters of contractors' associations. Ironworkers must be at least 18 years old. A high school diploma is preferred by employers and local apprenticeship committees.

Earnings: In 2012, median annual earnings of structural iron and steel workers in all industries were $46,140 ($22.18 per hour). The top 10% earned about $83,970 per year; the bottom 10% earned less than $26,970 per year. According to the International Association of Bridge, Structural, Ornamental, and Reinforcing Iron Workers, average hourly earnings, including benefits, for structural and reinforcing metal workers who belonged to a union and worked full time were 34 percent higher than the hourly earnings of nonunion workers.

Key Contacts: For information on apprenticeships or other work opportunities, contact local general contractors; a local of the International Association of Bridge, Structural, Ornamental, and Reinforcing Iron Workers Union; a local iron workers' joint union-management apprenticeship committee; a local or state chapter of the Associated Builders and Contractors or the Associated General Contractors of America; or the nearest office of your state employment service or apprenticeship agency.

For apprenticeship information, contact:

- **International Association of Bridge, Structural, Ornamental, and Reinforcing Iron Workers:** Apprenticeship Department, 1750 New York Avenue, NW, Suite 400, Washington, DC 20006. Website: www.ironworkers.org.

For general information about ironworkers, contact either of the following sources:

- **Associated Builders and Contractors:** 440 1st Street, NW, Suite 200, Washington, DC 20001. Website: www.abc.org.
- **Associated General Contractors of America:** 2300 Wilson Blvd., Suite 300, Arlington, VA 22201. Website: www.agc.org.

Ask Yourself

If some of the construction trades described in this chapter appeal to you, ask yourself the following questions:

1. Which construction trades am I most interested in pursuing?

_____

_____

2. What skills do I currently have that would be helpful in landing a job in those trades?

_____

_____

3. What additional education and trading do I need in order to land a job?

_____

_____

4. Where will I get that additional education and training?

_____

_____

5. Who could help me now in landing a job in the trade that interests me?

_____

_____

_____

6. What else do I need to know and do to get into this trade?

_____

_____

_____

_____

*   *   *

When completing the remaining chapters, ask yourself similar questions at the end of each chapter about the particular jobs or occupations featured in that chapter. In so doing, you'll get a better idea of how your interests and skills might best relate to each job. Better still, you'll begin developing an **action plan** for directing your post-release job search. You'll also begin identifying your additional education and training needs and focusing on key individuals who might be willing to extend you a helping hand for getting your career on a positive track.

5

Installation, Maintenance, and Repair Occupations

"If you want a safe, accessible, and rewarding occupational future – a job that is relatively recession-proof, difficult to offshore, requires basic education, and pays middle-class wages – be sure to look at installation, maintenance, and repair occupations."

THE INCREASED USE OF TECHNOLOGY and machinery requires more and more workers who are experts at installing, maintaining, and repairing equipment. Most of these jobs require some postsecondary education and training, such as attending specialized trade school classes, receiving on-the-job training, and acquiring certification. Individuals entering these fields can expect to regularly acquire additional education and training in order to keep up with the latest developments in their respective fields.

Most of the jobs profiled in this chapter are expected to grow substantially in the decade ahead as well as generate high median earnings for their workers. Many are attractive alternatives for installation- and repair-oriented individuals who are entering the job market but who do not have the requisite education credentials to enter other occupational fields. These also are some of the safest jobs – relatively recession-proof and nearly impossible to offshore. Entry into one of these jobs should lead to a relatively comfortable and secure employment future. Ex-offenders should seriously consider many of these job and career alternatives.

Aircraft and Avionics Equipment Mechanics & Service Technicians

- **Annual Earnings:** $55,230 ($26.55 per hour)
- **Education/Training:** Trade school, on-the-job training, and certificate
- **Outlook:** Little or no change – 2% increase from 2012 to 2022 (from 138,900 to 142,400 jobs)

Employment Outlook: Employment of aircraft and avionics equipment mechanics and technicians is projected to show little or no change from 2012 to 2022. Air traffic is expected to gradually increase over the coming decade. However, new aircraft are generally expected to require less maintenance than older aircraft. Airlines may continue to outsource maintenance work to specialized maintenance and repair shops both domestically and abroad. Increased specialization will allow maintenance facilities to use their resources more efficiently and therefore limit growth in the number of aircraft and avionics equipment mechanics and technicians.

Competition for aircraft and avionics equipment mechanic and technician jobs varies according to the type of job sought. In general, job opportunities will be best for mechanics who hold an Airframe (A) & Powerplant (P) certificate and have knowledge about the most cutting-edge technologies and composite materials. Familiarity with computers and digital systems will help provide the best opportunities. Bachelor's degree holders typically have an advantage when trying to enter the occupation and may find it easier to advance.

Nature of Work: Aircraft mechanics typically do the following:

- Examine replacement aircraft parts for defects
- Diagnose mechanical or electrical problems
- Read maintenance manuals to identify repair procedures
- Repair wings, brakes, electrical systems, and other aircraft components
- Replace defective parts using hand tools or power tools
- Test aircraft parts with gauges and other diagnostic equipment
- Inspect completed work to ensure that it meets performance standards
- Keep records of maintenance and repair work

Avionics technicians typically do the following:

- Test electronic instruments, using circuit testers, oscilloscopes, and voltmeters
- Interpret flight test data to diagnose malfunctions and performance problems
- Assemble components, such as electrical controls and junction boxes, and install software
- Install instrument panels, using hand tools, power tools, and soldering irons
- Repair or replace malfunctioning components
- Keep records of maintenance and repair work

Today's airplanes are highly complex machines that require reliable parts and service to fly safely. To keep an airplane in peak operating condition, aircraft and avionics equipment mechanics and technicians perform scheduled maintenance, make repairs, and complete inspections. They must follow detailed federal regulations set by the FAA that dictate maintenance schedules for a variety of different operations.

Working Conditions: Aircraft mechanics and avionics technicians held about 138,900 jobs in 2012. Approximately 88% were aircraft mechanics and the rest were avionics technicians. The majority worked for private companies and about 14% worked for the federal government. The industries that employed the most aircraft mechanics in 2012 were as follows:

- Support activities for air transportation — 26%
- Scheduled air transportation — 25%
- Aerospace product and parts manufacturing — 16%
- Federal government, excluding postal service — 15%
- Nonscheduled air transportation — 4%

The industries that employed the most avionics technicians in 2012 were as follows:

- Aerospace product and parts manufacturing — 30%
- Support activities for air transportation — 27%
- Federal government, excluding postal service — 13%
- Scheduled air transportation — 12%
- Professional, scientific, and technical services — 6%

Mechanics and technicians work in hangars, in repair stations, or on airfields. They must meet strict deadlines while maintaining safety standards. Most mechanics and technicians work near major airports. Mechanics may work outside, on the airfield, or in climate-controlled shops and hangars. Civilian mechanics employed by the U.S. Armed Forces work on military installations.

Education, Training, & Qualifications: The majority of mechanics who work on civilian aircraft are certified by the FAA as "airframe mechanic," "power plant mechanic," or "avionics repair specialist." The FAA requires at least 18 months of work experience for an airframe, power plant or avionics repairer's certificate. Completion of a program at an FAA-certified mechanic school can substitute for the work experience requirement. Applicants for all certificates also must pass written and oral tests and demonstrate that they can do the work authorized by the certificate. Although a few people become mechanics through on-the-job training, most learn their job in one of about 200 trade schools certified by the FAA. Some aircraft mechanics in the military acquire enough general experience to satisfy the work experience requirements for the FAA certificate. In general, however, jobs in the military services are too specialized to provide the broad experience required by the FAA. Courses in math and science are helpful, as they demonstrate many of the principles involved in the operation of aircraft. Development of writing skills is useful because mechanics are often required to submit reports.

Earnings: The median annual wage for aircraft mechanics and service technicians was $55,210 in 2012. The top 10% earned $76,660 per year; the bottom 10% earned $35,190. In 2012, the median annual wages for aircraft mechanics and service technicians in the top five industries in which these mechanics worked were as follows:

- Scheduled air transportation $59,110
- Federal government, excluding
  postal service $55,950
- Aerospace product and parts
  manufacturing $55,650
- Nonscheduled air transportation $54,910
- Support activities for air
  transportation $49,120

The median annual wage for avionics technicians was $55,350 in 2012. The top 10% earned $73,770 per year; the bottom 10% earned less than $39,150. In 2012, the median annual wages for avionics technicians in the top five industries in which these technicians worked were as follows:

- Aerospace product and parts
  manufacturing $60,780
- Professional, scientific, and
  technical services $59,730
- Scheduled air transportation $58,530
- Federal government, excluding
  postal service $54,090
- Support activities for air
  transportation $50,040

Mechanics and technicians usually work full time on rotating 8-hour shifts. Overtime and weekend work is often required. Day shifts are usually reserved for mechanics with the most seniority.

Key Contacts: For more information about aircraft and avionics equipment mechanics and service technicians, visit:

- **Federal Aviation Administration:** 800 Independence Avenue, SW, Washington, DC 20591. Website: www.faa.gov.
- **Professional Aviation Maintenance Association:** 400 North Washington Street, Suite 300, Alexandria, VA 22314. Website: http://pama.org.
- **Aircraft Mechanics Fraternal Association:** 14001 E. Iliff Avenue, Suite 217, Aurora, CO 80014. Website:www.amfanational.org.

- **National Center for Aerospace and Transportation Technologies:** P.O. Box 136818, Fort Worth, TX 76136. Website: www.ncatt.org.
- **Aviation Maintenance Magazine:** Website: www.avm-mag.com.
- **National Center for Aerospace & Transportation Technologies:** P.O. Box 136818, Fort Worth, TX 76136. Website: www.ncatt.org.
- **Professional Aviation Maintenance Association:** 400 Commonwealth Drive, Warren-dale, PA 15096. Website: www.pama.org.

Automotive Body and Glass Repairers

- **Annual Earnings:** $37,680 ($18.12 per hour)
- **Education/Training:** High school diploma or equivalent; technical school or apprenticeship training preferred
- **Outlook:** As fast as average – 13% growth from 2012 to 2022 (from 172,200 to 193,100 jobs)

Employment Outlook: Employment of automotive body and related repairers is expected to grow about as fast as average through the year 2022, and job opportunities are projected to be excellent due to a growing number of retirements in this occupation.

Employment of automotive body repairers is expected to grow 13% over the 2012-2022 decade. Demand for qualified body repairers will increase as the number of vehicles on the road continues to grow. Employment growth will continue to be in automotive body, paint, interior, and glass repair shops, with little or no change in automotive dealerships.

Nature of Work: Most of the damage resulting from everyday vehicle collisions can be repaired, and vehicles can be refinished to look and drive like new. Automotive body repairers, often called collision repair technicians, straighten bent bodies, remove dents, and replace crumpled parts that cannot be fixed. They repair all types of vehicles, and although some work on large trucks, businesses vehicles, or tractor-trailers, most work on cars and small trucks. They can work alone, with only general direction from supervisors, or as specialists on a repair team. In some shops, helpers or apprentices assist experienced repairers.

Working Conditions: Repairers work indoors in body shops that are noisy with the clatter of hammers against metal and the whine of power tools.

Most shops are well ventilated to disperse dust and paint fumes. Body repairers often work in awkward or cramped positions, and much of their work is strenuous and dirty.

Education, Training, & Qualifications: Automotive technology is rapidly becoming more sophisticated, and most employers prefer applicants who have completed a formal training program in automotive body repair or refinishing. Most new repairers complete at least part of this training on the job. Many repairers, particularly in urban areas, need a national certification to advance past entry-level work.

A high school diploma or GED is often all that is required to enter this occupation, but more specific education and training is needed to learn how to repair newer automobiles. Collision repair programs may be offered in high school or in postsecondary vocational schools and community colleges. Courses in electronics, physics, chemistry, English, computers, and mathematics provide a good background for a career as an automotive body repairer. Most training programs combine classroom instructions and hands-on practice.

Certification by the National Institute for Automotive Service Excellence (ASE), although voluntary, is the pervasive industry credential for non-entry-level automotive body repairers.

Earnings: Median annual earnings of automotive body and related repairers, including incentive pay, were $37,680 in 2012. The top 10% earned $63,300 a year; the bottom 10% earned less than $22,530 a year. Median annual earnings of automotive glass installers and repairers, including incentive pay, were $32,650 in 2012. The top 10% earned $47,730; the bottom 10% earned less than $20,500 a year.

The majority of body repairers employed by independent repair shops and automotive dealers are paid on an incentive basis. Under this system, body repairers are paid a set amount for various tasks, and earnings depend on both the amount of work assigned and how fast it is completed. Employers frequently guarantee workers a minimum weekly salary.

Key Contacts: For general information about automotive body repairer careers, contact the following sources:

- **Automotive Careers Today:** Website: www.autocareerstoday.org.
- **Automotive Service Association:** 8209 Mid Cities Blvd., North Richland Hills, TX 76182-4712. Website: www.asashop.org.

- **National Automotive Technicians Education Foundation:** 101 Blue Seal Drive, SE, Suite 101, Leesburg, VA 20175. Website: http://natef.org
- **National Glass Association:** 1945 Old Gallows Rd., Suite 750, Vienna, VA 22182. Website: www.glass.org.

For information on how to become a certified automotive body repairer, contact:

- **National Institute for Automotive Service Excellence (ASE):** 101 Blue Seal Drive, SE, Suite 101, Leesburg, VA 20175. Website: www.ase.com/HOME.aspx.

Automotive Service Technicians and Mechanics

- **Annual Earnings:** $36,610 ($17.60 per hour)
- **Education/Training:** High school or equivalent; training
- **Outlook:** As fast as average – 9% growth from 2012 to 2022 (from 701,100 to 761,500 jobs)

Employment Outlook: Employment of automotive service technicians and mechanics is expected to grow as fast as average in the decade ahead. Population growth will boost demand for motor vehicles, which will require regular maintenance and service. Growth of the labor force and in the number of families in which both spouses need vehicles to commute to work will contribute to increased vehicle sales and employment in this industry. Growth of personal income will also contribute to families owning multiple vehicles. Employment growth will continue to be concentrated in automobile dealerships and independent automotive repair shops. Many new jobs also will be created in small retail operations that offer after-warranty repairs, such as oil changes, brake repair, air-conditioner service, and other minor repairs. Most persons who enter the occupation can expect steady work, because changes in general economic conditions and developments in other industries have little effect on the automotive repair business.

Nature of Work: The ability to diagnose the source of a problem quickly and accurately requires good reasoning ability and a thorough knowledge of automobiles. The work of automotive service technicians and mechanics has evolved from mechanical repair to a high-tech job. Today, integrated electronic systems and complex computers run vehicles and measure their performance while on the road. Technicians must have the ability to work with electronic diagnostic equipment and computer-based technical reference materials.

Automotive service technicians and mechanics use their high-tech skills to inspect, maintain, and repair automobiles and light trucks that have gasoline engines. The increasing sophistication of automotive technology, including hybrid vehicles, now requires workers who can use computerized shop equipment and work with electronic components while maintaining their skills with traditional hand tools. Service technicians use a variety of tools in their work – power tools such as pneumatic wrenches to remove bolts quickly; machine tools like lathes and grinding machines to rebuild brakes; welding and flame-cutting equipment to remove and repair exhaust systems; and jacks and hoists to lift cars and engines. They also use common hand tools, such as screwdrivers, pliers, and wrenches, to work on small parts and in hard-to-reach places. Automotive service technicians in large shops have increasingly become specialized.

Automotive service technicians and mechanics held about 701,100 jobs in 2012. Automotive repair and maintenance shops and automotive dealers employed the majority of these workers – 29 percent each.

Working Conditions: About half of automotive service technicians work a standard 40-hour week, but almost 30% work more than 40 hours a week. Many of those working extended hours are self-employed technicians. To satisfy customer service needs, some service shops offer evening and weekend service. Generally, service technicians work indoors in well-ventilated and -lighted repair shops. However, some shops are drafty and noisy. Although technicians fix some problems with simple computerized adjustments, they frequently work with dirty and greasy parts, and in awkward positions. They often lift heavy parts and tools. Minor cuts, burns, and bruises are common, but technicians usually avoid serious accidents when the shop is kept clean and orderly and safety practices are observed.

Education, Training, & Qualifications: Automotive technology is rapidly increasing in sophistication, and most training authorities strongly recommend that persons seeking automotive service technician and mechanic jobs complete a formal training program in high school or in a postsecondary vocational school. However, some service technicians still learn the trade solely by assisting and learning from experienced workers.

Many high schools, community colleges, and vocational and technical schools offer automotive service technician training programs. The traditional postsecondary programs usually provide a thorough career preparation that expands upon the student's high school repair experience. Postsecondary automotive technician training programs vary greatly in format, but normally provide intensive career preparation through a combination of classroom instruction and hands-on practice. Some trade and technical school programs provide concentrated training for six months to a year, depending on how many hours the student attends each week. Community college programs normally spread the training over two years; supplement the automotive training with instruction in English, basic mathematics, computers, and other subjects; and award an associate degree or certificate. Some students earn repair certificates and opt to leave the program to begin their career before graduation. Recently, some programs have added to their curricula training on employability skills such as customer service and stress management. Employers find that these skills help technicians handle the additional responsibilities of dealing with the customers and parts vendors.

Most employers regard the successful completion of a vocational training program in automotive service technology as the best preparation for trainee positions. Experience working on motor vehicles in the armed forces or as a hobby also is valuable. Because of the complexity of new vehicles, a growing number of employers require the completion of high school and additional postsecondary training.

Earnings: Median annual earnings of automotive service technicians and mechanics, including those on commission, were $36,610 ($17.60 per hour) in 2012. The highest 10% earned more than $60,070; the bottom 10% earned less that $20,810. In 2012, the median annual wages for automotive service technicians in the top five industries employing these technicians were as follows:

- Government $47,240
- Automobile dealers $41,360
- Automotive repair and
  maintenance $33,230

- Automotive parts, accessories, and tire stores — $31,250
- Gasoline stations — $31,090

Many experienced technicians employed by automobile dealers and independent repair shops receive a commission related to the labor cost charged to the customer. Employers frequently guarantee commissioned mechanics and technicians a minimum weekly salary. Some technicians are members of labor unions.

Key Contacts: For more details about work opportunities, contact local automobile dealers and repair shops or local offices of the state employment service. The state employment service may also have information about training programs. A list of certified automotive service technician training programs can be obtained from:

- **National Automotive Technicians Education Foundation:** 101 Blue Seal Drive, Suite 101, Leesburg, VA 20175. Website: www.natef.org.

For a directory of accredited private trade and technical schools that offer programs in automotive service technician training, contact:

- **Accrediting Commission of Career Schools and Colleges of Technology:** 2101 Wilson Blvd., Suite 302, Arlington, VA 22201. Website: www.accsct.org.

For a list of public automotive service technician training programs, contact:

- **SkillsUSA:** 14001 SkillsUSA Way, Leesburg, VA 20176-5494. Website: www.skillsusa.org.

Information on automobile manufacturer-sponsored programs in automotive service technology can be obtained from:

- **Automotive Youth Educational Systems (AYES):** 101 Blue Seal Drive, Suite 101, Leesburg, VA 20175.

Information on how to become a certified automotive service technician is available from:

- **National Institute for Automotive Service Excellence (ASE):** 101 Blue Seal Drive SE, Suite 101, Leesburg, VA 20175. Website: www.asecert.org.

For general information about a career as an automotive service technician, contact:

- **National Automobile Dealers Association:** 8400 Westpark Drive, #1, McLean, VA 22102. Website: www.nada.org.

General Maintenance and Repair Workers

- **Annual Earnings:** $35,210 ($16.93 per hour)
- **Education/Training:** High school diploma or equivalent and training
- **Outlook:** As fast as average – 9% growth from 2012 to 2022 (from 1,325,100 to 1,450,300 jobs)

Employment Outlook: General maintenance and repair workers held 1.3 million jobs in 2012. They were employed in almost every industry. About one in five worked in manufacturing industries, almost evenly distributed through all sectors. About 19% worked in manufacturing industries, almost evenly distributed through all sectors, while about 10% worked for federal, state, and local governments. Others worked for wholesale and retail firms and for property management firms that operate office and apartment buildings.

Employment of general maintenance and repair workers is expected to grow about as fast as average (9% during the 2012-2022 decade) for all occupations. However, job openings should be plentiful. Maintenance and repair is a large occupation with significant turnover, and many job openings should result from the need to replace workers who transfer to other occupations or stop working for other reasons.

Employment is related to the number of buildings – for example, office and apartment buildings, stores, schools, hospitals, hotels, and factories – and the amount of equipment needing repair. However, as machinery becomes more advanced and requires less maintenance, the need for general maintenance and repair workers diminishes.

Nature of Work: Most craft workers specialize in one kind of work, such as plumbing or carpentry. General maintenance and repair workers, however, have skills in many different crafts. They repair and maintain machines, mechanical equipment, and buildings, and work on plumbing, electrical, and air-conditioning and heating systems. They build partitions, make plaster or drywall repairs, and fix or paint roofs, windows, doors, floors, woodwork, and other parts of building structures. They also maintain and repair specialized equipment and machinery found in cafeterias, laundries, hospitals, stores, offices, and factories. Typical duties include troubleshooting and fixing faulty electrical switches, repairing air-conditioning motors, and unclogging drains. New buildings sometimes have computer-controlled systems, requiring workers to acquire basic computer skills.

General maintenance and repair workers inspect and diagnose problems and determine the best way to correct them, frequently checking blueprints, repair manuals, and parts catalogs. They replace or fix work or broken parts, where necessary, or make adjustments to correct malfunctioning equipment and machines. General maintenance and repair workers also perform preventive maintenance and ensure that machines continue to run smoothly, building systems operate efficiently, and the physical condition of buildings does not deteriorate. Employees in small establishments, where they are often the only maintenance worker, make all repairs, except for very large or difficult jobs. In larger establishments, their duties may be limited to the general maintenance of everything in a workshop or a particular area.

Working Conditions: General maintenance and repair workers often carry out several different tasks in a single day, at any number of locations. They may work inside a single building or in several different buildings. They may have to stand for long periods, lift heavy objects, and work in uncomfortably hot or cold environments, in awkward and cramped positions, or on ladders. They are subject to electrical shock, burns, falls, cuts, and bruises. Most general maintenance workers put in a 40-hour week. Some work evening, night, or weekend shifts or are on call for emergency repairs. Those employed in small establishments often operate with only limited supervision. Those working in larger establishments frequently are under the direct supervision of an experienced worker.

Education, Training, & Qualifications: Many general maintenance and repair workers learn their skills informally on the job. They start as helpers, watching and learning from skilled maintenance workers. Some learn their skills by working as helpers to other repair or construction workers, including carpenters, electricians, or machinery repairers. Necessary skills also can be learned in high school shop classes and postsecondary trade or vocational schools. It generally takes from one to four years of on-the-job training or school, or a combination of both, to become fully qualified – depending on the skill level.

Graduation from high school is preferred for entry into this occupation. High school courses in mechanical drawing, electricity, woodworking, blueprint reading, science, mathematics, and computers are useful. Mechanical aptitude, the ability to use shop mathematics, and manual dexterity are important. Good health is necessary because the job involves a great deal of walking, standing, reaching, and heavy lifting. Many positions require the ability to work without direct supervision. Many general maintenance and repair workers in large organizations advance to maintenance supervisor or become a craftworker such as an electrician, a heating and air conditioning mechanic, or a plumber. Promotion opportunities are limited within small organizations.

Earnings: Median annual earnings of general maintenance and repair workers were $35,210 per year in 2012. The highest 10% earned more than $57,260 per year; the lowest 10% earned less than $20,920 per year. Some general maintenance and repair workers are members of unions. Many operate their own businesses as handymen.

Key Contacts: Information about job opportunities may be obtained from local employers and local offices of the state employment service. For information related to maintenance managers, contact:

- **Association of Certified Handyman Professionals:** Maitland, FL. Website: www.handymanassociation.org.

- **United Handyman Association:** Website: http://theuha.net.

Heating, Air-Conditioning, and Refrigeration Mechanics and Installers

- **Annual Earnings:** $43,640 ($20.98 per hour)
- **Education/Training:** 1-2 year postsecondary; technical school or apprenticeship training preferred
- **Outlook:** Faster than average – 21% growth from 2012 to 2022 (from 267,000 to 323,500 jobs)

Employment Outlook: Employment of heating, air-conditioning, and refrigeration mechanics and installers is expected to grow faster than average for all occupations through the 2012-2022 period. Job prospects are expected to be good, especially for those with technical school or formal apprenticeship training.

As population and economy grow, so does the demand for new residential, commercial, and industrial climate-control systems. Technicians who specialize in installation work may experience periods of unemployment when the level of new construction activity declines, but maintenance and repair work usually remains stable. In addition, the continuing focus on improving indoor air quality should contribute to the creation of more jobs for heating, air-conditioning, and refrigeration technicians. The growth of businesses that use refrigerated equipment – such as supermarkets and convenience stores – will also add to a growing need for technicians. In addition to openings created by employment growth, thousands of openings will result from the need to replace workers who transfer to other occupations or leave the labor force.

Nature of Work: Heating, air-conditioning, and refrigeration systems consist of many mechanical, electrical, and electronic components, such as motors, compressors, pumps, fans, ducts, pipes, thermostats, and switches. Technicians must be able to maintain, diagnose, and correct problems throughout the entire system. To do this, they adjust system controls to recommended settings and test the performance of the entire system using special tools and test equipment. Although they are trained to do both, technicians often specialize in either installation or maintenance and repair. Some specialize in one type of equipment – for example, oil burners, solar panels, or commercial refrigerators. Technicians may work for large or small contracting companies or directly for a manufacturer or wholesaler. Those working for smaller operations tend to do both installation and servicing, and work with heating, cooling, and refrigeration equipment. Depending on the size of the company, technicians may work solely on residential or commercial projects, although typically they service both. Service contracts – which involve work for particular customers on a regular basis – are becoming more common. Service agreements help to reduce the seasonal fluctuations of this work.

HVACR (heating, ventilation, air-conditioning, and refrigeration) mechanics and installers are adept at using a variety of tools, including hammers, wrenches, metal snips, electric drills, pipe cutters and benders, measurement gauges, and acetylene torches, to work with refrigerant lines and air ducts. They use voltmeters, thermometers, pressure gauges, manometers, and other testing devices to check airflow, refrigerant pressure, electrical circuits, burners, and other components.

Other craftworkers sometimes install or repair cooling and heating systems. For example, on a large air-conditioning installation job, especially where workers are covered by union contracts, duct work might be done by sheet metal workers and duct installers; electrical work by electricians; and installation of piping, condensers and other components by plumbers, pipefitters, and steamfitters.

Working Conditions: Heating, air-conditioning, and refrigeration mechanics and installers work in homes, stores, hospitals, office buildings, and factories – anywhere there is climate-control equipment. They may be assigned to specific job sites at the beginning of each day, or if they are making service calls, they may be dispatched to jobs by radio, telephone, or cell phones to coordinate schedules.

Technicians may work outside in cold or hot weather or in buildings that are uncomfortable because the air-conditioning or heating equipment is broken. Technicians might have to work in awkward or cramped positions and sometimes are required to work in high places. Hazards include electrical shock, burns, muscle strains, and other injuries from handling heavy equipment. Appropriate safety equipment is necessary when handling refrigerants because contact can cause skin damage, frostbite, or blindness. Inhalation of refrigerants when working in confined spaces also is a possible hazard.

The majority of mechanics and installers work at least a 40-hour week. During peak seasons they often work overtime or irregular hours. Maintenance workers, including those who provide maintenance services under contract, often work evening or weekend shifts and are on call. Most employers try to provide a full workweek year-round by scheduling both installation and maintenance work, and many manufacturers and contractors now provide or even require service contracts. In most shops that service both heating and air-conditioning equipment, employment is stable throughout the year.

Education, Training, & Qualifications: Because of the increasing sophistication of heating, air-conditioning, and refrigeration systems, employers prefer to hire those with technical school or apprenticeship training. Many mechanics and installers, however, still learn the trade informally on the job. Those who acquire their skills on the job usually begin by assisting experienced technicians.

Many secondary and postsecondary technical and trade schools, junior and community colleges, and the military offer month-long to 2-year programs in heating, air conditioning, and refrigeration. Students study theory, design, and equipment construction, as well as electronics. They also learn the basics of installation, maintenance, and repair. Courses in shop math, mechanical drawing, applied physics and chemistry, blueprint reading, and computer applications provide a good background for those interested in entering this occupation. Some knowledge of plumbing or electrical work also is helpful. A basic understanding of electronics is becoming more important because of the increasing use of this technology in equipment controls. Because technicians frequently deal directly with the public, they should be courteous and tactful, especially when dealing with an aggravated customer. They should also be in good physical condition because they sometimes have to lift and move heavy equipment.

Earnings: Median annual earnings of heating, air-conditioning, and refrigeration mechanics and installers were $43,640 ($20.98 per hour) in 2012. The top 10% earned $68,990 per year; the bottom 10% earned $27,330 per year. Apprentices usually begin at about 50% of the wage rate paid to experienced workers. In addition to typical benefits such as health insurance and pension plans, some employers pay for work-related training and provide uniforms, company vans, and tools. About 20% of workers are members of a union.

Key Contacts: For more information about opportunities for training and employment in this trade, contact local vocational and technical schools; local heating, air-conditioning, and refrigeration contractors; or the nearest office of the state employment service. For information on career opportunities, training, and technician certification, contact:

- **Air Conditioning Contractors of America (ACCA)**: 2800 Shirlington Road, Suite 300, Arlington, VA 22206. Website: www.acca.org.
- **Air-Conditioning, Heating, and Refrigeration Institute:** 2111 Wilson Blvd., Suite 500, Arlington, VA 22201. Website: www.ahrinet. org.
- **Refrigeration Service Engineers Society**: 1915 Rohlwing Road, Suite A, Rolling Meadows, IL 60008-1397. Website: www.rses.org.

- **Sheet Metal and Air Conditioning Contractors' National Association**: 4201 Lafayette Center Drive, Chantilly, VA 20151-1209. Website: www.smacna.org.
- **North American Technician Excellence**: 2111 Wilson Blvd., Suite 510, Arlington, VA 22203. Website: www.natex.org.

Line Installers and Repairers

- **Annual Earnings:** $58,210 ($27.99 per hour)
- **Education/Training:** High school diploma or equivalent
- **Outlook:** Slow growth but good – 7% increase from 2012 to 2022 (from 249.400 to 267,700 jobs)

Employment Outlook: Overall employment of line installers and repairers is expected to grow more slowly (7%) than average during the 2012-2022 decade, but retirements are expected to create very good job opportunities for new workers, particularly for electrical power-line installers. Growth will reflect an increasing demand for electricity and telecommunications services as the population grows. However, productivity gains – particularly in maintaining these networks – will keep employment growth slow. With the increasing competition in electrical distribution, many companies are contracting out construction of new lines. The introduction of new technologies, especially fiber optic cable, has increased the transmission capacity of telephone and cable television networks. Job growth also will stem from the maintenance and modernization of telecommunications networks. Jobs will be generated as telephone and cable television companies expand and improve networks that provide customers with high-speed access to data, video, and graphics. Line installers and repairers will be needed not only to construct and install networks, but also to maintain the ever-growing systems of wires and cables. Besides those due to employment growth, many job openings will result from the need to replace the large number of older workers reaching retirement age.

Employment of electrical power line installers and repairers is expected to grow about as fast as the average for all occupations. Despite consistently rising demand for electricity, power companies will cut costs by shifting more work to outside contractors and hire fewer installers and repairers.

Most new jobs for electrical power line installers and repairers are expected to arise among contracting firms in the construction industry. Because electrical power companies have reduced hiring and training in past years, opportunities are best for workers who possess experience and training.

Growth of wireless communications will also slow job increases for line installers and repairers in the long run. More households are switching to wireless delivery of their communications, video, and data services.

Nature of Work: Vast networks of wires and cables provide customers with electrical power and communication services. Networks of electrical power lines deliver electricity from generating plants to customers. Communication networks of telephone and cable television lines provide voice, video, and other communication services. These networks are constructed and maintained by line installers and repairers.

Line installers install new lines by constructing utility poles, towers, and underground trenches to carry the wires and cables. They use a variety of construction equipment, including digger derricks, trenchers, cable plows, and borers. When construction is complete, line installers string cable along the poles, towers, tunnels, and trenches. Other installation duties include setting up service for customers and installing network equipment.

In addition to installation, line installers and repairers also are responsible for maintenance of electrical, telecommunications, and cable television lines. Workers periodically travel in trucks, helicopters, and airplanes to visually inspect the wires and cables. Sensitive monitoring equipment can automatically detect malfunctions on the network, such as loss of current flow. When line repairers identify a problem, they travel to the location of the malfunction and repair or replace defective cables or equipment. Bad weather or natural disasters can cause extensive damage to networks. Line installers and repairers must respond quickly to these emergencies to restore critical utility and communication services. This can often involve working outdoors in adverse weather conditions.

Installation and repair work may require splicing, or joining together, separate pieces of cable. Many communication networks now use fiber optic cables instead of conventional wire or metal cables. Splicing fiber optic cable requires specialized equipment that carefully slices, matches, and aligns individual glass fibers. The fibers are joined by either electrical fusion (welding) or a mechanical fixture and gel (glue).

Working Conditions: Line installers and repairers must climb and maintain their balance while working on poles and towers. They lift equipment and work in a variety of positions, such as stooping or kneeling. Their work often requires that they drive utility vehicles, travel long distances, and work outdoors under a variety of weather conditions. Many line installers and repairers work a 40-hour week; however, emergencies may require overtime work. For example, when severe weather damages electrical and communication lines, line installers and repairers may work long and irregular hours to restore service.

Line installers and repairers encounter serious hazards on their jobs and must follow safety procedures to minimize potential danger. They wear safety equipment when entering utility holes and test for the presence of gas before going underground. Electric power line workers have the most hazardous jobs. High-voltage power lines can cause electrocution, and line installers and repairers must consequently use electrically insulated protective devices and tools when working with live cables. Power lines are typically higher than telephone and cable television lines, increasing the risk of severe injury due to falls. To prevent these injuries, line installers and repairers must use fall-protection equipment when working on poles or towers.

Education, Training, & Qualifications: Line installers and repairers are trained on the job, and employers require at least a high school diploma. Employers also prefer technical knowledge of electricity, electronics, and experience obtained through vocational/technical programs, community colleges, or the armed forces. Prospective employees should possess a basic knowledge of algebra and trigonometry, and mechanical ability. Customer service and interpersonal skills also are important. Because the work entails lifting heavy objects (many employers require applicants to be able to lift at least 50 pounds), climbing, and other physical activity, applicants should have stamina, strength, and coordination, and must be unafraid of heights. The ability to distinguish colors is necessary because wires and cables may be color-coded.

Many community or technical colleges offer programs in telecommunications, electronics, and/or electricity. Some schools, working with local companies, offer 1-year certificate programs that emphasize hands-on field work; graduates get preferential treatment in the hiring process at companies participating in the program. More advanced 2-year associate degree programs provide students with a broader knowledge of telecommunications and electrical utilities through courses in electricity, electronics, fiber optics, and microwave transmission.

Electrical line installers and repairers complete formal apprenticeships or employer training programs. These are sometimes administered jointly by the employer and the union representing the workers. Government safety regulations strictly define the training and education requirements for apprentice electrical line installers.

Line installers and repairers in telephone and cable television companies receive several years of on-the-job training. They also may attend training or take courses provided by equipment manufacturers, schools, unions, or industry training organizations.

Entry-level line installers may be hired as ground workers, helpers, or tree trimmers, who clear branches from telephone and power lines. These workers may advance to positions stringing cable and performing service installations. With experience, they may advance to more sophisticated maintenance and repair positions responsible for increasingly larger portions of the network. Promotion to supervisory or training positions also is possible, but more advanced supervisory positions often require a college diploma.

Earnings: Earnings for line installers and repairers are higher than those in most other occupations that do not require postsecondary education. Median annual earnings for electrical power line installers and repairers were $58,210 ($27.99 per hour) in 2012. The top 10% earned $83,590 per year; the bottom 10% earned $36,500 per year.

Most line installers and repairers belong to unions, principally the Communications Workers of America, the International Brotherhood of Electrical Workers, and the Utility Workers Union of America. For these workers, union contracts set wage rates, wage increases, and the time needed to advance from one job level to the next.

Key Contacts: For more details about employment opportunities, contact the telephone, cable television, or electrical power companies in your community. For general information and some ed-

ucational resources on line installer and repairer jobs, contact:

- **American Public Power Association:** 2451 Crystal Drive, Suite 1000, Arlington, VA 22202-4804. Website: www.publicpower.org.
- **International Brotherhood of Electrical Workers:** 900 Seventh Street, NW, Washington, DC 20001. Website: www.ibew.org.
- **Telecommunications Industry Association:** 1320 North Courthouse Road, Suite 200, Arlington, VA 22201. Website: www.tiaonline.org
- **The Fiber Optic Association:** 1119 S. Mission Road, #355, Fallbrook, CA 92028. Website: www.thefoa.org.
- **National Joint Apprenticeship and Training Committee:** 301 Prince George's Blvd., Upper Marlboro, MD 20774. Website: www.njatc.org.

Small Engine Mechanics

- **Annual Earnings:** $32,640 ($15.69 per hour)
- **Education/Training:** High school diploma or equivalent; vocational training program/on-the-job training
- **Outlook:** Good, but slower than average – 6% increase from 2012 to 2022 (from 68,200 to 72,000 jobs)

Employment Outlook: Employment of small engine mechanics is expected to grow slower than average for all occupations during the 2012-2022 decade – 6% growth. Most of the job openings are expected to be replacement jobs, because many experienced small engine mechanics are expected to transfer to other occupations, retire, or stop working for other reasons. Job prospects should be especially favorable for persons who complete formal training programs. Growth of personal disposal income should provide consumers with more discretionary dollars to buy motorboats, lawn and garden power equipment, and motorcycles. While advancements in technology will lengthen the interval between routine maintenance, the need for qualified mechanics to perform this service will increase. Employment of motorcycle mechanics should increase as the popularity of motorcycles rebounds. More people will be entering the 40-and-older age group – those responsible for the largest segment of marine craft purchases. These potential buyers will expand the market for motorboats, maintaining the demand for qualified mechanics.

Nature of Work: Small engine repair mechanics repair and service power equipment ranging from racing motorcycles to chain saws. Like large engines, small engines require periodic service to minimize the chance of breakdowns and keep them operating at peak performance. When a piece of equipment breaks down, mechanics use various techniques to diagnose the source and extent of the problem. The mark of a skilled mechanic is the ability to diagnose mechanical, fuel, and electrical problems and to make repairs in a minimal amount of time. Quick and accurate diagnosis requires problem-solving ability and a thorough knowledge of the equipment's operation.

In larger repair shops, mechanics may use special computerized diagnostic testing equipment as a preliminary tool in analyzing equipment. After pinpointing the problem, the mechanic makes the needed adjustments, repairs, or replacements. Some jobs require minor adjustments. A complete engine overhaul, on the other hand, requires a number of hours to disassemble the engine and replace worn valves, pistons, bearings, and other internal parts.

Working Conditions: Small engine mechanics usually work in repair shops that are well lighted and ventilated, but are sometimes noisy when engines are tested. Motorboat mechanics may work outdoors at docks or marinas, as well as in all weather conditions, when making repairs aboard boats. They may work in cramped or awkward positions to reach a boat's engine.

During the winter months in the northern United States, mechanics may work fewer than 40 hours a week, because the amount of repair and service work declines when lawnmowers, motorboats, and motorcycles are not in use. Many mechanics work only during the busy spring and summer seasons. However, many schedule time-consuming engine overhauls or work on snowmobiles and snow-blowers during winter downtime. Mechanics may work considerably more than 40 hours a week when demand is strong.

Education, Training, & Qualifications: Due to the increasing complexity of motorcycles and motorboats, most employers prefer to hire mechanics who graduate from formal training programs for small engine mechanics. Because the number of these specialized postsecondary programs is lim-

ited, most mechanics learn their skills on the job or while working in related occupations. For trainee jobs, employers hire persons with mechanical aptitude who are knowledgeable about the fundamentals of small two- and four-stroke engines. Many trainees develop an interest in mechanics and acquire some basic skills through working on automobiles, motorcycles, motorboats, or outdoor power equipment as a hobby. Others may be introduced to mechanics through vocational automotive training in high school or one of many postsecondary institutions.

Most employers prefer to hire high school graduates for trainee mechanic positions, but will accept applicants with less education if they possess adequate reading, writing, and arithmetic skills.

Knowledge of basic electronics is essential for small engine mechanics, because electronic components control an engine's performance, the vehicle's instruments displays, and a variety of other functions of motorcycles, motorboats, and outdoor power equipment. The skills used as a small engine mechanic generally transfer to other occupations, such as automobile, diesel, or heavy vehicle and mobile equipment mechanics, Experienced mechanics with leadership ability may advance to shop supervisor or service manager jobs. Mechanics with sales ability sometimes become sales representatives or open their own repair shops.

Earnings: Median annual earnings of small engine mechanics were $32,640 ($15.69 per hour) in 2012. The top 10% earned $51,040 per year; the bottom 10% earned $20,490 per year. Median annual wages for specialty occupations in 2012 were as follows:

- Motorboat mechanics and
  service technicians $35,530
- Motorcycle mechanics $33,140
- Outdoor power equipment
  and other small engine mechanics $30,510

Median annual wages for specialty occupations in May 2012 were as follows:

- $35,530 for motorboat mechanics and service technicians
- $33,140 for motorcycle mechanics
- $30,510 for outdoor power equipment and other small engine mechanics

Most small engine mechanics work full time during regular business hours. However, seasonal work hours often fluctuate. They are busiest during the spring and summer, when demand for work on equipment from lawnmowers to boats is the highest. During the peak seasons, some mechanics work considerable overtime hours. In contrast, some mechanics are not busy during the winter, when demand for small engine work is low. As a result, during these months they work only part time. Many employers schedule major repair work such as an engine rebuild to be performed during the off-season, to try to keep work consistent. Mechanics employed in large shops often receive benefits, such as health insurance, sick leave, and paid vacation time. Conversely, those in small repair shops usually receive few benefits. Some employers pay for work-related training and help mechanics purchase new tools.

Key Contacts: To learn about work opportunities, contact local motorcycle, motorboat, and lawn and garden equipment dealers, boatyards, and marinas. Local offices of the state employment service also may have information about employment and training opportunities. For more information on motorboat mechanics and training programs, visit:

- **Association of Marine Technicians:** Marine Career Training Institute of North America, 513 River Estates Parkway, Canton, GA 30115-3019. Website: www.am-tech.org.

For more information on outdoor power equipment and other small engine mechanics and training programs, visit:

- **Equipment & Engine Training Council:** 3880 Press Wallace Dr., York, SC 29745. Website: www.eetc.org.

6

Science, Math, Engineering, and Technology Jobs

"STEM careers are well worth pursuing. They emphasize good educations, excellent incomes, and learning the latest information and skills to get and keep jobs in these fields."

WHILE THE U.S. ECONOMY is not currently experiencing a major shortage of scientists and engineers, nonetheless, job opportunities for scientists and engineers should be good to excellent throughout the coming decade. Indeed, the popular STEM careers – science, technology, engineering, and math – are in high demand throughout the U.S. economy and are increasingly promoted in today's educational system. The popularity of these jobs emphasizes an important employment trend – the increasing demand for formal education and training, especially at the bachelor's and master's levels. If you get a degree in a STEM field, your career will be relatively secure and you can expect to make a very decent living.

The U.S. economy should continue to move in the direction of more science and technology. The electronics revolution will continue unabated as it spreads through all areas of life. More and more money is expected to be invested by both government and private industry in research and development in order to develop a more internationally competitive economy.

While decreased defense spending in the 1990s did have an adverse effect on some scientific and engineering jobs tied to defense industries, the overall picture for the coming decade looks good, especially for those in the biological sciences, chemistry, mathematics, geology, meteorology, and civil, electronics, and mechanical engineering. As more public money is spent on developing national security and a more adequate infrastructure of roads, bridges, airports, tunnels, rapid transit, and water supply and sewage systems, opportunities for engineering technicians should improve considerably. Assuming manufacturing industries will continue to grow in the decade ahead, opportunities for mechanical engineering technicians should be good. The future especially looks good for electronics and environmental engineering technicians.

Ex-offenders who have the educational training and aptitude to pursue careers in these fields should do very well in the decade ahead. Most are stable, good paying jobs, which require some advanced education, especially two-year associate's degrees readily available through community colleges.

Computer Support Specialists

- **Annual Earnings:** $48,900 ($23.51 per hour)
- **Education/Training:** Associate's degree to bachelor's degree
- **Outlook:** Faster than average – 17% growth from 2012 to 2022 (from 722,400 to 845,400 jobs)

Employment Outlook: Employment of computer support specialists is projected to grow 17% from 2012 to 2022, faster than the average for all occupations. More support services will be needed as organizations upgrade their computer equipment and software. Computer support staff will be needed to respond to the installation and repair requirements of increasingly complex computer equipment and software. However, a rise in cloud computing could increase the productivity of computer support specialists, slowing their growth at many firms. Growth will be highest at firms that provide cloud-computing technology. Employment of support specialists in computer systems design and related firms is projected to grow 49% from 2012 to 2022. Some lower level tech support jobs, commonly found in call centers, may be sent to countries that have lower wage rates. However, a recent trend to move jobs to lower cost regions of the U.S. may offset some loss of jobs to other countries.

Nature of Work: Computer support specialists provide help and advice to people and organizations using computer software or equipment. Some, called computer network support specialists, support information technology (IT) employees within their organization. Others, called computer user support specialists, assist non-IT users who are having computer problems.

Computer network support specialists typically do the following:

- Test and evaluate existing network systems
- Perform regular maintenance to ensure that networks operate correctly
- Troubleshoot local area networks (LANs), wide area networks (WANs), and Internet systems

Also called technical support specialists, they usually work in their organizations IT department. They help IT staff analyze, troubleshoot, and evaluate computer network problems. They play an important role in the daily upkeep of their organization's networks by finding solutions to problems as they occur. Technical support spe-

cialists may provide assistance to the organization's computer users through phone, email, or in-person visits. They often work under network and computer systems administrators, who handle more complex tasks.

Computer user support specialists typically do the following:

- Pay attention to customers when they describe their computer problems
- Ask customers questions to properly diagnose the problem
- Walk customers through the recommended problem-solving steps
- Set up or repair computer equipment and related devices
- Train users to work with new computer hardware or software, such as printers, word-processing software, and email
- Assist users in installing software
- Provide others in the organization with information about what gives customers the most trouble and about other concerns customers have

Computer user support specialists, also called help-desk technicians, usually provide technical help to non-IT computer users. They respond to phone and email requests for help. Sometimes they make site visits so that they can solve a problem in person.

Work Environment: Computer support specialists held about 722,400 jobs in 2012. They work in many different industries, including information technology (IT), education, finance, health care, and telecommunication. Many help-desk technicians work for outside support service firms on a contract basis and provide help to a range of businesses and consumers.

The industries that employed the most computer network support specialists in 2012 were as follows:

- Computer systems design and related services   20%
- Telecommunications   10%
- Finance and insurance   8%
- Education services; state, local, and private   8%

The industries that employed the most computer user support specialists in 2012 were as follows:

- Computer systems design and related services   19%
- Educational services; state, local, and private   14%

- Information   11%
- Wholesale trade   8%

Faster computer networks are making it possible for some support specialists, particularly help-desk technicians, to work from a home office. However, a few specialized help-desk technicians may have to travel to a client's location to solve a problem.

Education, Training, & Qualifications: Computer user support specialist jobs do not necessarily require a postsecondary degree. Applicants who have taken some computer-related classes are often qualified. For computer network support specialists, many employers accept applicants with an associate's degree, although some prefer applicants to have a bachelor's degree. Large software companies that provide support to business users who buy their products or services often require a bachelor's degree. More technical positions are likely to require a degree in a field such as computer science, engineering, or information science, but for others, the applicant's field of study is less important. Computer support specialists are expected to continue their education throughout their careers

Earnings: The median annual wage for computer network support specialists was $59,090 in 2012. The top 10% earned $96,850 a year; the bottom 10% less than $34,930. In 2012, the median annual wages for computer network support specialists in the top four industries in which these specialists worked were as follows:

- Telecommunications $64,780
- Finance and insurance $62,750
- Computer systems design and
  related services $60,050
- Educational services; state, local,
  and private $51,920

The median annual wage for computer user support specialists was $46,420 in 2012. The top 10% earned $77,430; the bottom 10% earned less than $27,620. In 2012, median annual wages for computer user support specialists in the top four industries in which these specialists worked were as follows:

- Wholesale trade $49,150
- Information $47,950
- Computer systems design and
  related services $46,690
- Educational services; state, local,
  and private $43,620

Most computer support specialists have full-time work schedules; however, many do not work typical 9-to-5 jobs. Because computer support is important for businesses, support specialists must be available 24 hours a day. As a result, many support specialists must work nights or weekends.

Key Contacts: For more information about computer support specialists, visit:

- **Technology Services Industry Association:** 17065 Camino San Bernardo, Suite 200, San Diego, CA 92127. Website: www.tsia.com.
- **Help Desk Institute (HDI):** 121 South Tejon, Suite 1100, Colorado Springs, CO 80903. Website: www.thinkhdi.com.
- **Association of Support Professionals:** 38954 Proctor Blvd., #398, Sandy, OR 97055. Website: http://asponline.com.

Cost Estimators

- **Annual Earnings:** $58,860 ($28.30 per hour)
- **Education/Training:** Bachelor's degree
- **Outlook:** Much faster than average – 26% increase from 2012 to 2022 (from 202,200 to 255,200 jobs)

Employment Outlook: Employment of cost estimators is projected to grow 26% from 2012 to 2022, much faster than the average for all occupations. Demand for cost estimators is expected to be strong because companies need accurate cost projections to ensure that their products and services are profitable. For this reason, cost estimators are essential to companies. Growth in the construction industry will create the majority of new jobs. In particular, the construction and repair of infrastructure, including roads, bridges, airports, and subway systems, will drive demand for qualified estimators.

Nature of Work: Cost estimators collect and analyze data in order to estimate the time, money, materials, and labor required to manufacture a product, construct a building, or provide a service. They generally specialize in a particular industry or type of product. They typically do the following:

- Identify and quantify cost factors, such as production time, materials, and labor expenses
- Read blueprints and technical documents in order to prepare estimates
- Collaborate with engineers, architects, clients, and contractors on estimates

- Use computer software to calculate estimates
- Recommend ways to make a product more cost effective or profitable
- Develop project plans for the duration of the project
- Accurately predicting the cost, size, and duration of future construction and manufacturing projects is vital to the survival of businesses. Cost estimators' calculations give managers or investors this information.

Cost estimators use computer software, including databases, to simulate building construction. Cost estimators often use a computer database with information on the costs of other, similar projects.

Work Environment: Cost estimators held about 202,200 jobs in 2012. The industries that employed the most cost estimators in 2012 were as follows:

- Construction of buildings   16%
- Building equipment contractors   16%
- Manufacturing   14%
- Foundation, structure, and building exterior contractors   8%

Although cost estimators work mostly in offices, they often visit construction sites and factory floors. Depending on the industry, these visits may involve frequent travel. Cost estimators need to meet deadlines in order to prepare bids. Inaccurate estimates can cause a firm to lose a bid or to lose money on a job that otherwise could have been profitable.

Education, Training, & Qualifications: Increasingly, employers prefer candidates who have a bachelor's degree. A strong background in mathematics is essential. Construction cost estimators generally need a bachelor's degree in an industry-related field, such as construction management, building science, or engineering. Those interested in estimating manufacturing costs typically need a bachelor's degree in engineering, physical sciences, mathematics, or statistics. Some employers accept candidates with backgrounds in business-related disciplines, such as accounting, finance, and business.

Earnings: The median annual wage for cost estimators was $58,860 in 2012. The top 10% earned $96,670 a year; the bottom 10% earned less than $34,520. Cost estimators usually work full time. Some, however, are required to work overtime in order to meet deadlines.

Key Contacts: For more information about cost estimators, visit

- **Association for the Advancement of Cost Engineering International:** 1265 Suncrest Towne Centre Drive, Morgantown, WV 26505-1876. Website: www.aacei.org.
- **American Society of Professional Estimators:** 2525 Perimeter Place Drive, Suite 103 Nashville, TN 37214. Website: www.aspenational.org.
- **International Cost Estimating and Analysis Association:** 8221 Old Courthouse Road, Suite 106, Vienna, VA 22182. Website: www.iceaaonline.org.

Database Administrators

- **Annual Earnings:** $77,080 ($37.06 per hour)
- **Education/Training:** Bachelor's degree
- **Outlook:** Faster than average – 15% growth from 2012 to 2022 (from 118,700 to 136,600 jobs)

Employment Outlook: Employment of database administrators (DBAs) is projected to grow 15% from 2012 to 2022, faster than the average for all occupations. Growth in this occupation will be driven by the increased data needs of companies in all sectors of the economy. Database administrators will be needed to organize and present data in a way that makes it easy for analysts and other stakeholders to understand. However, employment growth may be slowed by new software tools that increase the productivity of DBAs. The increasing popularity of database-as-a-service, which allows database administration to be done by a third party over the Internet, could increase the employment of DBAs at cloud computing firms in the computer systems design and related services industry. Employment of DBAs is projected to grow 48% in this industry from 2012 to 2022.

Nature of Work: Database administrators use specialized software to store and organize data, such as financial information and customer shipping records. They make sure that data are available to users and are secure from unauthorized access. Database administrators typically do the following:

- Identify user needs to create and administer databases
- Ensure that the database operates efficiently and without error

- Make and test modifications to the database structure when needed
- Maintain the database and update permissions
- Merge old databases into new ones
- Backup and restore data to prevent data loss
- Ensure that organizational data is secure

Database administrators make sure that data analysts can easily use the database to find the information they need and that the system performs as it should. DBAs sometimes work with an organization's management to understand the company's data needs and to plan the goals of the database. Database administrators are responsible for backing up systems to prevent data loss in case of a power outage or other disaster. They also ensure the integrity of the database, guaranteeing that the data stored in it come from reliable sources.

Work Environment: Database administrators held about 118,700 jobs in 2012. They were employed in many types of industries. The largest number work for computer systems design and related services firms, such as Internet service providers and data-processing firms. Other DBAs are employed by firms with large databases, such as insurance companies and banks, both of which keep track of vast amounts of personal and financial data for their clients. Some DBAs administer databases for retail companies that keep track of their buyers' credit card and shipping information; others work for health care firms and manage patients' medical records.

The industries that employed the most database administrators in 2012 were as follows:

- Computer systems design and related services   16%
- Finance and insurance   13%
- Information   11%
- Educational services; state, local, and private   10%
- Management of companies and enterprises   8%

Education, Training, & Qualifications: Most database administrators have a bachelor's degree in management information systems (MIS) or a computer-related field. Firms with large databases may prefer applicants who have a master's degree focusing on data or database management, typically either in computer science, information systems, or information technology. Database administrators need an understanding of database languages, the most common of which is Structured Query Language, commonly called SQL. Most database systems use some variation of SQL, and a DBA will need to become familiar with whichever programming language the firm uses.

Earnings: The median annual wage for database administrators was $77,080 in 2012. The top 10% earned $118,720 a year; the bottom 10% earned less than $42,930. In 2012, the median annual wages for database administrators the top five industries in which these administrators worked were as follows:

- Finance and insurance $85,880
- Computer systems design and related services $84,550
- Management of companies and enterprises $82,290
- Information $81,800
- Educational services; state, local, and private $63,620

Almost all database administrators work full time. About a quarter worked more than 40 hours per week in 2012.

Key Contacts: For more information about database administrators, visit:

- **Association for Computing Machinery:** 2 Penn Plaza, Suite 701, New York, NY 10121. Website: www.acm.org.
- **IEEE:** 2001 L Street, NW, Suite 700, Washington, DC 20036-4928. Website: www.com puter.org.
- **Computing Research Association:** 1828 L Street, NW, Suite 800, Washington, DC 20036. Website: www.cra.org.

Drafters

- **Annual Earnings:** $49,630 ($23.86 per hour)
- **Education/Training:** Technical training to associate degree
- **Outlook:** Little or no change in the decade ahead – 1% increase from 2012 to 2022 (from 199,800 to 202,000 jobs

Employment Outlook: Employment of drafters is expected to grow slower than average for occupations in the coming decade. Industrial growth and increasingly complex design problems associated with new products and manufacturing processes will increase the demand for drafting services. Drafters also are beginning to break out of the traditional drafting role and increasingly do work traditionally performed by engineers and architects, thus also increasing demand for drafters. However, the greater use of CADD equipment by drafters, as well as by architects and engineers, should limit demand for less skilled drafters, resulting in slower-than-average overall employment growth.

Nature of Work: Drafters prepare technical drawings and plans used by production and construction workers to build everything from manufactured products, such as toys, toasters, industrial machinery, and spacecraft, to structures, such as houses, office buildings, and oil and gas pipelines. Their drawings provide visual guidelines, show the technical details of the products and structures, and specify dimensions, materials, and procedures. Drafters fill in technical details, using drawings, rough sketches, specifications, codes, and calculations previously made by engineers, surveyors, architects, or scientists.

Working Conditions: Most drafters work a standard 40-hour week; only a small number work part time. Drafters usually work in comfortable offices furnished to accommodate their tasks. Because they spend long periods in front of computer terminals doing detailed work, drafters may be susceptible to eyestrain, back discomfort, and hand and wrist problems.

Education, Training, & Qualifications: Employers prefer applicants who have completed postsecondary school training in drafting, which is offered by technical institutes, community colleges, and some four-year colleges and universities. Employers are most interested in applicants with well-developed drafting and mechanical-drawing skills; knowledge of drafting standards, mathematics, science, and engineering technology; and a solid background in computer-aided design and drafting (CADD) techniques.

Earnings: Earnings for drafters vary by specialty and level of responsibility. Median annual earnings of architectural and civil drafters were $49,630 ($23.86 per hour) in 2012. The top 10% earned $77,770 per year; the bottom 10% earned $32,190 per year.

Key Contacts: Information on training and certification for drafting and related fields is available from:

- **Accrediting Commission of Career Schools and Colleges:** 2101 Wilson Blvd., Suite 302, Arlington, VA 22201. Website: www.accsc.org.

- **American Design Drafting Association:** 105 E. Main Street, Newbern, TN 38059. Website: www.adda.org.

Electrical and Electronics Engineering Technicians

- **Annual Earnings:** $57,850 ($27.81 per hour)
- **Education/Training:** Associate degree
- **Outlook:** Little or no change – 1% growth from 2012 to 2022 (146,000 jobs)

Employment Outlook: Overall employment of electrical and electronics engineering technicians is expected to remain stable in the coming decade. Competitive pressures will force companies to improve and update manufacturing facilities and product designs, resulting in more jobs for engineering technicians. However, the growing use of advanced technologies, such as computer simulation and computer-aided design and drafting (CADD) will continue to increase productivity and limit job growth.

Nature of Work: Engineering technicians use the principles and theories of science, engineering, and mathematics to solve technical problems in research and development, manufacturing, sales, construction, inspection, and maintenance. Their work is more limited in scope and more practically oriented than that of scientists and engineers. Many engineering technicians assist engineers and scientists, especially in research and development. Others work in quality control – inspecting products and processes, conducting tests, or collecting data. In manufacturing, they may assist in product design, development, or production. Most engineering technicians specialize in certain areas, learning skills and working in the same disciplines as engineers. Occupational titles, therefore, tend to reflect those of engineers. Electrical and electronics engineering technicians held 146,000 jobs in 2012.

Working Conditions: Most engineering technicians work at least 40 hours a week in laboratories, offices, or manufacturing or industrial plants, or on construction sites. Some may be exposed to hazards from equipment, chemicals, or toxic materials.

Education, Training, & Qualifications: Although it may be possible to qualify for certain engineering technician jobs without formal training, most employers prefer to hire someone with a least a two-year associate degree in engineering technology. Training is available at technical institutes, community colleges, extension divisions of colleges and universities, and public and private vocational-technical schools, and in the armed forces.

Earnings: Median annual earnings of engineering technicians averaged $57,850 ($27.81 per hour). The top 10% earned $83,120 a year; the bottom 10% earned $34,560. Average annual wages vary in the top five industries:

- Federal government, excluding
  postal service $75,690
- Postal service $62,180
- Architectural, engineering,
  and related services $56,610
- Navigational, measuring,
  electromedical, and control
  instruments manufacturing $52,130
- Semiconductor and other
  electronic component
  manufacturing $52,050

Key Contacts: For more information on training and certification of engineering technicians, contact:

- **American Society for Engineering Education:** 1818 N Street, NW, Suite 600, Washington, DC 20036-2479. Website: www.asee.org
- **National Institute for Certification in Engineering Technologies (NICET):** 1420 King Street, Alexandria, VA 22314-2794. Website: www.nicet.org.
- **Accreditation Board for Engineering and Technology, Inc.:** 415 North Charles Street, Baltimore, MD 21201. Website: www.abet.org.

Electrical and Electronics Installers and Repairers

- **Annual Earnings:** $51,220 ($24.63 per hour)
- **Education/Training:** Postsecondary non-degree award; training
- **Outlook:** Little or no change – 1% increase from 2012 to 2022 (from 144,700 to 145,600 jobs)

Employment Outlook: Overall employment of electrical and electronics installers and repairers is expected to remain relatively unchanged compared to all occupations in the decade ahead, but it varies by occupational specialty. Average employment growth is projected for electrical and electronics installers and repairers of commercial and industrial equipment. Employment of motor vehicle electronic equipment installers and repairers also is expected to grow as fast as the average. Employment of electric motor, power tool, and related repairers is expected to grow more slowly than average. Employment of electrical and electronic installers and repairers of transportation equipment is expected to grow more slowly than the average, due to declining industry employment in rail transportation, aerospace product and parts manufacturing, and ship- and boat-building. Employment of electrical and electronics installers and repairers of powerhouse, substation, and relay is expected to decline slightly.

Nature of Work: Electrical and electronics installers and repairers install, maintain, and repair complex pieces of electronic equipment used in business, government, and other organizations. The nature of their work varies depending on their occupational specialty. In 2012 electrical and electronics installers and repairers held about 144,700 jobs in their occupational specialties:

	2012	2022	Growth
■ Electrical and electronics repairers, commercial and industrial equipment	69,000	71,300	+3
■ Electric motor, power tool, and related repairers	20,700	19,900	-4
■ Electrical and electronics repairers, powerhouse, substation, and relay	24,500	24,500	0
■ Electrical and electronics installers and repairers, motor vehicles	14,600	13,700	-6
■ Electrical and electronics installers and repairers, transportation equipment	15,900	16,200	2

Many repairers worked for utilities, building equipment contractors, machinery and equipment repair shops, wholesalers, the federal government, retailers of automotive parts and accessories, rail transportation companies, and manufacturers of electrical, electronic, and transportation equipment.

Working Conditions: Many electrical and electronics installers and repairers work on factory floors, where they are subject to noise, dirt, vibration, and heat. Bench technicians work primarily in repair shops, where the surroundings are relatively quiet, comfortable, and well lighted. Installers and repairers may have to do heavy lifting and work in a variety of positions.

Education, Training, & Qualifications: Knowledge of electrical equipment and electronics is necessary for employment. Many applicants gain this knowledge through programs lasting one to two years at vocational schools or community colleges, although some less skilled repairers may have only a high school diploma. Entry-level repairers may work closely with more experienced technicians who provide technical guidance. Various organizations provide certification, including ACES International, the Consumer Electronics Association, the Electronics Technicians Association International, and the International Society of Certified Electronics Technicians. Repairers may specialize – in industrial electronics, for example. To receive certification, repairers must pass qualifying exams corresponding to their level of training and experience.

Earnings: Median annual earnings of electrical and electronics repairers, commercial and industrial equipment were $51,220 in 2012 ($24.63 per hour). The top 10% earned $75,740 per year; the bottom 10% earned $28,340. Average annual earnings varied by specialty:

- Electrical and electronics repairers, powerhouse, substation, and relay $68,810
- Electrical and electronics repairers, commercial and industrial equipment $52,650
- Electrical and electronics installers and repairers, transportation equipment $51,240
- Electric motor, power tool, and related repairers $36,240
- Electrical and electronics installers and repairers, motor vehicles $31,340

Key Contacts: For information on careers and certification, contact the following organizations:
- **Electronics Technicians Association International:** 5 Depot Street, Greencastle, IN 46135. Website: www.eta-i.org.
- **International Society of Certified Electronics Technicians:** 3000-A Landers Street, Fort Worth, TX 76107-5642. Website: www.iscet.org.

Information Security Analysts

- **Annual Earnings:** $86,170 ($41.43 per hour)
- **Education/Training:** Bachelor's degree
- **Outlook:** Much faster than average – 37% increase from 2012 to 2022 (from 75,100 to 102,500 jobs)

Employment Outlook: This is a really hot field given the explosive growth of security issues in U.S. organizations relating to computer networks and systems, especially the increase in cyberattacks. Employment of information security analysts is projected to grow 37% from 2012 to 2022, much faster than the average for all occupations. Demand for information security analysts is expected to be very high as these analysts will be needed to come up with innovative solutions to prevent hackers from stealing critical information or creating havoc on computer networks.

Nature of Work: Information security analysts typically do the following:
- Monitor their organizations networks for security breaches and investigate a violation when one occurs
- Install and use software, such as firewalls and data encryption programs, to protect sensitive information
- Prepare reports that document security breaches and the extent of the damage caused by the breaches
- Conduct penetration testing, which is when analysts simulate attacks to look for vulnerabilities in their systems before they can be exploited
- Develop security standards and best practices for their organization
- Help computer users when they need to install or learn about new security products and procedures

Information security analysts must continually adapt to stay a step ahead of cyberattackers. Because information security is important, these workers usually report directly to upper management. Many information security analysts work with an organization's computer and information systems manager or chief technology officer (CTO) to design security or disaster recovery systems.

Working Conditions: Information security analysts held about 75,100 jobs in 2012. Most analysts work for computer companies, consulting firms, and business and financial companies. The industries that employed the most information security analysts in 2012 were as follows:

- Computer systems design and related services 27%
- Finance and insurance 19%
- Information 10%
- Management of companies and enterprises 8%

Education, Training, & Qualifications: Information security analysts usually need at least a bachelor's degree in computer science, programming, or a related field. As information security continues to develop as a career field, many schools are responding with information security programs for prospective job seekers. These programs may become a common path for entry into the occupation. Currently, a well-rounded computer education is preferred. Employers of information security analysts sometimes prefer applicants who have a Master's of Business Administration (MBA) in information systems.

Earnings: The median annual wage for information security analysts was $86,170 in 2012. The top 10% earned more than $135,600; the lowest 10% earned less than $49,960. In 2012, the median annual wages for information security analysts in the top four industries in which these analysts worked were as follows:

- Finance and insurance $92,080
- Information $91,400
- Computer systems design and related services $88,270
- Management of companies and enterprises $81,130

Most information security analysts work full time. Information security analysts sometimes have to be on call outside of normal business hours in case of an emergency at their organization.

Very few information security analysts are self-employed.

Key Contacts: For more information about computer careers, visit

- **Association for Computing Machinery:** 2 Penn Plaza, Suite 701, New York, NY 10121. Website: www.acm.org.
- **IEEE:** 2001 L Street, NW, Suite 700, Washington, DC 20036-4928. Website: www.com puter.org.
- **Computing Research Association:** 1828 L Street, NW, Suite 800, Washington, DC 20036. Website: www.cra.org.

For information about opportunities for women pursuing information technology careers, visit

- **National Center for Women & Information Technology:** 231 ATLAS Building, University of Colorado, 1125 18th Street, Boulder, CO 80309. Website: www.ncwit.org.

Operations Research Analysts

- **Annual Earnings:** $72,100 ($34.66 per hour)
- Education/Training: Bachelor's degree
- Outlook: Much faster than average – 27% growth from 2012 to 2022 (from 73,200 to 92,700 jobs)

Employment Outlook: Employment of operations research analysts is projected to grow 27% from 2012 to 2022, much faster than the average for all occupations. As technology advances and companies seek efficiency and cost savings, demand for operations research analysis should continue to grow. Operations research analysts will continue to be needed to provide support for the armed forces and to assist in the development and implementation of policies and programs in other areas of government. Technological advances have made it faster and easier for organizations to get data. In addition, improvements in analytical software have made operations research more affordable and more applicable to a wider range of areas. More companies are expected to use operations research analysts to help them turn data into valuable information that managers can use in order to make better decisions in all aspects of their business. For example, operations research analysts will be needed to help businesses improve their manufacturing operations and logistics.

Nature of Work: Operations research analysts typically do the following:

- Identify and define business problems, such as those in production, logistics, or sales
- Collect and organize information from a variety of sources, such as computer databases
- Gather input from workers involved in all aspects of the problem or from others who have specialized knowledge, so that they can help solve the problem
- Examine information to figure out what is relevant to the problem and what methods should be used to analyze it
- Use statistical analysis or simulations to analyze information and develop practical solutions to business problems
- Advise managers and other decision makers on the impacts of various courses of action to take in order to address a problem
- Write memos, reports, and other documents, outlining their findings and recommendations for managers, executives, and other officials

Operations research analysts are involved in all aspects of an organization. They help managers decide how to allocate resources, develop production schedules, manage the supply chain, and set prices. For example, they may help decide how to organize products in supermarkets or help companies figure out the most effective way to ship and distribute products. Analysts must first identify and understand the problem to be solved or the processes to be improved. Analysts typically collect relevant data from the field and interview clients or managers involved in the business processes. Analysts show the implications of pursuing different actions and may assist in achieving a consensus on how to proceed. Operations research analysts use sophisticated computer software, such as databases and statistical programs, and modeling packages, to analyze and solve problems.

Working Conditions: Operations research analysts held about 73,200 jobs in 2012. The industries that employed the most operations research analysts in 2012 were as follows:

- Finance and insurance   25%
- Computer systems design
  and related services   10%
- Manufacturing   8%
- State and local government,
  excluding education and hospitals   8%
- Management of companies
  and enterprises   8%

Most operations research analysts in the federal government work for the Department of Defense, which also employs a large number of analysts through private consulting firms. Operations research analysts spend most of their time in offices. Many also spend some time in the field, gathering information and analyzing processes through direct observation. Analysts may travel to work with clients and company executives and to attend conferences. Because problems are complex and often require expertise from many disciplines, most analysts work on teams. Once a manager reaches a final decision, these teams may work with others in the organization to ensure that the plan is successful. Because they work on projects that are of immediate interest to top managers, operations research analysts often are under pressure to meet deadlines.

Education, Training, & Qualifications: Although some employers prefer to hire applicants with a master's degree, many entry-level positions are available for those with a bachelor's degree. Although some schools offer bachelor's and advanced degree programs in operations research, many analysts typically have degrees in other technical or quantitative fields, such as engineering, computer science, mathematics, or physics. Because operations research is based on quantitative analysis, students need extensive course work in mathematics. Courses include statistics, calculus, and linear algebra. Course work in computer science is important because analysts rely on advanced statistical and database software to analyze and model data. Courses in other areas, such as engineering, economics, and political science, are useful because operations research is a multidisciplinary field with a wide variety of applications. Continuing education is important for operations research analysts. Keeping up with advances in technology, software tools, and improved analytical methods is vital.

Earnings: The median annual wage for operations research analysts was $72,100 in 2012. The top 10% earned more than $129,490 a year; the bottom 10% earned less than $40,550. In 2012, the median annual wages for operations research analysts in the top five industries in which these analysts worked were as follows:

- Manufacturing $79,630
- Computer systems design
  and related services $74,490
- Management of companies
  and enterprises $72,630
- Finance and insurance $67,480
- State and local government,
  excluding education and hospitals $56,670

Almost all operations research analysts work full time. About 1 in 5 worked more than 40 hours per week in 2012.

Key Contacts: For more information about operations research analysts, visit:

- **Institute for Operations Research and the Management Sciences:** 5521 Research Park Drive, Suite 200, Catonsville, MD 21228. Website: www.informs.org.
- **Military Operations Research Society:** 2111 Wilson Blvd., Suite 700, Arlington, VA 22201. Website: www.mors.org.

7

Production Occupations

"Many production jobs in manufacturing are in decline. While popular with ex-offenders, these jobs might be best viewed as transitional work experiences for those who want to develop a stable and rewarding career."

THIS CHAPTER OUTLINES three production jobs for people re-entering the workforce. Many ex-offenders find good job opportunities in what are often high turnover occupations, which constantly demand more workers. Most of these jobs require some postsecondary education and training. Some are best entered through on-the-job training and apprenticeships. Most are skilled occupations that pay modest wages.

Since most of our production jobs are plentiful, you should have little difficulty finding and changing jobs in these fields. Similar to the jobs outlined in Chapter 5, the jobs profiled here are relatively safe from offshoring. Most of these jobs also are becoming increasingly technical and automated. Technology will continue to transform these workplaces, and workers will be required to learn new skills through on-the-job training programs.

At the same time, many production jobs in manufacturing are either declining or experiencing limited growth and wages are relatively low or flat. For example, bakers, butchers, meat cutters, meat packers, laundry and dry-cleaning workers, and printing workers are not well paid, and working conditions in these occupations are often difficult. For ex-offenders, many of these jobs offer transitional work experiences.

Machinists and Tool and Die Makers

- **Annual Earnings:** $40,910 ($19.67 per hour)
- **Education/Training:** High school diploma or equivalent; apprenticeship
- **Outlook:** Slower than average – 7% growth from 2012 to 2022 (from 476,200 to 509,900 jobs)

Employment Outlook: Overall employment of machinists and tool and die makers is projected to grow 7% from 2012 to 2022, slower than the average for all occupations. Employment growth will vary by specialty. Employment of machinists is projected to grow 9% from 2012 to 2022, about as fast as the average for all occupations. Despite improvements in technologies, such as computer

numerically controlled (CNC) machine tools, autoloaders, high-speed machining, and lights-out manufacturing, machinists will still be required to set up, monitor, and maintain these automated systems. In addition, employers will continue to need machinists, who have a wide range of skills and are capable of performing modern production techniques, in a machine shop. Manufacturers will continue to rely heavily on skilled machinists, as they invest in new equipment, modify production techniques, and implement product design changes more rapidly. Employment of tool and die makers is projected to show little or no change from 2012 to 2022. Although foreign competition in manufacturing and advances in automation, including CNC machine tools and computer-aided design, should improve worker productivity, tool and die makers will still be needed to program CNC machines. There also will be a need for tool and die makers to manufacture small production orders and special-order parts.

Nature of Work: Machinists typically do the following:

- Work from blueprints, sketches or computer-aided design (CAD), and computer-aided-manufacturing (CAM) files
- Set up, operate, and disassemble manual, automatic, and computer-numeric controlled (CNC) machine tools
- Align, secure, and adjust cutting tools and workpieces
- Monitor the feed and speed of machines
- Turn, mill, drill, shape, and grind machine parts to specifications
- Measure, examine, and test completed products for defects
- Smooth the surfaces of parts or products
- Present finished workpieces to customers and make modifications if needed

Tool and die makers typically do the following:

- Read blueprints, sketches, specifications, or CAD and CAM files for making tools and dies
- Compute and verify dimensions, sizes, shapes, and tolerances of workpieces
- Set up, operate, and disassemble conventional, manual, and computer-numeric controlled (CNC) machine tools
- File, grind, and adjust parts so that they fit together properly
- Test completed tools and dies to ensure that they meet specifications
- Smooth and polish the surfaces of tools and dies

Machinists use machine tools, such as lathes, milling machines, and grinders, to produce precision metal parts. These tools are either manually controlled or computer numerically controlled (CNC). CNC machines control the cutting tool speed and do all necessary cuts to create a part. The machinist determines the cutting path, the speed of the cut, and the feed rate by programming instructions into the CNC machine. Many machinists must be able to use both manual and computer-controlled machinery in their jobs.

Work Environment: Machinists and tool and die makers held about 476,200 jobs in 2012. The vast majority worked in manufacturing. The industries that employed the most machinists and tool and die makers in 2012 were as follows:

- Machinery manufacturing   20%
- Machine shops   19%
- Transportation equipment manufacturing   15%

Machinists and tool and die makers work in machine shops, tool rooms, and factories, where work areas are usually well ventilated. Most machinists and tool and die makers work full time during regular business hours. However, overtime is somewhat common. Because many manufacturers run machinery for long hours, evening and weekend work is also common.

Education, Training, & Qualifications: Machinists and tool and die makers must have a high school diploma or equivalent. In high school, students should take math courses, especially trigonometry and geometry. They also should take courses in blueprint reading, metalworking, and drafting, if available. Some advanced positions, such as those in the aircraft manufacturing industry, require the use of advanced applied calculus and physics. The increasing use of computer-controlled machinery requires machinists and tool and die makers to have basic computer skills before entering a training program. Some community colleges and technical schools have 2-year programs that train students to become machinists. These programs usually teach design and blueprint reading, how to use a variety of welding and cutting tools, and the programming and function of computer numerically controlled (CNC) machines. Apprenticeship programs, typically sponsored by a manufacturer, are an excellent way to become a machinist or tool and die maker, but they are often hard to get into. Apprentices usually must have a high school diploma or equivalent, and most have taken algebra and trigonometry classes. A growing number of machinists and tool and die makers receive their technical training from community and technical colleges. In this setting, employees learn while employed by a manufacturer that supports the employee's training goals and provides the needed on-the-job training.

Key Contacts: For more information about machinists and tool and die makers, including training and certification, visit:

- **Fabricators & Manufacturers Association, International (FMA):** 833 Featherstone Road, Rockford, IL 61107. Website: www. fmanet.org.
- **National Institute for Metalworking Skills (NIMS):** 10565 Fairfax Boulevard, Suite 203, Fairfax, VA 22030. Website: www.nims-skills.org.

For general information about manufacturing careers, including machinery and tool and die makers, visit:

- **American Mold Builders Association (AMBA):** 7321 Shadeland Station Way, #285, Indianapolis, IN 46256. Website: www.amba.org.
- **Association for Manufacturing Technology (AMT):** 7901 Westpark Drive, McLean, Virginia 22102-4206. Website: www.amtonline.org.
- **National Tooling and Machining Association (NTMA):** 1357 Rockside Road, Cleveland, OH 44134. Website: www.ntma.org.
- **Precision Machined Products Association (PMPA):** 6880 West Snowville Road, Suite 200, Brecksville, OH 44141. Website: www.pmpa.org.
- **Precision Metalforming Association (PMA):** 6363 Oak Tree Blvd., Independence, OH 44131-2500. Website: www.pma.org/home.

Painting and Coating Workers

- **Annual Earnings:** $32,850 ($15.79 per hour)
- **Education/Training:** Moderate-term on-the-job training
- **Outlook:** Slower than average – 4% growth from 2012 to 2022 (from 149,700 to 155,200 jobs)

Employment Outlook: Overall employment of painting and coating workers is expected to grow 4% from 2012 to 2022, slower than average for all occupations. Employment growth will vary by specialty and industry. As with many skilled manufacturing jobs, employers often report difficulty finding qualified workers. Therefore, job opportunities should be very good for those with painting experience.

Nature of Work: Millions of items ranging from cars to candy are covered by paint, plastic, varnish, chocolate, or some other type of coating solution. Spray machine operators use spray guns to coat metal, wood, ceramic, fabric, paper, and food products with paint and other coating solutions. Some factories use automated painting systems that are operated by coating, painting, and spraying machine setters, operators, and tenders. Individuals who paint, coat, or decorate articles such as furniture, glass, pottery, toys, cakes, and books are known as painting, coating, and decorating workers. Transportation equipment painters, also called automotive painters, who work in repair shops are among the most highly skilled manual spray operators because they perform intricate, detailed work and mix paints to match the original color, a task that is especially difficult if the color has faded.

Painting and coating workers held about 149,700 jobs in 2012. Approximately 70 percent of wage-and-salary workers were employed by manufacturing establishments. Less that 4 percent were self-employed.

Working Conditions: Painting and coating workers typically work indoors and may be exposed to dangerous fumes from paint and coating solutions, although, in general, workers' exposure to hazardous chemicals has decreased because of regulations limiting emissions of volatile organic compound and other hazardous air pollutants.

Education, Training, & Qualifications: Most workers acquire their skills on the job; training usually lasts from a few days to several months, but becoming skilled in all aspects of painting can require 1 to 2 years of training.

Training for beginning painting and coating machine setters, operators, and tenders and for painting, coating, and decorating workers, may last from a few days to a couple of months.

Becoming skilled in all aspects of painting usually requires 1 to 2 years of on-the-job training and sometimes requires some formal classroom instruction.

Earnings: Median annual earnings of wage-and-salary coating, painting, and spraying machine setters, operators, and tenders were $32,850 ($15.79 per hour) in 2012. The top 10% earned more than $54,600 a year; the bottom 10% earned less than $20,870. In 2012, median annual wages for painting and coating occupations were as follows:

- $39,600 for transportation equipment painters
- $30,530 for coating, painting, and spraying machine setters, operators, and tenders
- $27,790 for painting, coating, and decorating workers

Many automotive painters who work for motor vehicle dealers and independent automotive repair shops get a commission. Employers frequently guarantee commissioned painters a minimum weekly salary.

Key Contacts: For a director of certified automotive painting programs, contact:

- **National Automotive Technicians Education Foundation:** 101 Blue Seal Dr., SE, Suite 101, Leesburg, VA 20175. Website: www.natef.org.
- **National Institute for Automotive Service Excellence:** 101 Blue Seal Dr., SE, Suite 101, Leesburg, VA 20175. Website: www.ase.com.

Welders, Cutters, Solderers, and Brazers

- **Annual Earnings:** $36,300 ($17.45 per hour)
- **Education/Training:** High school diploma or equivalent
- **Outlook:** Slower than average growth – 6% growth from 2012 to 2012 (from 357,400 to 378,200 jobs)

Employment Outlook: Employment of welders, cutters, solderers, and brazers is expected to grow about 6% from 2012 to 2022, which is slower than average for all occupations. However, job prospects should be excellent, as many potential entrants who could be welders may prefer to attend college or do work that has more comfortable working conditions. In addition, many openings will occur as workers retire or leave the occupation for other reasons.

The major factor affecting employment of welders is the economic health of the industries in which they work. Because almost every manufacturing industry uses welding at some stage of manufacturing or in the repair and maintenance of equipment, a strong economy will keep demand for welders high. A downturn affecting industries such as auto manufacturing, construction, or petroleum, however, would have a negative impact on the employment of welders in those areas, and could cause some layoffs. Levels of government funding for shipbuilding as well as for infrastructure repairs and improvements are expected to be another important determinant of the future number of welding jobs.

Regardless of the state of the economy, the pressures to improve productivity and hold down labor costs are leading many companies to invest more in automation, especially computer-controlled and robotically controlled welding machinery. This will reduce the demand for some low-skilled welders, cutters, solderers, and brazers because these simple, repetitive jobs are being automated. The growing use of automation, however, should increase demand for higher skilled welding, sol-

dering, and brazing machine setters, operators, and tenders. Welders working on construction projects or in equipment repair will not be affected by technology change to the same extent, because their jobs are not as easily automated.

Nature of Work: Welding is the most common way of permanently joining metal parts. In this process, heat is applied to metal pieces, melting and fusing them to form a permanent bond. Because of its strength, welding is used in shipbuilding, automobile manufacturing and repair, aerospace applications, and thousands of other manufacturing activities. Welding is also used to join beams when constructing buildings, bridges, and other structures, and to join pipes in pipelines, power plants, and refineries.

Welders use many types of welding equipment set up in a variety of positions, such as flat, vertical, horizontal, and overhead. They may perform manual welding, in which the work is entirely controlled by the welder, or semiautomatic welding, in which the welder uses machinery, such as a wire feeder, to perform welding tasks. Skilled welding, soldering, and brazing workers generally plan their work from drawings or specifications or use their knowledge of fluxes and base metals to analyze the parts to be joined. These workers then select and set up welding equipment, execute the planned welds, and examine welds to ensure that they meet standards or specifications. Highly skilled welders often are trained to work with a wide variety of materials in addition to steel, such as titanium, aluminum, or plastics. Some welders have more limited duties. They perform routine jobs that already have been planned and laid out and do not require extensive knowledge or welding techniques.

Working Conditions: Welding, cutting, soldering, and brazing workers often are exposed to a number of hazards, including the intense light created, poisonous fumes, and very hot materials. They wear safety shoes, goggles, hoods with protective lenses, and other devices designed to prevent burns and eye injuries and to protect them from falling objects. They normally work in well-ventilated areas to limit their exposure to fumes. Automated welding, cutting, soldering, and brazing machine operators are not exposed to as many dangers, however, and a face shield or goggles provide adequate protection for these workers.

Welders and cutters may work outdoors, often in inclement weather, or indoors, sometimes in a confined area designed to contain sparks and glare. Outdoors, they may work on a scaffold or platform high off the ground. In addition, they may be required to lift heavy objects and work in a variety of awkward positions, while bending, stooping, or standing to perform work overhead.

Although about 55% of welders, solderers, and brazers work a 40-hour week, overtime is common, and some welders work up to 70 hours per week. Welders also may work in shifts as long as 12 hours. Some welders, cutters, solderers, brazers, and machine operators work in factories that operate around the clock, necessitating shift work.

Education, Training, & Qualifications: Training for welding, cutting, soldering, and brazing workers can range from a few weeks of school or on-the-job training for low-skilled positions to several years of combined school and on-the-job training for highly skilled jobs. Formal training is available in high schools, vocational schools, and postsecondary institutions, such as vocational technical institutes, community colleges, and private welding schools. The military services operate welding schools as well. Some employers provide training. Courses in blueprint reading, shop mathematics, mechanical drawing, physics, chemistry, and metallurgy are helpful. Knowledge of computers is gaining importance, especially for welding, soldering, and brazing machine operators, who are becoming responsible for the programming of computer-controlled machines, including robots.

Welding, soldering, and brazing workers need good eyesight, hand-eye coordination, and manual dexterity. They should be able to concentrate on detailed work for long periods and be able to bend, stoop, and work in awkward positions. In addition, welders increasingly need to be willing to receive training and perform tasks in other production jobs.

Earnings: Median annual earnings of welders, cutters, solderers, and brazers were $36,300 ($17.45 per hour) in 2012. The top 10% earned $56,130 a year; the bottom 10% earned less than $24,720. Wages for welders, cutters, solderers, and brazers vary with the worker's experience and skill level, the industry, and the size of the company. Although most welders, solderers, cutters, and brazers work full time, overtime is common. Many manufacturing firms have two or three 8- to 12-hour shifts each day, allowing the firm to continue production around the clock if needed. As a result, welders, cutters, solderers, and brazers may work evenings and weekends.

Key Contacts: For information on training opportunities and jobs for welding, cutting, soldering, and brazing workers, contact local employers, the local office of the state employment service, or schools providing welding, soldering, and brazing training. Information on career opportunities in welding is available from:

- **American Welding Society**: 8669 NW 36th Street, # 130, Miami, Florida 33166-6672. Website: www.aws.org.
- **Fabricators & Manufacturers Association, International:** 833 Featherstone Road, Rockford, IL 61107. Website: http://fmanet.org.
- **Institute for Printed Circuits:** 3000 Lakeside Drive, 105 N, Bannockburn, IL 60015. Website: www.ipc.org.
- **Precision Machined Products Association:** 6880 West Snowville Road, Suite 200, Brecksville, OH 44141. Website: www.pmpa.org.

Production Occupations in Decline

The production occupations listed on the next page have long been popular with ex-offenders. However, in the coming decade, the U.S. Department of Labor projects significant declines in employment related to these fields. Much of the decline is due to increased productivity caused by automation and offshoring of jobs to countries offering cheap labor. While you'll still find excellent opportunities available in these fields, nonetheless, you need to be aware that finding and keeping a job in these fields may be difficult. Worst of all, many of these jobs do not have a good future for someone looking for career advancement in the long run. Several other declining occupations, mainly in manufacturing, are outlined on page 8.

Production Occupations

- Assemblers and fabricators
- Bakers
- Machine setters, operators, and tenders – metal and plastic

Printing Occupations

- Bookbinders and bindery workers
- Prepress technicians and workers
- Printing machine operators

Other Production Occupations

- Apparel manufacturing
- Butchers, meat cutters, and meat packers
- Laundry and dry-cleaning workers
- Food and tobacco processing workers
- Textile, apparel, and furnishings occupations
- Photographic process workers and processing machine operators
- Semiconductor processors

For more information on these occupations, please review the current editions of the ***Occupational Outlook Handbook*** (OOH) and the ***O*NET Dictionary of Occupational Titles*** (O*NET). Online versions of these key reference books can be found here:

- www.bls.gov/ooh (*OOH*)
- www.onetcenter.org (*O*NET*)

8

Transportation and Material Moving Occupations

While these are not high-paying jobs, they are plentiful and can lead to long-term job security. These jobs also are relatively recession-proof and difficult to offshore."

IF MANY OF YOUR INTERESTS and skills relate to transportation and material moving occupations – both on land and on sea – be sure to survey the jobs outlined in this chapter. Many job and career opportunities are available for those who enjoy these lines of work and the variable work settings. While these are not high-paying jobs, they are plentiful and can lead to long-term job security. Similar to many jobs profiled in previous chapters, the transportation and material moving occupations described here are some of today's "safest" jobs – relatively recession-proof and difficult to offshore.

Since most of the following jobs require a basic education and a limited amount of training, they are especially attractive for individuals re-entering the job market who need to quickly find a job but who may have limited work experience. Many of these jobs especially appeal to ex-offenders. Most of these jobs require a high school diploma and some specialized training. A few jobs, especially bus, truck, and taxi drivers, require a license and a good driving record. Some very high-paying jobs, such as air traffic controller and ship captains, require security clearances, which pose problems for many ex-offenders. Some jobs, such as taxi driver, are undergoing major transformations with the rise of disruptive competitive forces organized around the application of innovative high-tech communication and management technologies, such as the ride-sharing companies operated by Uber, Lyft, SideCar, Carma, and Taxi Magic.

If you are re-entering the job market with little work experience, few marketable skills, and red flags in your background, consider getting started in one of the jobs profiled in this chapter. Lower-paying entry-level jobs in this occupational field may provide important first steps for your new work life.

Bus Drivers

- **Annual Earnings:** $29,550 ($14.21 per hour)
- **Education/Training:** High school diploma or equivalent; commercial driver's license
- **Outlook:** As fast as average – 9% growth from 2012 to 2022 (from 654,300 to 712,200 jobs)

Employment Outlook: Persons seeking jobs as bus drivers should encounter many opportunities. Individuals who have good driving records and who are willing to work part time or an irregular schedule should have the best job prospects. School bus driving jobs, particularly in rapidly growing suburban areas, should be the easiest to acquire because most are part-time positions with high turnover and minimal training requirements. However, depending on one's offense, ex-offenders may be prohibited from acquiring jobs related to children and education. Those seeking higher paying intercity and public transit bus driver positions may encounter competition. Employment prospects for motorcoach drivers will fluctuate with the cyclical nature of the economy, as demand for motorcoach services is very dependent on tourism.

Employment of bus drivers is expected to increase about as fast as the average for all occupations through the year 2022, primarily to meet the transportation needs of the growing general population and the school-age population. Many additional job openings are expected to occur each year because of the need to replace workers who take jobs in other occupations or who retire.

Nature of Work: Bus drivers are essential in providing passengers with an alternative to their automobiles or other forms of transportation. Intercity bus drivers transport people between regions of a state or the country; local-transit bus drivers do so within a metropolitan area or county; motorcoach drivers take clients on charter excursions and tours; and school bus drivers take youngsters to and from school and related events. Drivers pick up and drop off passengers at bus stops, stations, or, in the case of students, at regularly scheduled neighborhood locations based on strict time schedules. Drivers must operate vehicles safely, especially when traffic is heavier than normal. However, they cannot let light traffic put them ahead of schedule so that they miss passengers.

Local-transit and intercity bus drivers report to their assigned terminal or garage where they stock up on tickets or transfers and prepare trip report forms. In some transportation firms, maintenance departments are responsible for keeping vehicles in good condition. In other firms, drivers may be responsible for keeping their vehicles in good condition. During their shift, these drivers collect fares; answer questions about schedules, routes, and transfer points; and sometimes announce stops.

Motorcoach drivers transport passengers on charter trips and sightseeing tours. Drivers routinely interact with clients and tour guides to make the trip as comfortable and informative as possible. They are responsible for keeping to strict schedules, adhering to the guidelines of the tour's itinerary, and ensuring the overall success of the trip. These drivers act as a customer service representative, tour guide, program director, and safety guide. Trips frequently last more than one day. The driver may be away for more than a week if assigned to an extended tour.

School bus drivers usually drive the same routes each day, stopping to pick up pupils in the morning and return them to their homes in the afternoon. Some school bus drivers also transport students and teachers on field trips or to sporting events. In addition to driving, some school bus drivers work part-time in the school system as janitors, mechanics, or classroom assistants when not driving buses.

Working Conditions: Driving a bus through heavy traffic while dealing with passengers is more stressful and fatiguing than physically strenuous. Intercity bus drivers may work nights, weekends, and holidays and often spend nights away from home, during which they stay in hotels at company expense. Drivers with seniority and regular routes have routine weekly work schedules, but others do not have regular schedules and must be prepared to work on short notice. They report for work only when called for a charter assignment or to drive extra buses on a regular route.

School bus drivers work only when school is in session. Many work 20 hours a week or less, driving one or two routes in the morning and afternoon. Drivers taking field or athletic trips, or who also have midday kindergarten routes, may work more hours a week.

Regular local-transit bus drivers usually have a five-day workweek; Saturdays and Sundays are considered regular workdays. Some drivers work evenings and after midnight. To accommodate commuters, many work split shifts – for example, 6am to 10am and 3pm to 7pm with time off in between. Tour and charter bus drivers may work any day and all hours of the day, including weekends and holidays. Their hours are dictated by the charter trips booked and the scheduled prearranged itinerary of tours. However, all bus drivers must comply with the limits placed on drivers by the Department of Transportation's rules and regulations concerning hours of service.

Education, Training, & Qualifications: Qualifications and standards for bus drivers are established by state and federal regulations. Federal regulations require drivers who operate commercial vehicles to hold a commercial driver's license (CDL) from the state in which they live. To qualify for a commercial driver's license, applicants must pass a written test on rules and regulations and then demonstrate that they can operate a bus safely. A national databank permanently records all driving violations incurred by persons who hold commercial licenses. A state may not issue a CDL to a driver who has already had a license suspended or revoked in another state. A driver with a CDL must accompany trainees until the trainees get their own CDL. There are physical requirements mandated for bus drivers as well. Age requirements may vary by state and all drivers must be able to read and speak English well enough to read road signs, prepare reports, and communicate with law enforcement officials and the public. Many employers prefer high school graduates and require a written test of ability to follow complex bus schedules. Because bus drivers deal with passengers, they must be courteous. They need an even temperament and emotional stability because driving in heavy, fast-moving, or stop-and-go traffic and dealing with passengers can be stressful.

Many companies and school systems give driver trainees instruction in Department of Transportation and company work rules, safety regulations, state and municipal driving regulations, and safe driving practices. During training, drivers practice driving on set courses.

Opportunities for promotion are generally limited. However, experienced drivers may become supervisors or dispatchers, assigning buses to drivers, checking whether drivers are on schedule, rerouting buses to avoid blocked streets or other problems, and dispatching extra vehicles and service crews to scenes of accidents and breakdowns. A few drivers may become managers. Promotion in publicly owned bus systems is often by competitive civil service examination. Some motorcoach drivers purchase their own equipment and open their own business.

Earnings: Median annual earnings of transit and intercity bus drivers were $29,550 in 2012. The top 10% earned more than $59,480 a year; the bottom 10% earned less than $21,320.

The benefits bus drivers receive from their employers vary greatly. Most intercity and local-transit bus drivers receive paid health and life insurance, sick leave, vacation leave, and free bus rides on any of the regular routes of their line or system. School bus drivers receive sick leave, and many are covered by health and life insurance and pension plans. Because they do not generally work when school is not in session, they do not get va-

cation leave. Most intercity and many local transit bus drivers are members of the Amalgamated Transit Union.

Key Contacts: For information on employment opportunities, contact local transit systems, intercity bus lines, school systems, or the local office of the state employment service. General information on school bus driving is available from:

- **National School Transportation Association:** 122 South Royal Street, Alexandria, VA 22314. Website: www.yellowbuses.org.

- **National Association of State Directors of Pupil Transportation Services:** 8205 Bristol Court, Tallahassee, FL 32311. Website: www.nasdpts.org.

General information on local-transit bus driving is available from:

- **American Public Transportation Association:** 1666 K Street NW, 11th Floor, Washington, DC 20006. Website: www.apta.com.

General information on motorcoach driving is available from:

- **United Motorcoach Association:** 113 S. West St., 4th Floor, Alexandria, VA 22314. Website: www.uma.org.

Cargo and Freight Agents

- **Annual Earnings:** $39,720
- **Education/Training:** High school diploma or equivalent
- **Outlook:** As fast as average – 14% growth from 2012 to 2022 (from 79,500 to 91,000 jobs)

Employment Outlook: Employment of cargo and freight agents is expected to grow as fast as average for all occupations in the decade ahead in response to the continuing growth of cargo traffic and next-day shipping services.

Nature of Work: Cargo and freight agents arrange for and track incoming and outgoing cargo and freight shipments in airline, train, and trucking terminals or on shipping docks. They take orders from customers and arrange pickup of freight and cargo for delivery to loading platforms. They prepare and examine bills of lading to determine shipping charges and tariffs.

Working Conditions: Cargo and freight agents work in a variety of settings. Some work in warehouses, stockrooms, or shipping and receiving rooms while others may spend time in cold storage rooms or outside on loading platforms, where they are exposed to the weather.

Education, Training, & Qualifications: A high school diploma is usually sufficient for entry in these positions.

Earnings: The median annual earnings in 2012 for cargo and freight agents were $39,720.

Key Contacts: Information on job opportunities for cargo and freight agents is available from local employers and local offices of the state employment service.

Delivery Truck Drivers and Driver/Sales Workers

- **Annual Earnings:** $27,530 ($13.23 per hour)
- **Education/Training:** High school diploma or equivalent
- **Outlook:** Slower than average – 5% growth from 2012 to 2022 (from 1,273,600 to 1,342,400 jobs)

Employment Outlook: Employment of light truck or delivery services drivers is projected to grow 4% from 2012 to 2022, slower than the average for all occupations. Employment of driver/sales workers is projected to grow 9% over the same period, about as fast as the average for all occupations. Improved routing through GPS technology can make existing truck drivers more productive, which may limit the demand for additional drivers. With improved routing, drivers can be more efficient, navigating better in traffic and spending less time idling at each stop. Additionally, higher diesel prices could cause companies to limit their hiring of new drivers and increase the company's focus on technological solutions. The limits on hiring will be especially true for drivers at large shipping companies. However, as the economy grows, the need for more deliveries is expected to increase. From the distribution of warehouse goods to the delivery of packages to households, nearly all goods are brought to their final destination by delivery drivers.

Nature of Work: Delivery truck drivers and driver/sales workers typically do the following:

- Load and unload their cargo
- Report any incidents they encounter on the road to a dispatcher

- Follow all applicable traffic laws
- Report serious mechanical problems to the appropriate personnel
- Keep their truck and associated equipment clean and in good working order
- Accept payments for the shipment
- Handle paperwork, such as receipts or delivery confirmation notices

Most drivers plan their routes. Some have a regular daily or weekly delivery schedule. Others have different routes each day. These drivers generally receive instructions to go to a delivery location at a particular time, and it is up to them to determine the best route. They must have a thorough understanding of an area's street grid and know which roads allow trucks and which do not.

Work Environment: Most delivery drivers work for couriers and express delivery services. Light truck drivers or delivery service drivers held about 841,600 jobs in 2012. The industries that employed the most light truck or delivery service drivers in 2012 were as follows:

- Retail trade   20%
- Couriers and messengers   20%
- Wholesale trade   17%

Driver/sales workers held about 432,000 jobs in 2012. The industries that employed the most driver/sales workers in 2012 were as follows:

- Restaurants and other eating places   32%
- Wholesale trade   29%
- Retail trade   13%

Delivery truck drivers and driver/sales workers have physically demanding jobs. Driving a truck for long periods of time can be tiring. When loading and unloading cargo, drivers do a lot of lifting, carrying, and walking.

Education, Training, & Qualifications: Delivery truck drivers and driver/sales workers typically enter their occupations with a high school diploma or equivalent. Companies train new delivery truck drivers and driver/sales workers on the job. This may include training from a driver-mentor who rides along with a new employee to ensure that he/she is able to operate a truck safely on crowded streets. New drivers also have training to learn company policies about package drop-offs, returns, taking payment, and what to do with damaged goods. Driver/sales workers must learn detailed information about the products they offer. Their company also may teach them proper sales techniques, such as how to approach potential new customers. All delivery drivers must have a driver's license.

Earnings: The median annual wage for driver/sales workers was $22,670 in 2012. The top 10% earned $46,240 annually; the bottom 10% earned less than $16,780. In 2012, the median annual wages for driver/sales workers in the top three industries in which these drivers worked were as follows:

- Wholesale trade $30,170
- Retail trade $25,490
- Restaurants and other eating places $18,330

The median annual wage for light truck or delivery service drivers was $29,390 in 2012. The top 10% earned $62,520 annually; the bottom 10% earned less than $18,190.

In 2012, the median annual wages for light truck or delivery service drivers in the top 3 industries in which these drivers worked were as follows:

- Couriers and messengers $55,130
- Wholesale trade $27,750
- Retail trade $23,060

Most drivers work full time, and many work additional hours. Those who work on regular routes sometimes must begin work very early in the morning or work late at night. For example, a driver who delivers bread to a deli every day must be there before the deli opens. Drivers often work weekends and holidays.

Key Contacts: For more information about truck drivers, including delivery truck drivers and driver/sales workers, visit:

- **American Trucking Associations:** 950 North Glebe Road, Suite 210, Arlington, VA 22203-4181. Website: www.trucking.org.
- **Professional Truck Driver Institute:** 555 E. Braddock Road, Alexandria, VA 22314. Website: www.ptdi.org.

Hand Laborers and Material Movers

- **Annual Earnings:** $22,970 ($11.04 per hour)
- **Education/Training:** Less than high school; short-term on-the-job training
- **Outlook:** As fast as average – 10% growth from 2012 to 2022 (from 3,428,800 to 3,870,500 jobs)

Employment Outlook: This is a very large quick-and-easy entry-level occupation for transitioning ex-offenders. While the jobs don't pay well, they do not require a great deal of education and training or extensive background checks. Projected employment changes for specific groups of workers within this occupation are as follows:

- Employment of refuse and recyclable material collectors is projected to grow 16% from 2012 to 2022. Trash collection will continue to grow as populations grow, and collectors will be needed to remove trash. An increase in recycling collection is expected to drive the rapid growth of this occupation.

- Employment of cleaners of vehicles and equipment is projected to grow 11% from 2012 to 2022. Growth in automobile dealers, an industry in which many of these workers are employed, is expected to drive employment growth of cleaners of vehicles and equipment. However, a decline in the use of full-service car washes in favor of automatic conveyors may limit job growth somewhat.

- Employment of laborers and hand, freight, stock, and material movers is projected to grow 11% from 2012 to 2022. The need for warehouses is expected to grow as consumer spending increases. However, greater automation will increase the efficiency of hand material movers. Most warehouses are installing equipment, such as high-speed conveyors and sorting systems and robotic pickers, that decreases the number of workers needed.

- Employment of hand packers and packagers is projected to grow 6% from 2012 to 2022. A decline in the use of baggers in grocery stores, where many hand packers and packagers are employed, is expected to dampen growth in this occupation. The growing number of cashiers who also bag groceries is contributing to the decline in baggers. However, those employed in warehouses are expected to see some employment growth as the industry grows.

- Employment of machine feeders and offbearers is projected to show little or no change from 2012 to 2022. These workers are heavily employed in declining manufacturing industries in which automation is further decreasing the need for them. In addition, other workers who operate the machines are increasingly doing the tasks of machine feeders and offbearers.

Nature of Work: Hand laborers and material movers typically do the following:

- Manually move material from one place to another
- Pack or wrap material by hand
- Keep a record of the material they move
- Use signals, when necessary, to assist machine operators who are moving larger pieces of material
- Ensure a clean and orderly workplace

In warehouses and wholesale and retail operations, hand material movers work closely with material moving machine operators and material recording clerks. Automatic sensors and tags are increasingly being used to track items that allow hand material movers to work faster. Some workers are employed in manufacturing industries in which they load material onto conveyor belts or other machines.

Work Environment: Hand laborers and material movers held about 3.4 million jobs in 2012. They work in a variety of industries. Laborers and hand, freight, stock, and material movers held about 2.2 million jobs in 2012. The industries that employed the most laborers and hand, freight, stock, and material movers in 2012 were as follows:

- Employment services   18%
- Merchant wholesalers, nondurable goods   8%
- Warehousing and storage   8%
- Merchant wholesalers, durable goods   8%

Hand packers and packagers held about 666,900 jobs in 2012. The industries that employed the most hand packers and packagers in 2012 were as follows:

- Grocery stores   23%
- Employment services   16%
- Food manufacturing   10%
- Merchant wholesalers, nondurable goods   8%
- Warehousing and storage   7%

Cleaners of vehicles and equipment held about 325,200 jobs in 2012. The industries that employed the most cleaners of vehicles and equipment in 2012 were as follows:

- Other automotive repair and maintenance   34%
- Automobile dealers   22%
- Food manufacturing   6%

Refuse and recyclable material collectors held about 133,200 jobs in 2012. The industries that

employed the most refuse and recyclable material collectors in 2012 were as follows:

- Waste collection   40%
- Local government, excluding education and hospitals   34%
- Waste treatment and disposal and waste management services   11%

Machine feeders and offbearers held about 106,100 jobs in 2012. The industries that employed the most machine feeders and offbearers in 2012 were as follows:

- Food manufacturing   12%
- Wood product manufacturing   10%
- Paper manufacturing   8%
- Plastics and rubber products manufacturing   7%

The work of hand laborers and material movers is usually repetitive and physically demanding. Workers may lift and carry heavy objects. They bend, kneel, crouch, or crawl in awkward positions.

Education, Training, & Qualifications: Some employers may prefer to hire workers who have a high school diploma, although it is generally not required for these jobs. Most of these positions require less than 1 month of on-the-job training. Some workers need only a few days of training. Certain hand freight, stock, and material movers and refuse and recyclable material collectors have up to 3 months of training. Most training is done by a supervisor or a more experienced worker who decides when trainees are ready to work on their own. Workers learn safety rules as part of their training. Many of these rules are standardized through the Occupational Safety and Health Administration (OSHA). Workers who handle hazardous materials receive additional training.

Refuse and recyclable material collectors who drive a truck that surpasses a certain size have to have a commercial driver's license (CDL). Getting a CDL requires passing written, skills, and vision tests.

Earnings: The median annual wage for hand laborers and material movers was $22,970 in 2012. The top 10% earned more than $38,410 a year; the bottom 10% earned less than $17,100. Median wages for hand laborers and material moving occupations in 2012 were as follows:

- $32,930 for refuse and recyclable material collectors
- $27,120 for machine feeders and offbearers

- $23,890 for laborers and hand freight, stock, and material movers
- $19,910 for hand packers and packagers
- $19,850 for cleaners of vehicles and equipment

Most people in these occupations work full time. Almost a quarter of laborers and hand, freight, stock, and material movers and packers and packagers work part time, a somewhat higher percentage than that of other occupations. In addition, most workers have 8-hour shifts, although longer shifts and overtime are common. Because materials are shipped around the clock, some workers, especially those in warehousing, work overnight shifts.

Key Contacts: For more information about hand laborers and material movers, visit:

- **MHI:** 8720 Red Oak Blvd., Suite 201, Charlotte, NC 28217-3996. Website: www.mhi.org.
- **The Warehousing Education and Research Council:** 1100 Jorie Boulevard, Suite 170, Oak Brook, IL 60523. Website: www.werc.org.

Heavy and Tractor-Trailer Truck Drivers

- **Annual Earnings:** $38,200 ($18.37 per hour)
- **Education/Training:** 1-2 year postsecondary; short-term on-the-job training
- **Outlook:** As fast as average – 11% growth from 2012 to 2022 (from 1,701,500 to 1,893,400 jobs)

Employment Outlook: Employment of heavy and tractor-trailer truck drivers is projected to grow 11% from 2012 to 2022, about as fast as the average of all occupations. As the economy grows, the demand for goods will increase, and more truck drivers will be needed to keep supply chains moving. Trucks transport most of the freight in the U.S., so as households and businesses increase their spending, the trucking industry will grow. If fuel prices rise, some companies may switch their shipping to rail to lower costs. However, rail is unlikely to take much market share away from trucks, because even with high diesel prices for truck fuel, trucks are more efficient for short distances. Additionally, many products need to be delivered within the short time frame that only trucks can operate in. Demand for truck drivers is expected to increase in oil and gas industries as more drivers become needed to transport materials to and from mining sites.

Nature of Work: Heavy and tractor-trailer truck drivers typically do the following:

- Drive long distances
- Report to a dispatcher any incidents encountered on the road
- Follow all applicable traffic laws
- Inspect their trailer before and after the trip, and record any defects they find
- Keep a log of their activities
- Report serious mechanical problems to the appropriate personnel
- Keep their truck and associated equipment clean and in good working order

Most heavy and tractor-trailer truck drivers plan their own routes. They may use satellite tracking to help them plan. Before leaving, a driver usually is told a delivery location and time, but it is up to the driver to determine how to get the cargo there. A driver must know which roads allow trucks and which do not. Drivers also must plan legally required rest periods into their trip. Some drivers have one or two routes that they drive regularly, and others drivers take many different routes throughout the country. Companies sometimes use two drivers, known as teams, on long runs to minimize downtime. On these team runs, one driver sleeps in a berth behind the cab while the other drives. Some heavy truck drivers transport hazardous materials, such as chemical waste, and thus have to take special precautions when driving. Also, these drivers normally carry specialized safety equipment in case of an accident. Other drivers, such as those carrying liquids, oversized loads, or cars, must follow rules that apply specifically to them. Some long-haul truck drivers, called "owner-operators," buy or lease trucks and go into business for themselves. They then have business tasks, including finding and keeping clients and doing administrative work such as accounting, in addition to their driving tasks.

Work Environment: Some truck drivers travel far from home and can be on the road for long periods at a time. Heavy and tractor-trailer truck drivers held about 1.7 million jobs in 2012. Many heavy and tractor-trailer truck drivers are employed in general freight trucking. The industries that employed the most truck drivers in 2012 were as follows:

- General freight trucking   34%
- Specialized freight trucking   13%

- Merchant wholesales, nondurable goods   8%

Working as a long-haul truck driver is a major lifestyle choice because these drivers can be away from home for days or weeks at a time. They spend much of this time alone. Truck driving can be a physically demanding job as well. Driving for many hours straight can be tiring, and some drivers must load and unload cargo.

Education, Training, & Qualifications: Most companies require their truck drivers to have a high school diploma or equivalent. Many companies require drivers to attend professional truck-driving schools, where they take training courses to learn how to maneuver large vehicles on highways or through crowded streets. During these classes, drivers also learn the federal laws and regulations governing interstate truck driving. Students attend either a private truck-driving school or a program at a community college that lasts between 3 and 6 months. Upon finishing these classes, drivers receive a certificate of completion. The U.S. Department of Transportation is considering requiring all newly hired interstate truck drivers to take a truck-driving course. The Professional Truck Driver Institute (PTDI) certifies a small percentage of driver-training courses at truck-driver training schools that meet both the industry standards and the U.S. Department of Transportation guidelines for training tractor-trailer drivers.

All long-haul truck drivers must have a commercial driver's license (CDL). Qualifications for obtaining a CDL vary by state but generally include passing both a knowledge test and a driving test. States have the right to refuse to issue a CDL to anyone who has had a CDL suspended by another state.

Earnings: The median annual wage for heavy and tractor-trailer truck drivers was $38,200 in 2012. The top 10% earned more than $58,910 annually; the bottom 10% earned less than $25,110. In 2012, the median annual wages for heavy and tractor-trailer drivers in the top three industries in which these drivers worked were as follows:

- General freight trucking $40,360
- Merchant wholesalers,
  nondurable goods $39,630
- Specialized freight trucking $37,710

Drivers of heavy trucks and tractor-trailers are usually paid by how many miles they have driven, plus bonuses. The per-mile rate varies from employer to employer and may depend on the type of cargo and the experience of the driver. Some long-distance drivers, especially owner-operators, are paid a share of the revenue from shipping.

Key Contacts: For more information about truck drivers, visit:

- **American Trucking Association:** 950 North Glebe Road, Suite 210, Arlington, VA 22203-4181. Website: www.trucking.org.
- **Federal Motor Carrier Safety Administration:** 1200 New Jersey Avenue, SE, Washington, DC 20590. Website: www.fmcsa.dot.gov.

For more information about truck-driving schools and programs, visit:

- **Commercial Vehicle Training Association:** 7005 Backlick Court, Suite 100, Springfield, VA 22151. Website: http://cvta.org.
- **National Association of Publicly Funded Truck Driving Schools:** 1324 S 220 W Avenue, Sand Springs, OK 74063. Website: http://napftds.org.
- **Professional Truck Driver Institute:** 555 Braddock Road, Alexandria, VA 22314. Website: www.ptdi.org.

Taxi Drivers and Chauffeurs

- **Annual Earnings:** $22,820 ($10.97 per hour)
- **Education/Training:** Less than high school; taxi driver's license
- **Outlook:** Faster than average – 16% growth from 2012 to 2022 (from 233,000 to 269,200 jobs)

Employment Outlook: Persons seeking jobs as taxi drivers and chauffeurs should encounter good opportunities, because of the need to replace the many people who work in this occupation for short periods and then transfer to other occupations or leave the labor force. Opportunities should be best for persons with good driving records and the ability to work flexible schedules. Employment of taxi drivers and chauffeurs is expected to grow faster than average for all occupations through the year 2022, as local and suburban travel increases with population growth. Employment growth also will stem from federal legislation requiring services for persons with disabilities. Rapidly growing metropolitan areas should offer the best job opportunities. The number of job openings can fluctuate with the cycle of the overall economy because the demand for taxi and limousine transportation depends on travel and tourism. Extra drivers may be hired during holiday seasons and peak travel and tourist times. At the same time, this industry is going through some challenging times given the increasing defection of traditional taxi customers to the innovative ride-sharing companies, such as Uber, Lyft, SideCar, Carma, and Taxi Magic.

Nature of Work: Taxi drivers help passengers get to and from their homes, workplaces, and recreational pursuits such as dining, entertainment, and shopping. At the start of their driving shift, taxi drivers usually report to a taxicab service or garage where they are assigned an automobile modified for commercial passenger use. Taxi drivers pick up passengers in one of three ways: "cruising" the streets to pick up random passengers; prearranged pickups; and picking up passengers from taxi stands established in highly trafficked areas.

Drivers should be familiar with the streets in the areas they serve so they can use the most efficient route to destinations. They should know the location of frequently requested destinations, such as airports, bus and railroad terminals, convention centers, hotels, and other points of interest. In case of emergency, the driver should also know the location of fire and police stations and hospitals. Upon reaching the destination, drivers determine the fare and announce it to the rider. Fares may include a surcharge for additional passengers, a fee for handling luggage, or a drop charge. Each jurisdiction determines the rate and structure of the fare system of zones through which the taxi passes during a trip. Passengers usually add a tip to the fare.

Chauffeurs operate limousines, vans and private cars for limousine companies, private businesses, government agencies, and wealthy individuals. Chauffeur service differs from taxi service in that all trips are prearranged. Many chauffeurs transport customers in large vans between hotels and airports, bus, or train terminals. Others drive luxury vehicles such as limousines, to business events, entertainment venues, and social events. Still others provide full-time personal transportation for wealthy families and private companies. Chauffeurs cater to passengers with attentive customer service and a special regard for detail. They help riders into the car by holding open doors, holding umbrellas when it is raining, and loading packages and luggage into the trunk of the car. A growing number of chauffeurs work as full-service executive assistants, simultaneously acting as driver, secretary, and itinerary planner.

Working Conditions: Taxi drivers and chauffeurs occasionally have to load and unload heavy luggage and packages. Driving for long periods can be tiring and uncomfortable, especially in densely populated urban areas. Drivers must be alert to conditions on the road, especially in heavy and congested traffic or in bad weather. Taxi drivers also risk robbery because they work alone and often carry large amounts of cash.

Work hours vary greatly. Some jobs offer full-time or part-time employment with work hours that can change from day to day or remain the same every day. It is often necessary for drivers to report to work on short notice. Chauffeurs who work for a single employer may be on call much of the time. Evening and weekend work are common for limousine and taxicab services. The needs of the client or employer dictate the work schedule for chauffeurs. The work of taxi drivers is much less structured. Working free of supervision, they may break for a meal or a rest whenever their vehicle is unoccupied. Many taxi drivers and chauffeurs like the independent, unsupervised work of driving their automobile. This occupation is attractive to individuals seeking flexible work schedules, such as college and postgraduate students, and to anyone seeking a second source of income.

Full-time taxi drivers usually work one shift a day, which may last from eight to 12 hours. Part-time drivers may work half a shift each day, or work a full shift once or twice a week. Drivers may work shifts at all times of the day and night, because most taxi companies offer services 24 hours a day. Early morning and late night shifts are common. Drivers work long hours during holidays, weekends, and other special times during which demand for their services may be heavier. Independent drivers, however, often set their own hours and schedules.

Design improvements in newer cabs have reduced some of the stress and increased the comfort and efficiency of drivers. Many regulatory bodies overseeing taxi and chauffeur services require standard amenities such as air-conditioning and general upkeep of the vehicles. Modern taxicabs also are equipped with sophisticated tracking devices, fare meters, and dispatching equipment. Satellites and tracking systems link many of these state-of-the-art vehicles with company headquarters. In a matter of seconds, dispatchers can deliver directions, traffic advisories, weather reports, and other important communication to drivers anywhere in the transporting area. The satellite link also allows dispatchers to track vehicle location, fuel consumption, and engine performance. Drivers can easily communicate with dispatchers to discuss delivery schedules and courses of action should there be mechanical problems. For instance, automated dispatch systems help dispatchers locate the closest driver to a customer in order to maximize efficiency and quality of service. When threatened with crime or violence, drivers may have special "trouble lights" to alert authorities to emergencies and ensure that help arrives quickly.

Taxi drivers and chauffeurs meet many different types of people. Dealing with rude customers and waiting for passengers requires patience.

Education, Training, & Qualifications: Persons interested in driving a limousine or taxicab must first have a regular automobile driver's license. They also must acquire a chauffeur or taxi driver's license, commonly called a "hack" license. Local governments set license standards and requirements for taxi drivers and chauffeurs that include minimum qualifications for driving experience and training. Local authorities generally require applicants for a hack license to pass a written exam or complete a training program that may require up to 80 hours of classroom instruction.

To qualify through either an exam or training program, applicants must know local geography, motor vehicle laws, safe driving practices, regulations governing taxicabs, and display some aptitude for customer service. Many taxi and limousine companies set higher standards than required by law. It is common for companies to review applicants' medical, credit, criminal, and driving records. In addition, many companies require a higher minimum age than that which is legally required and prefer that drivers be high school graduates.

In small and medium-sized communities, drivers are sometimes able to buy their taxi, limousine, or other type of automobile and go into business for themselves. These independent owner-drivers are required to have an additional permit allowing them to operate their vehicle as a company. Some big cities limit the number of operating permits. In these cities, drivers become owner-drivers by buying permits from owner-drivers who leave the business. Although many owner-drivers are suc-

cessful, some fail to cover expenses and eventually lose their permit and automobile. Good business sense and courses in accounting, business, and business arithmetic can help an owner-driver to become successful. Knowledge of mechanics enables owner-drivers to perform their own routine maintenance and minor repairs to cut expenses.

Earnings: Earnings of taxi drivers and chauffeurs vary greatly, depending upon such factors as the number of hours worked, customers' tips, and geographic location. Median annual earnings of salaried taxi drivers and chauffeurs, including tips, were $22,820 ($10.97 per hour) in 2012. The top 10% earned more than $37,200 per year; the bottom 10% earned less than $17,050. Taxi drivers and chauffeurs who lease their car from a company may pay a fee for the use of the car. This fee covers storage, insurance, and maintenance costs.

Key Contacts: Information on licensing and registration of taxi drivers and chauffeurs is available from local government agencies that regulate taxicabs. For information about work opportunities as a taxi driver or chauffeur, contact local taxi or limousine companies or state employment service offices or contact:

- **Taxicab, Limousine, and Paratransit Association:** 3200 Tower Oaks Blvd., Suite 220, Rockville, MD 20852. Website: www.tipa.org.

For general information about the work of limousine drivers, contact:

- **National Limousine Association:** 49 South Maple Ave., Marlton, NJ 08053. Website: www.limo.org

Water Transportation Occupations

- **Annual Earnings:** $48,980 ($23.55 per hour)
- **Education/Training:** From high school and equivalent through bachelor's degree plus certifications and licenses.
- **Outlook:** As fast as average – 13% growth from 2012 to 2022 (from 81,600 to 92,500 jobs)

Employment Outlook: Employment of water transportation occupations is projected to grow 13% from 2012 to 2022, about as fast as the average for all occupations. Employment of captains, mates, and pilots of water vessels is projected to grow 14%. Employment of ship engineers is projected to grow 8%. Employment of sailors and marine oilers is projected to grow 16% from 2012 to 2022.

As the economy recovers, the demand for waterway freight shipping will grow, increasing the need for these workers. Job growth is likely to be concentrated on inland rivers and the Great Lakes. This will be driven by the demand for commodities such as iron ore, grain, and petroleum. In addition, the need to supply offshore oil platforms will drive growth of supply ships. However, growth in domestic waterways freight may be limited by an increase in intermodal shipping. Intermodal shipping means that shippers use more than one method to transport a good. An increase in intermodal shipping may send some freight from barges to trains. For some products, rail is a more direct route from the Midwest to a coastal port, which saves time and money.

Jobs in coastal shipping will likely continue to decline, as more companies use foreign vessels to transport goods internationally. However, there is a limit to the decline because federal laws and subsidies ensure that there will always be a fleet of merchant ships with U.S. flags. Keeping a fleet of merchant ships is considered important for the nation's defense.

The popularity of river cruises as a type of vacation is growing. This trend may lead to more opportunities for workers on inland rivers such as the Mississippi or Ohio River. However, most ocean-going cruise ships go to international destinations, and these ships generally do not employ U.S. workers.

Employment of motorboat operators is projected to grow 6% from 2012 to 2022. Demand for these workers will be driven by growth in tourism and recreational activities, where they are primarily employed.

Nature of Work: Workers in water transportation occupations operate and maintain vessels that take cargo and people over water. These vessels travel to and from foreign ports across the ocean, to domestic ports along the coasts, across the Great Lakes, and along the country's many inland waterways. Water transportation workers typically do the following:

- Operate and maintain non-military vessels
- Follow their vessel's strict chain of command
- Ensure the safety of all people and cargo on board

These workers, sometimes called **merchant mariners**, work on a variety of ships. Some operate large deep-sea container ships to transport manufactured goods around the world. Others work on bulk carriers that move heavy commodities, such as coal or iron ore, across the oceans and over the Great Lakes. Still others work on both large and small tankers that carry oil and other liquid products around the country and the world. Others work on supply ships that transport equipment and supplies to offshore oil and gas platforms. Workers on tugboats help barges and other boats maneuver in small harbors and at sea. Salvage vessels that offer emergency services also employ merchant mariners. Cruise ships employ a large number of water transportation workers, and some merchant mariners work on ferries to transport passengers along shorter distances.

A typical deep sea merchant ship, large coastal ship, or Great Lakes merchant ship employs a captain and chief engineer, along with three mates, three assistant engineers, and a number of sailors and marine oilers. Smaller vessels that operate in harbors or rivers may have a smaller crew. The specific complement of mariners is dependent on US Coast Guard regulations.

Also, there are other workers on ships, such as cooks, electricians, and mechanics. For more information, see the profiles on cooks, electricians, and general maintenance and repair workers.

Captains, sometimes called **masters**, have overall command of a vessel. They have the final responsibility for the safety of the crew, cargo, and passengers. Captains typically do the following:

- Supervise the work of other officers and the crew
- Ensure that proper safety procedures are followed
- Prepare a maintenance and repair budget
- Oversee the loading and unloading of cargo or passengers
- Keep logs and other records that track the ship's movements and activities
- Interact with passengers on cruise ships

Mates, or **deck officers**, direct the operation of a vessel while the captain is off duty. Large ships have three officers, called first, second, and third mates. The first mate has the highest authority and takes command of the ship if the captain is incapacitated. Usually, the first mate is in charge of the cargo and/or passengers, the second mate is in charge of navigation, and the third mate is in charge of safety. On smaller vessels, there may be only one mate who handles all of the responsibilities. Deck officers typically do the following:

- Alternate watches with the captain and other officers
- Supervise and coordinate the activities of the deck crew
- Assist with docking the ship
- Monitor the ship's position, using charts and other navigational aides
- Determine the speed and direction of the vessel
- Inspect the cargo hold during loading, to ensure that the cargo is stowed according to specifications
- Make announcements to passengers, when needed

Pilots guide ships in harbors, on rivers, and on other confined waterways. They are not part of a ship's crew but go aboard a ship to guide it through a particular waterway that they are familiar with. They work in places where a high degree of familiarity with local tides, currents, and hazards is needed. Some, called **harbor pilots**, work for ports and help many ships coming into the harbor during the day. When coming into a commercial port, a captain will often have to turn control of the vessel over to a pilot, who can safely guide it into the harbor. Pilots typically do the following:

- Board an unfamiliar ship from a small boat in the open water, often using a ladder
- Confer with a ship's captain about the vessel's destination and any special requirements it has
- Establish a positive working relationship with a vessel's captain and deck officers
- Receive mooring instructions from shore dispatchers

Sailors, or **deckhands**, operate and maintain the vessel and deck equipment. They make up the deck crew and keep all parts of a ship, other than areas related to the engine and motor, in good working order. New deckhands are called **ordinary seamen** and do the least-complicated tasks. Experienced deckhands are called **able seamen** and usually make up most of a crew. Some large ships have a **boatswain**, who is the chief of the deck crew. Sailors typically do the following:

- Stand watch, looking for other vessels or obstructions in their ship's path, and for navigational aids, such as buoys and lighthouses

- Steer the ship and measure water depth in shallow water
- Do routine maintenance, such as painting the deck and chipping away rust
- Keep the inside of the ship clean
- Handle lines when docking or departing
- Tie barges together when they are being towed
- Load and unload cargo
- Help passengers, when needed

Ship engineers operate and maintain a vessel's propulsion system. This includes the engine, boilers, generators, pumps, and other machinery. Large vessels usually carry a **chief engineer**, who has command of the engine room and its crew, and a first, second, and third assistant engineer. The assistant engineer oversees the engine and related machinery when the chief engineer is off duty. Small ships may only have one engineer. Engineers typically do the following:

- Maintain the electrical, refrigeration, and ventilation systems of a ship
- Start the engine and regulate the vessel's speed, based on the captain's orders
- Record information in an engineering log
- Keep an inventory of mechanical parts and supplies
- Do routine maintenance checks throughout the day
- Calculate refueling requirements

Marine oilers work in the engine room, helping the engineers keep the propulsion system in working order. They are the engine room equivalent of sailors. New oilers are usually called **wipers,** or **pumpmen,** on vessels handling liquid cargo. With experience, a wiper can become a Qualified Member of the Engine Department (QMED). Marine oilers typically do the following:

- Lubricate gears, shafts, bearings, and other parts of the engine or motor
- Read pressure and temperature gauges and record data
- Help engineers with repairs to machinery
- Connect hoses, operate pumps, and clean tanks
- May assist the deck crew with loading or unloading of cargo

Motorboat operators run small, motor-driven boats that only carry a few passengers. They work for a variety of services, such as fishing charters, tours, and harbor patrols. Motorboat operators typically do the following:

- Check and change the oil and other fluids on their boat
- Pick up passengers and help them board the boat
- May act as a tour guide

Work Environment: Workers in water transportation occupations held about 81,600 jobs in 2012. The industries that employed the most water transportation workers in 2012 were as follows:

- Deep sea, coastal, and great lakes water transportation
- Inland water transportation
- Support activities for water transportation
- Government
- Scenic and sightseeing transportation, water

Workers in water transportation occupations usually work for long periods on small and cramped ships, which can be uncomfortable. Many people decide life at sea is not for them because of difficult conditions onboard ships and long periods away from home. However, companies try to provide a pleasant living condition aboard their vessels. Most vessels are now air-conditioned and include comfortable living quarters. Many also include entertainment systems with satellite TV and Internet connections. Large ships usually have one or two full-time cooks as well.

Education, Training, & Qualifications: Most deck officers, engineers, and pilots have a bachelor's degree from a merchant marine academy. The academy programs offer a bachelor's degree and a Merchant Marine Credential (MMC) with an endorsement as a third mate or third assistant engineer. Graduates of these programs can also choose to receive a commission as an ensign in the U.S. Naval Reserve, Merchant Marine Reserve, or U.S. Coast Guard Reserve. Non-officers, such as sailors or marine oilers, usually do not need a degree.

Ordinary seamen, wipers, and other entry-level mariners get on-the-job training for 6 months to a year. Length of training depends on the size and type of ship and waterway they work on. For example, workers on deep sea vessels need more complex training than those whose ships travel on a river.

All mariners working on ships with U.S. flags must have a Transportation Worker Identification Credential (TWIC) from the Transportation Security Administration. This credential states that a person is a U.S. citizen or permanent resident and has passed a security screening. Most mariners must also have a Merchant Marine Credential (MMC). They can apply for an MMC at a U.S. Coast Guard regional examination center. Entry-level employees, such as ordinary seamen or wipers, do not have to pass a written exam. However, some have to pass physical, hearing, and vision tests, and all must undergo a drug screening, to get their MMC. They also have to take a class on shipboard safety. Crew members can apply for endorsements to their MMC that allow them to move into more advanced positions.

Wipers can get an endorsement to become a Qualified Member of the Engine Department (QMED) after 6 months of experience by passing a written test. Ordinary seamen can get an able seamen endorsement after 6 months to 1 year of experience, depending on the type of ship they work on, by passing a written test. Able seamen can complete a number of training and testing requirements, after at least 3 years of experience in the deck department, to get an endorsement as a third mate. Experience and testing requirements increase with the size and complexity of the ship.

Officers who graduate from a maritime academy receive an MMC with a third mate or third assistant engineer endorsement, depending on which department they are trained in. To move up each step of the occupation ladder, from third mate/third assistant engineer to second to first and then to captain or chief engineer, requires 365 days of experience at the previous level. A second mate or second assistant engineer who wants to move to first mate/first assistant engineer also must complete a 12-week training course and pass an exam.

Pilots are licensed by the state in which they work. The U.S. Coast Guard licenses pilots on the Great Lakes. The requirements for these licenses vary, depending on where a pilot works.

Earnings: The median annual wage for water transportation occupations was $48,980 in 2012. The top 10% earned more than $105,440 annually; the bottom 10% earned less than $24,920. Median annual wages for water transportation occupations in 2012 were as follows:

- $70,890 for ship engineers
- $66,150 for captains, mates, and pilots of water vessels
- $38,190 for sailors and marine oilers
- $35,190 for motorboat operators

In 2012, the median annual wages for water transportation workers in the top five industries in which these workers worked were as follows:

- Support activities for water
  transportation $59,290
- Deep sea, coastal, and great
  lakes water transportation $50,230
- Deep sea, coastal, and great
  lakes water transportation $47,600
- Government $47,600
- Inland water transportation $46,780
- Scenic and sightseeing
  transportation, water $35,190

Workers on deep sea ships can spend months at a time away from home. Workers on supply ships have shorter trips, usually lasting for a few hours to a month. Tugboats and barges travel along the coasts and on inland waterways and are usually away for 2 to 3 weeks at a time. Those who work on the Great Lakes have longer trips, around 2 months, but often do not work in the winter when the lakes freeze. Crews on all vessels often work long hours, 7 days a week. Ferry workers and motorboat operators usually are away only for a few hours at a time and return home each night. Many ferry and motorboat operators service ships for vacation destinations and have seasonal schedules.

Key Contacts: For more information about water transportation occupations, including employment and training information, visit:

- **Maritime Administration, U.S. Department of Transportation:** 1200 New Jersey Avenue, SE, Washington, DC 20590. Website: www. marad.dot.gov.

For more information about licensing requirements, visit:

- **The U.S. Coast Guard:** 2703 Martin Luther King Jr. Ave., SE, Washington, DC. Website: www.uscg.mil.

For information about jobs on inland and coastal waterways on barges, tugboats, and towboats, visit:

- **The American Waterways Operators:** 801 North Quincy Street, Suite 200, Arlington, VA 22203. Website: www.americanwaterways.com.
- **Lake Carriers' Association:** 20325 Center Ridge Road, Suite 720, Rocky River, OH 44116. Website: www.lcaships.com.
- **Passenger Vessel Association:** 103 Oronoco Street, Suite 200, Alexandria, VA 22314. Website: www.passengervessel.com.

9

Travel and Hospitality Jobs

"This industry is especially noted for focusing on performance and promoting talent from within its ranks. Many jobs only require basic skills, interest, motivation, drive, and a willingness to learn. Going from a doorman to a general manager is not a joke – it happens frequently!"

FEW INDUSTRIES PROVIDE as many great job and career opportunities for people without a four-year degree and those re-entering the job market than the travel and hospitality industry. Highly segmented, this industry encompasses everything from airlines, cruise lines, tour operators, and car rental agencies to hotels, resorts, and rail services. The travel and hospitality industry is especially noted for focusing on performance and promoting talent from within its ranks. Indeed, many general managers of major hotels began their careers at the very bottom – doorman, front desk clerk, or porter – and were promoted within to increasingly responsible positions.

Many entry-level positions within this industry only require a high school diploma and demonstrated ability to learn and achieve goals. Similar to other industries, employers within the travel and hospitality industry increasingly require candidates to have higher levels of education and training for entry into and advancement within this industry. Many vocational education schools, community colleges, and universities offer specialized short- and long-term programs in travel and hospitality. For anyone without a four-year degree, the travel and hospitality industry offers some of the more rewarding short- and long-term job and career opportunities.

Many of the jobs defining this exciting industry cross-cut other industries and only require basic skills, interest, motivation, drive, and a willingness to learn. If many of the jobs outlined in previous chapters are less than appealing to you, chances are you may find your dream job in one of the many segments that define the relatively open and inviting travel and hospitality industry. This also is an example of an industry undergoing tremendous economic stress and restructuring. It's often during such times that new opportunities arise for enterprising individuals who are willing to invest their futures in what may well be some exciting career opportunities.

The Industry and Its Many Players

The travel industry is much more than the stereotypical travel agent arranging tickets, tours, and hotels for tour groups and anxious tourists. This is a highly segmented industry consisting of a network of mutually dependent players – airlines, hotels, resorts, cruise lines, restaurants, wholesalers, incentive groups, retail tour agents, car rental companies, catering firms, meeting planners, corporate travel offices, educators, journalists, photographers, and travel writers. These, as well as a host of related organizations, individuals, and jobs, are focused on the business of moving and managing people from one location to another.

The travel industry is a challenging, exciting, and highly entrepreneurial industry. Its many players report a high degree of job satisfaction. Indeed, many claim to have found *"the best job in the world"* – and with all the perks to prove it! Public relations directors in major hotels, for example, often meet and entertain celebrities, work closely with the local business community, and participate in numerous community activities – a worklife many still can't believe they "fell into" in the travel industry.

While many of the businesses, such as major airlines and hotel chains, are huge corporations, most travel-related businesses appear big but are actually small and highly entrepreneurial. They appear big because they are connected to one another through efficient communication and marketing systems, which place everyone within a mutually interdependent network of business transactions. It's the type of business where there is a high degree of competition as well as a high degree of mutual dependence and cooperation. Individuals working in this industry manage to advance their careers by moving from one player to another with relative ease.

The major segments or sub-industries and players within the travel industry include operators, suppliers, promoters, and supporters:

- accommodations and lodging industry
- advertising
- advertising agencies
- airlines
- airport and aviation management groups
- bus lines
- car rentals
- computer support services
- convention and meeting planners
- corporate travel managers
- cruise lines
- culture and arts promotion groups
- government tourist promotion offices
- incentive travel companies
- public relations
- publishing and journalism
- rail services
- research and marketing groups
- resorts and spas
- restaurants
- sales and marketing
- theme parks
- tour guiding
- tour operators
- tourist sites and attractions
- travel agencies and operators
- travel clubs
- travel education and training
- travel insurance
- travel websites (e-travel)
- travel writers and photographers

While some of these players are experiencing major restructuring and downsizing, such as travel agencies and operators, others are experiencing major growth, such as cruise lines and e-travel.

Not surprisingly, the travel industry employs numerous types of workers from accountants, computer specialists, and lawyers to market researchers, artists, and doctors. Many people also are able to freelance in this industry as part- and full-time professionals serving as wholesalers, travel agents, writers, photographers, trainers, and consultants.

Air Traffic Controllers

- **Annual Earnings:** $122,530 ($58.91 per hour)
- **Education/Training:** Associate degree and work experience
- **Outlook:** Little or no change – 1% growth from 2012 to 2022 (from 25,000 to 25,400 jobs)

Employment Outlook: Employment of air traffic controllers is expected to experience little or no growth during the 2012-2022 decade. Most employment opportunities will result from the need to replace workers who retire. The Federal Aviation Administration (FAA) has not reduced – and does not expect to reduce – the overall number of controllers, although total air traffic has fallen since 2000. Even though air traffic is expected to increase, employment growth will not keep pace, because the FAA already has enough personnel capacity. In addition, federal budget constraints should limit the hiring of new controllers. In the long term, the NextGen satellite-based system is expected to allow individual controllers to handle more air traffic.

Job opportunities will be best for individuals with prior experience or those who are in their early 20s and have completed an AT-CTI study program. Competition for air traffic controller jobs is expected to be very strong, as many people will apply for a relatively few number of jobs. Those who are willing to live anywhere in the country will have an advantage.

Nature of Work: Air traffic controllers coordinate the movement of air traffic to ensure that planes stay a safe distance apart. Their primary concern is safety, but controllers also must direct planes efficiently to minimize delays. Some regulate airport traffic; others regulate flights between airports. Both airport tower and en route controllers usually control several planes at a time. Often they have to make quick decisions about completely different activities.

Work Environment: Controllers work a basic 40-hour week; however, they may work additional hours for which they receive overtime pay or equal time off. Because most control towers and centers operate 24 hours a day, seven days a week, controllers rotate night and weekend shifts. During busy times, controllers must work rapidly and efficiently. Total concentration is required to keep track of several planes at the same time and to make certain that all pilots receive correct instructions. The mental stress of being responsible for the safety of several aircraft and their passengers can be exhausting for some persons.

Education, Training, & Qualifications: To become an air traffic controller, a person must enroll in an FAA-approved education program and pass a pre-employment test that measures his/her ability to learn the controller's duties in order to qualify for job openings in the air traffic control system. (Exceptions are air traffic controllers with prior experience and military veterans.) The pre-employment test is currently offered only to students enrolled in an FAA-approved education program. In addition, applicants must have three years of full-time work experience or four years of college, or an equivalent combination of both.

Upon successful completion of an FAA-approved program, individuals who receive a school recommendation and who meet the basic qualification requirements, including age limit and achievement of a qualifying score on the FAA pre-employment test, become eligible for employment as an air traffic controller. Candidates must also pass a medical exam, drug screening, and security clearance before they can be hired. Upon selection, employees attend the FAA Academy in Oklahoma City for 12 weeks of training, during which they learn the fundamentals of the airway system, FAA regulations, controller equipment, and aircraft performance characteristics, as well as more specialized tasks. After they graduate, it takes several years of progressively more responsible work experience, interspersed with considerable classroom instruction and independent study, to become a fully licensed controller.

Earnings: This is one of the highest paid jobs for people without a four-year degree. Median annual earnings of air traffic controllers in 2012 were $122,530. The top 10% earned $171,340 per year; the bottom 10% earned $64,930. Both the worker's job responsibilities and complexity of the particular facility determine a controller's pay. For example, controllers who work at FAA's busiest air traffic control facilities earn higher pay.

Key Contacts: For more information about air traffic controllers, visit:

- **Federal Aviation Administration:** 800 Independence Avenue, SW, Washington, DC 20591. Website: www.faa.gov.
- **National Air Traffic Controllers Association:** 1325 Massachusetts Avenue, NW, Washington, DC 20005. Website: www.natca.org.

Chefs and Head Cooks

- **Annual Earnings:** $42,480 ($20.42 per hour)
- **Education/Training:** High school diploma or equivalent
- **Outlook:** Slower than average – 5% growth from 2012 to 2022 (from 115,400 to 121,400 jobs)

Employment Outlook: Employment of chefs and head cooks is projected to grow 5% from 2012 to 2022, slower than the average for all occupations. Population and income growth are expected to result in greater demand for high-quality dishes at a variety of dining venues, including many upscale establishments. However, employment growth should be limited, as many restaurants, in an effort to lower costs, choose to hire cooks or other food service workers to perform the work normally done by higher-paid chefs and head cooks.

Job opportunities should be best for chefs and head cooks with several years of work experience. The majority of job openings will result from the need to replace workers who leave the occupation. The fast pace, long hours, and high energy levels required for these jobs often lead to a high rate of turnover.

There will be strong competition for jobs at upscale restaurants, hotels, and casinos, where the pay is typically highest. Workers with a combination of business skills, previous work experience, and creativity should have the best job prospects.

Nature of Work: Chefs and head cooks typically do the following:

- Check freshness of food and ingredients
- Supervise and coordinate activities of cooks and other food preparation workers
- Develop recipes and determine how to present the food
- Plan menus and ensure uniform serving sizes and quality of meals
- Inspect supplies, equipment, and work areas for cleanliness and functionality
- Hire, train, and supervise cooks and other food preparation workers
- Order and maintain inventory of food and supplies
- Monitor sanitation practices and follow kitchen safety standards

Chefs and head cooks use a variety of kitchen and cooking equipment, including step-in coolers, high-quality knives, meat slicers, and grinders. They also have access to large quantities of meats, spices, and produce. Some chefs use scheduling and purchasing software to help them in their administrative tasks.

Some chefs run their own restaurant or catering business. These chefs are often busy with kitchen and office work and have little time to interact with diners.

The following are examples of types of chefs and head cooks:

- **Executive chefs, head cooks, and chefs de cuisine** are primarily responsible for overseeing the operation of a kitchen. They coordinate the work of sous chefs and other cooks, who prepare most of the meals. Executive chefs also have many duties beyond the kitchen. They design the menu, review food and beverage purchases, and often train

cooks and other food preparation workers. Some executive chefs primarily handle administrative tasks and may spend less time in the kitchen.

- **Sous chefs** are a kitchen's second-in-command. They supervise the restaurant's cooks, prepare meals, and report results to the head chefs. In the absence of the head chef, sous chefs run the kitchen.
- **Private household chefs** typically work full time for one client, such as a corporate executive, university president, or diplomat, who regularly entertains as part of his or her official duties.

Work Environment: Chefs and head cooks held about 115,400 jobs in 2012. The industries that employed the most chefs and head cooks in 2012 were as follows:

- Restaurants and other eating places   46%
- Traveler accommodations   11%
- Special food services   10%
- Other amusement and recreation industries   6%

Chefs and head cooks work in restaurants, hotels, private households, and other food service facilities, all of which must be kept clean and sanitary. Chefs and head cooks usually stand for long periods and work in a fast-paced environment.

About 13% of chefs and head cooks were self-employed in 2012. Because some self-employed chefs run their own restaurant or catering business, their work can be additionally stressful. For example, outside the kitchen, they often spend long hours managing all aspects of the business, to ensure that bills and salaries are paid and that the business is profitable.

Education, Training, & Qualifications: A growing number of chefs and head cooks receive formal training at community colleges, technical schools, culinary arts schools, and 4-year colleges. Students in culinary programs spend most of their time in kitchens practicing their cooking skills. Programs cover all aspects of kitchen work, including menu planning, food sanitation procedures, and purchasing and inventory methods. Most training programs also require students to gain experience in a commercial kitchen through an internship or apprenticeship program.

Most chefs and head cooks start working in other positions, such as line cooks, learning cooking skills from the chefs they work for. Many spend years working in kitchens before learning enough to get promoted to chef or head cook positions.

Some chefs and head cooks train on the job, where they learn the same skills as in a formal education program. Some train in mentorship programs, where they work under the direction of an experienced chef. Executive chefs, head cooks, and sous chefs who work in fine-dining restaurants often have many years of training and experience.

Some chefs and head cooks learn through apprenticeship programs sponsored by professional culinary institutes, industry associations, and trade unions in coordination with the U.S. Department of Labor. Apprenticeship programs generally last about 2 years and combine instructions and on-the-job training. Apprentices must complete at least 1,000 hours of both instructions and paid on-the-job training. Courses typically cover food sanitation and safety, basic knife skills, and equipment operation. Apprentices spend the rest of the training learning practical skills in a commercial kitchen under a chef's supervision.

Earnings: The median annual wage for chefs and head cooks was $42,480 in 2012. The top 10% earned $74,120 a year; the bottom 10% earned less than $24,530. In 2012, the median annual wages for chefs and head cooks in the top four industries employing these workers were as follows:

- Traveler accommodations $48,210
- Other amusement and recreation industries $47,490
- Special food services $42,960
- Restaurants and other eating places $39,790

About 13% of chefs and head cooks were self-employed in 2012. Some self-employed chefs run their own restaurant or catering business.

The level of pay for chefs and head cooks varies greatly by region and employer. Pay is usually highest in upscale restaurants and hotels, where many executive chefs work, as well as in major metropolitan and resort areas.

Most chefs and head cooks work full time and often work early mornings, late evenings, weekends, and holidays. Many executive chefs and chefs who run their own business work 12-hour days, because they oversee the delivery of food products early in the day and use the afternoon to prepare special menu items.

Key Contacts: For information on career opportunities and educational programs for chefs, cooks, and other kitchen workers, contact local employers, local offices of the state employment service, or:

- **American Culinary Federation:** 180 Center Place Way, St. Augustine, FL 32095. Website: www.acfchefs.org.
- **International Council on Hotel, Restaurant, and Institutional Education:** 2810 North Parham Road, Suite 230, Richmond, VA 23294. Website: www.chrie.org.
- **National Restaurant Association:** 2055 L Street, NW, Suite 700, Washington, DC 20036. Website: www.restaurant.org.

For information on becoming a private chef, visit:

- **American Personal and Private Chef Association:** Website: www.personalchef.com.

Cruise Line Jobs

- **Annual Earnings:** Varies
- **Education/Training:** High school diploma to college
- **Outlook:** Excellent

Employment Outlook: Job opportunities with cruise lines should increase at a faster rate than most jobs for the decade ahead as more and more cruise ships come on line to accommodate the increased demand for cruise vacations. Indeed, the cruise industry has experienced phenomenal growth during the past decade as interest in cruise vacations has increased and as more and more mega-cruise ships have come on line. Each year cruise ships carry nearly 8 million North American passengers. The number of passengers is likely to double over the coming decade as more and more people choose cruise ships as their favorite mode of vacation-resort travel. In response to this projected growth in passengers, nearly 50 new cruise ships have come on line during the past five years. Such growth translates into more and more jobs in this much sought-after industry.

Cruise ship jobs are highly competitive. Operating like large resorts whose main purpose is to pamper their guests during three- to 14-day cruises, most cruise ships maintain a high staff-per-passenger ratio. They hire for every type of department and position you would find in five-star resorts – housekeeping, kitchen, entertainment, health, fitness, tours, gaming, guest relations, engineering, maintenance, hair salon, and gift shop. They hire accountants, cooks, waiters, engineers, casino operators, pursers, photographers, massage therapists, cosmetologists, doctors, nurses, entertainers, youth counselors, water sports instructors, fitness instructors, and lecturers. However, they disproportionately hire crew members from Europe and Asia who traditionally occupy these lower-paying jobs.

Nature of Work: There are many myths about cruise line jobs. The biggest myths are that these jobs are all fun and games, they pay well, and there are plenty of opportunities available onboard for Americans. The realities are that most cruise line jobs involve hard work and do not pay well, and few Americans find jobs onboard. Cruise ship jobs involve long hours, a great deal of stress, a willingness to work with a diverse multinational team, an ability to please all types of passengers, and the willingness to give exceptional and exacting service. Above all, you must be people-oriented, tolerant, flexible, and handle stress well. You must have the disposition of a servant – the customer is always right, even though he or she may be a jerk!

If you have a family, an onboard cruise ship job is likely to involve long separations. For many Americans, it's the type of job best enjoyed by young single individuals who regard these cruise ship jobs as short-term travel positions or entry-level positions for moving within the larger travel and hospitality industry. Many Americans will spend three to five years working with cruise lines – accumulating valuable travel and resort experience – before "settling down" to more stable family-oriented jobs on shore.

Few Americans work onboard, and those that do tend to be found in a very limited number of "American" positions – entertainment, gift shop, youth counselor, physical fitness, and sports. You won't find many Americans piloting ships, managing restaurants, serving tables, cooking food, or making beds. These positions tend to be dominated by other nationals. Most American involvement with the cruise ship industry tends to be on shore – in marketing, sales, and computer reservation systems.

Americans tend to be disproportionately found in the entertainment, physical fitness, public relations, youth counseling, spa, shop, casino, and marketing and sales end of cruise ship jobs. Despite all the glamour, cruise ship pay and lifestyles simply are not sufficiently attractive for many Americans to continue long-term in this industry. Americans also are not noted for their talent in dispensing exceptional, exacting, and high level service that is the hallmark of many cruise lines.

Many Americans typically pursue cruise ship jobs in the hopes of moving on to other jobs on shore within the travel and hospitality industry, especially with hotels, resorts, restaurants, casinos, and night clubs. A cruise ship job is often a short stop along the way to other more rewarding jobs and careers.

Breaking into the cruise industry is relatively easy given the high turnover rate of personnel and the availability of numerous entry-level positions. Functioning as a combination floating city, resort, and hotel, most cruise ships operate with a staff of 300 to 900 who provide a wide range of services. As a result, cruise lines are constantly hiring for all types of positions. The most common shipboard opportunities include:

- **Front desk/purser's desk:** Positions include chief purser, assistant purser, guest services staff members.
- **Boutiques/shops:** sales staff and cashiers.
- **Restaurants and bars:** Chef, sous chef, pastry cook, baker, wine steward, buffet staff, food and beverage staff, bartender, maitre d', wait staff, busboy, butcher, ice carver, dishwasher.
- **Casino:** Cashier, dealer, slot technician.
- **Salon and spa:** Massage therapist, cosmetologist, hair stylist, nail technician, masseur/masseuse.
- **Show lounges:** Dancer, singer, comedian, magician, lecturer, sound technician, band member, disk jockey, and other types of entertainers.
- **Activities:** Youth counselor, activities coordinator, instructor (yoga, chess, bridge, diving, golf, tennis, dance, water sports), shore excursion, sports director, swimming pool/deck attendant.
- **Operations:** Computer specialist, electrician, machinist, painter.
- **Photography:** Photographer.
- **Medical:** Physician, dentist, nurse.

The cruise industry is a great entry point into the travel industry. Most positions require little or no experience, though a few positions require many years of experience. If you target your job search, make the right contacts, and are persistent, you may be able to land a job with a cruise line.

As you conduct a job search, you should be aware that many onboard positions are not controlled by the cruise lines. Gift shops, beauty salons, casinos, sports and recreation, and entertainment are often concessions operated by contractors or concessionaires. For example, dancers, musicians, singers, massage therapists, cosmetologists, and medical doctors are often hired through firms that control these onboard concessions. If a position you desire relates to these concessions, you will need to make employment contacts with the appropriate concessionaire rather than the cruise line.

Most cruise lines require an online application or a mailed, faxed, or e-mailed resume and cover letter. Another approach is to send a copy of your resume, along with an accompanying cover letter, directly to the personnel office of a cruise line. Specify on the envelope or in the attention line whether you are applying for a "shipside" or a "shoreside" position, identify which department you wish to work for, and/or call ahead to get the name of the department or person you should address your correspondence to.

Cruise lines recruit individuals for both shoreside and shipboard positions. The three largest cruise lines, which employ the largest staffs, include the following:

- **Carnival Cruise Lines** www.carnival.com
- **Princess Cruises** www.princess.com
- **Royal Caribbean International** www.royalcaribbean.com

Be sure to familiarize yourself with each cruise line's operations. For example, the Disney Cruise Lines and Carnival Cruises are very family- and youth-oriented, requiring many youth counselors. Crystal and Seabourn Cruises are very upscale, offering many five-star amenities and the services of spa personnel and academic lecturers. Norwegian Cruise Lines is noted for its sports programs and theme cruises. If you survey the companies' websites, you'll get a good idea of various opportunities available with such companies. Best of all, you can apply for jobs online 24 hours a day! One of the best books on the cruise industry is Douglas Ward's *Berlitz Cruising and Cruise Ships* (Berlitz). For reviews of various cruise lines and cruise ships, be sure to visit www.cruisecritic.com as well as individual cruise lines featured on www.glassdoor.com.

Key Contacts: Several websites offer books and application packages for cruise ship jobs, which include job search tips and addresses of major cruise employers and employment firms:

- **All Cruise Jobs** www.allcruisejobs.com
- **Cruise Line Jobs** www.cruiselinesjob.com
- **Cruise Ship Entertainment Jobs** www.cruiseshipentertainment.com
- **CruiseJobFinder** www.cruisejobfinder.com
- **Cruise Ship Jobs** www.hcareers.com/cruise-ship-jobs

Food and Beverage Servicing and Related Workers

- **Annual Earnings:** $18,400 ($8.84 per hour) plus tips
- **Education/Training:** Less than high school
- **Outlook:** As fast as average – 12% growth from 2012 to 2022 (from 4,438,100 to 4,962,300 jobs)

Employment Outlook: Overall employment of food and beverage serving and related workers is projected to grow 12% from 2012 to 2022, about as fast as the average for all occupations. Employment growth, however, will vary by specialty. Employment of nonrestaurant servers, such as those who deliver food trays in hotels, in hospitals, in residential care facilities, and at catered events, is projected to grow 20% from 2012 to 2022, faster than the average for all occupations.

Employment of combined food preparation and serving workers, which includes fast-food workers, is projected to grow 14% from 2012 to 2022, about as fast as the average for all occupations.

Employment of dining room and cafeteria attendants, counter attendants, and hosts and hostesses is projected to grow 8% from 2012 to 2022, about as fast as the average for all occupations.

As a growing population continues to dine out, purchase carryout meals, or have food delivered, more restaurants, particularly fast-food and casual dining restaurants, will open, increasing demand for food and beverage serving workers, including fast-food workers.

In addition, nontraditional food service operations, such as those found inside grocery stores and cafeterias in hospitals and residential care facilities, will serve more prepared meals. Because these workers are essential to the operation of a food-serving establishment, they will continue to be in demand.

Nature of Work: Food and beverage serving and related workers typically do the following:

- Greet customers and answer their questions about menu items and specials
- Take food or drink orders from customers

- Prepare food and drink orders, such as sandwiches, salads, and coffee
- Relay customers' orders to other kitchen staff
- Serve food and drinks to customers at a counter, at a stand, or in a hotel room
- Clean assigned work areas, dining tables, or serving counters
- Replenish and stock service stations, cabinets, and tables
- Set tables or prepare food trays for new customers

Food and beverage serving and related workers are the front line of customer service in restaurants, cafeterias, and other food service establishments. Depending on the establishment, they take customers' food and drink orders and serve food and beverages. Most work as part of a team, helping coworkers to improve workflow and customer service. The job titles of food and beverage serving and related workers vary with where they work and what they do.

Working Conditions: Food and beverage workers are on their feet most of the time and often have to carry heavy trays of food, dishes, and glassware. During busy dining periods, they are under pressure to serve customers quickly. Many food and beverage workers are expected to work evenings, weekends, and holidays; some work split shifts. Although some food and beverage workers work 40 hours or more per week, the majority are employed part-time.

Education, Training, & Qualifications: There are no specific educational requirements for food and beverage service jobs. Although many employers prefer to hire high school graduates for waiter, waitress, bartender, host, and hostess positions, completion of high school is generally not required for fast-food workers, or dining room attendants and bartender helpers. For many persons, these jobs serve as a source of immediate income rather than a career. Most food and beverage workers pick up their skills on the job by observing and working with more experienced workers.

Earnings: This is one of the least paid occupations featured in this book. However, it's also one that has a very high turnover (some restaurants literally turn over 100% of their wait staff every year!) and thus has numerous openings for people in transitional or supplementary income situations.

The median hourly wage for food and beverage serving and related workers was $8.84 in 2012. The top 10% earned $11.63 per hours; the bottom 10% earned less than $7.76 per hour. In 2012, median hourly wages for food and beverage serving and related workers were as follows:

- $9.44 for food servers, nonrestaurant
- $8.93 for hosts and hostesses, restaurant, lounge, and coffee shop
- $8.92 for counter attendants, cafeteria, food concession, and coffee shop
- $8.89 for dining room and cafeteria attendants and bartender helpers
- $8.78 for combined food preparation and serving workers, including fast food
- $9.76 for food preparation and serving related workers, all other

Although some workers in this occupation earn tips, most get their earnings from hourly wages alone. Many entry-level or inexperienced workers earn the federal minimum wage ($7.25 per hour as of July 24, 2009). However, many others earn more per hour because they work in states that set minimum wages higher than the federal minimum.

Some food and beverage serving workers receive customers' tips. In some restaurants, workers contribute all or a portion of their tips to a tip pool, which is distributed among qualifying workers. Tip pools allow workers who do not usually receive tips directly from customers, such as dining room attendants, to be part of a team and to share in the rewards for good service.

Some states have exceptions to their minimum-wage laws for tipped employees in certain specific circumstances. According to the Fair Labor Standards Act, tipped employees are employees who regularly receive more than $30 a month in tips. The employer may consider tips as part of wages, but must pay at least $2.13 an hour in direct wages. The Wage and Hour Division of the U.S. Department of Labor maintains a website listing minimum wages for tipped employees by state.

About half of all food and beverage serving and related workers were employed part time in 2012. Because food service and drinking establishments typically have long dining hours, early morning, late evening, weekend, and holidays work is common. Those who work in school cafeterias have more regular hours and may work only during the school year, which is usually 9 to 10 months.

Employers often provide free meals and furnish uniforms, but some may deduct the cost from the worker's wages.

Key Contacts: For information on food and beverage service jobs, contact:

- **International Council on Hotel, Restaurant, and Institutional Education:** 2810 North Parham Road, Suite 230, Richmond, VA 23294. Website: www.chrie.org.

- **National Restaurant Association:** 2055 L St. NW, Suite 700, Washington, DC 20036. Website: www.restaurant.org.

Food Service Managers

- **Annual Earnings:** $47,960 ($23.06 per hour)
- **Education/Training:** High school diploma or equivalent and some experience
- **Outlook:** Little or no change – 2% growth from 2012 to 2022 (from 321,400 to 326,400 jobs)

Employment Outlook: Employment of food service managers is projected to show little or no change from 2012 to 2022. Population and income growth are expected to result in greater demand for food at a variety of dining establishments. People will continue to dine out, purchase take-out meals, or have food delivered to their homes or workplaces. In response, more restaurants will open, and cafeterias, catering services, and nontraditional food services, such as those found inside grocery or retail stores, will serve more prepared dishes.

However, employment growth should be limited as companies that operate restaurants and other food service establishments continue to consolidate managerial functions and use first-line supervisors to perform the work normally done by managers.

Job opportunities should be best for food service managers with several years of work experience in a restaurant or food service establishment. Most job openings will result from the need to replace managers who retire or transfer to other occupations.

Jobseekers with a combination of work experience in food service and a bachelor's degree in hospitality, restaurant, or food service management should have an edge when competing for jobs at upscale restaurants.

Nature of Work: Food service managers typically do the following:

- Interview, hire, train, oversee, and sometimes fire employees

- Manage the inventory and order food and beverages, equipment, and supplies

- Oversee food preparation, portion sizes, and the overall presentation of food

- Inspect supplies, equipment, and work areas

- Ensure employees comply with health and food safety standards and regulations

- Investigate and resolve complaints regarding food quality or service

- Schedule staff hours and assign duties

- Maintain budgets and payroll records and review financial transactions

- Establish standards for personnel performance and customer service

Besides coordinating activities of the kitchen and dining room staff, managers ensure that customers are served properly and in a timely manner. They monitor orders in the kitchen and, if needed, they work with the chef to remedy any delays in service. Some food service managers, including those who manage their own business, deal with suppliers and arrange for delivery of food and beverages and other supplies. Some also plan or approve menus and set prices for food and beverage items.

Food service managers are responsible for all functions of the business, related to employees. For example, most managers interview, hire, train, and sometimes fire employees. Managers also schedule work hours, making sure that enough workers are present to cover each shift. During busy periods, they may expedite the service by helping to serve customers, cashiering, or cleaning tables.

Food service managers also plan and arrange for cleaning and maintenance services of the equipment and facility. For example, they arrange for linen service, heavy cleaning when the dining room and kitchen are not in use, trash removal, and pest control when needed.

In addition, managers perform many administrative tasks, such as keeping employee records; preparing the payroll; and completing paperwork to comply with licensing, tax and wage, unemployment compensation, and Social Security laws. Although they sometimes assign these tasks to an assistant manager or bookkeeper, most managers are responsible for the accuracy of business records.

Full-service restaurants (those with table service) may have a management team that includes a general manager, one or more assistant managers, and an executive chef. Managers add up the cash and charge slips and secure them in a safe place. Many managers also lock up the establishment; check that ovens, grills, and lights are off; and switch on the alarm system.

Work Environment: Food service managers held about 321,400 jobs in 2012. About 40% were self-employed. Food service managers typically work in restaurants, including fine-dining and fast-food chains and franchises. Others work in hotels, catering, and other establishments, such as cafeterias in schools, hospitals, factories, or offices. Many food service managers work long hours, and the job is often hectic. Dealing with unhappy customers can sometimes be stressful.

Most food service managers work full time. Managers at fine-dining and fast-food restaurants often work long hours. Managers of institutional food service facilities in schools, factories, or office buildings usually work traditional business hours. Those who oversee multiple locations of a chain or franchise may be called in on short notice, including evenings, weekends, and holidays.

Education, Training, & Qualifications: Many restaurant and food service manager positions are filled by promoting experienced food and beverage preparation and service workers. Waiters, waitresses, chefs, and fast-food workers who have demonstrated their potential for handling increased responsibility sometimes advance to assistant manager or management trainee jobs when openings occur. However, most food service management companies and restaurant chains recruit management trainees from among graduates of two- and four-year college programs. They prefer to hire persons with degrees in restaurant and institutional food service management. A bachelor's degree in restaurant and food service management provides especially strong preparation for a career in this occupation.

Earnings: The median annual wage for food service managers was $47,960 in 2012. The top 10% earned $81,030 per year; the bottom 10% earned less than $30,820. In 2012, median annual wages for food service managers in the top five industries employing these managers were as follows:

- Traveler accommodation $54,850
- Special food services $54,210
- Nursing care facilities $49,650
- Elementary and secondary schools $49,440
- Restaurants and other eating places $46,360

Key Contacts: For more information about food service managers, including a directory of college programs in food service, visit:

- **National Restaurant Association:** 2055 L Street, NW, Suite 700, Washington, DC 20036. Website: www.restaurant.org.

For more information about food service managers and certification as a Foodservice Management Professional, visit:

- **National Restaurant Association Educational Foundation:** 2055 L Street, NW, Suite 700, Washington, DC 20036. Website: www.nraef.org.

Hotel, Motel, and Resort Desk Clerks

- **Annual Earnings:** $22,180 ($10.67 per hour)
- **Education/Training:** On-the-job training
- **Outlook:** Faster than average – 8-14% growth from 2012 to 2022 (from 232,000 to 260,000 jobs)

Employment Outlook: Employment is expected to grow faster than average for most occupations in the decade ahead as the number of hotels, motels, and other lodging establishments increases in response to increased business travel and tourism. Opportunities for part-time work should be plentiful. Employment of desk clerks is sensitive to cyclical swings in the economy. During recessions, vacation and business travel declines, and hotels and motels need fewer clerks.

Nature of Work: Hotel and motel desk clerks may register guests, assign rooms, and answer questions about available services, checkout times, the local community, and other matters. Because most smaller hotels and motels have minimal staffs, the clerk also may function as a bookkeeper, advance reservation agent, cashier, and/or telephone operator.

Working Conditions: Hotel and motel desk clerks are on their feet most of the time. During holidays and other busy periods, these clerks may find the work hectic due to the large number of guests or travelers who must be served. When service does not flow smoothly – because of mishandled reservations, for example – these clerks act as a buffer between the establishment and its customers.

Education, Training, & Qualifications: A high school diploma or its equivalent usually is required. Hotel and motel desk clerk job orientation is usually brief and includes an explanation of the job duties and information about the establishment, such as room location and available services. They start work on the job under the guidance of a supervisor or experienced clerk. They may need additional training in data processing or office machine operations to use computerized reservation, room assignment, and billing systems.

Earnings: In 2012, the average annual earnings of full-time hotel and motel clerks were around $22,180 ($10.67 per hour). The top 10% earned $30,460 a year; the bottom 10% earned $16,780. Earnings depend on the location, size, and type of establishment in which they work. Large luxury hotels and those located in metropolitan and resort areas generally pay clerks more than less expensive ones and those located in less populated areas. In general, hotels pay higher salaries than motels or other types of lodging establishments.

Key Contacts: Information on careers in the lodging industry may be obtained from:

- **American Hotel and Lodging Educational Institute:** 800 N. Magnolia Ave., Suite 300, Orlando, FL 32803. Website: www.ahlei.org.

- **American Hotel & Lodging Association:** 1250 I Street, NW, Suite 1100, Washington, DC 20005. Website: www.ahla.com.

For general information about food service managers, visit:

- **Society for Hospitality and Foodservice Management:** 328 E. Main Street, Louisville, KY 40202. Website: www.sfm-online.org.

Meeting, Convention, and Event Planners

- **Annual Earnings:** $45,810 ($22.02 per hour)
- **Education/Training:** Bachelor's degree
- **Outlook:** Much faster than average – 33% increase from 2012 to 2022 (from 94,200 to 125,500 jobs)

Employment Outlook: As businesses and organizations become increasingly international, meetings and conventions are expected to become even more important. For organizations with geographically separate offices and members, meetings are the only time they can bring everyone together. Despite the spread of online communication, face-to-face interaction continues to be preferred by many people. Candidates with a bachelor's degree in hospitality or tourism management should have the best job opportunities. A

Certified Meeting Professional (CMP) credential is also viewed favorably by potential employers. Those who have experience with virtual meeting software and social media outlets also should have an advantage.

Nature of Work: Meeting, convention, and event planners typically do the following:

- Meet with clients to understand the purpose of the meeting or event
- Plan the scope of the event, including time, location, and cost
- Solicit bids from venues and service providers (for example, florists or photographers)
- Inspect venues to ensure that they meet the client's requirements
- Coordinate event services such as rooms, transportation, and food service
- Monitor event activities to ensure the client and event attendees are satisfied
- Review event bills and approve payment

Whether it is a wedding, educational conference, or business convention, meetings and events bring people together for a common purpose. Meeting, convention, and event planners work to ensure that this purpose is achieved efficiently and seamlessly. They coordinate every detail of events, from beginning to end. Before a meeting, for example, planners will meet with clients to estimate attendance and determine the meeting's purpose. During the meeting, they handle meeting logistics, such as registering guests and organizing audio/visual equipment for speakers. After the meeting, they may survey attendees to find out how the event was received.

Meeting, convention, and event planners also search for potential meeting sites, such as hotels and convention centers. They consider the lodging and services that the facility can provide, how easy it will be for people to get there, and the attractions that the surrounding area has to offer. More recently, planners also consider whether an online meeting can achieve the same objectives as a face-to-face meeting in certain cases. Once a location is selected, planners arrange the meeting space and support services. For example, providing services such as wheelchair accessibility, interpreters, and other accommodations may be required. They may also negotiate contracts with suppliers to provide meals for attendees and coordinate plans with on-site staff. In addition, they organize speakers, entertainment, and activities. Meeting, convention, and event planners manage the finances of meetings and conventions within a budget set by their clients.

Work Environment: Meeting, convention, and event planners held about 94,200 jobs in 2012. Most worked for private companies; about 1 in 6 were self-employed. Meeting, convention, and event planners spend most of their time in offices. During meetings and events, they usually work on-site at hotels or convention centers. They travel regularly to attend the events they organize and to visit prospective meeting sites. Planners regularly collaborate with clients, hospitality workers, and meeting attendees. Their work can be fast-paced and demanding. Planners oversee many aspects of an event at the same time and face numerous deadlines. Most meeting, convention, and event planners work full time. In addition, many are required to work long, irregular hours in the time leading up to a major event. During meetings or conventions, planners may have very long work days. They sometimes work on weekends.

Education, Training, & Qualifications: Many employers prefer applicants who have a bachelor's degree and some work experience in hotels or planning. The proportion of planners with a bachelor's degree is increasing because work responsibilities are becoming more complex and because there are more college degree programs related to hospitality or tourism management. If an applicant's degree is not related to these fields, employers are likely to require at least 1 to 2 years of related experience. Meeting, convention, and event planners often come from a variety of academic disciplines. Some related undergraduate majors include marketing, public relations, communications, and business. Planners who have studied hospitality management may start out with greater responsibilities than those from other academic disciplines.

Earnings: The median annual wage for meeting, convention, and event planners was $45,810 in 2012. The top 10% earned $79,270 a year; the bottom 10% earned less than $26,560.

Key Contacts: For more information about meeting, convention, and event planners, including information about certification and industry trends, visit:

- **Convention Industry Council:** 700 N. Fairfax Street, Suite 510, Alexandria, VA 22314. Website: www.conventionindustry.org.

- **Meeting Professionals International:** 3030 Lyndon B. Johnson Freeway, Suite 1700, Dallas, Texas 75234-2759. Website: www.mpiweb.org.

- **Professional Convention Management Association:** 35 East Wacker Drive, Suite 500, Chicago, IL 60601. Website: www.pcma.org.

- **Society of Government Meeting Professionals:** PO Box 321025, Alexandria, VA 22320. Website: www.sgmp.org.

10

52 More Jobs for Ex-Offenders

*"It's not rocket science. **Education** is the key to building a resilient career, making good money, and experiencing long-term job security. Whatever you do, always **invest in yourself first** by acquiring more education and training. While you don't need a Ph.D., you at least need a GED or high school diploma plus additional education for enhancing your investment!"*

THIS FINAL CHAPTER SUMMARIZES in abbreviated form 52 additional jobs ex-offenders should consider as possible career alternatives. Detailed information on each of these jobs, including required skills, work environment, salaries, and training, can be found in the U.S. Department of Labor's biannual *Occupational Outlook Handbook* (www.bls.gov/ooh) and the *O*NET Dictionary of Occupational Titles* (www.onetonline.org).

Employment Restrictions Revisited

Please note that not all of the jobs featured here are open to any ex-offender. The degree of openness will depend on your particular offense, which will most certainly be revealed in a thorough background check and review of your rap sheet. Therefore, it's incumbent upon you to investigate what types of employment restrictions, such as those outlined in Chapter 3, may pertain to your history. There's a big difference, for example, in employment restrictions on "youthful indiscretions" (a minor drug offense, vandalism, public drunkenness) and indebtedness (failure to pay child support) that resulted in jail time or got escalated to prison time versus employment restrictions for armed robbery, fraud, aggravated assault, arson, kidnapping, rape, and murder that resulted in serious prison time. If you've committed any of the latter group of toxic offenses, you may have difficulty landing many of the jobs featured in this book.

Computer and Internet Jobs

Despite a great deal of talk about offshoring information technology jobs, the computer and Internet industries will generate a large number of jobs within the U.S. during the coming decade. These remain some of the hottest industries for anyone wishing to hitch themselves to a very promising career future. Indeed, next to health care, the fastest growing occupations – increasing the number of jobs by over 35% – will be in the computer industry:

- network systems and data communications analysts
- computer software engineers
- database administrators
- computer systems analysts

- network and computer systems administrators
- computer and information systems managers
- software developers
- cybersecurity

That's the good news. The bad news affects people without a four-year degree, because most of these growing computer- and Internet-related occupations require at least a bachelor's degree. In fact, entry into these high-demand fields requires a great deal of formal education at the bachelor's level and beyond. Computer software engineers, for example, must have a bachelor's degree to qualify for the more than 200 certification programs that constitute part of the formal continuing education track for computer software engineers. Given the right education and training in various computer fields, one should experience long-term job security, career advancement, job mobility, and relatively high salaries and generous benefits in these fields. Computer engineers and computer systems analysts are found on most lists of the hottest jobs in the decade ahead. Many of these workers constantly respond to the technology needs of today's hottest employers, who are found in health and medical care fields. If you want to fast-track your career, make good money, and experience long-term job security, these are the fields to be in for the coming decade. But, first, you need to take stock of your educational credentials. Do you have what it takes to enter these stellar fields? Do you want to work with smart, successful, and driven people? What do you need to do to get your educational house in order? **Breaking news (also see page 14):** Inmates may soon (2016) be eligible for federal Pell grants to pursue a college education!

There's also good news here for people with less than a bachelor's degree. Thousands of computer-related job opportunities are available for those without a four-year degree. Many of these jobs require short-term training courses, certification, or a two-year associate degree acquired through a junior or community college. For the most part, these jobs relate to the serving and maintenance of computers, computer support services, and computer applications. Given the rapidly changing nature of computer technology, individuals in these fields are constantly being retrained in the latest hardware and systems applications. Consequently, the distinction between people with or without a four-year degree becomes less important than the distinction between people with or without the latest training.

Computer, ATM, and Office Machine Repairers

- **Annual Earnings:** $36,620 ($17.60 per hour)
- **Education/Training:** Some college, no degree
- **Outlook:** Slower than average – 4% growth from 2012 to 2022 (from 133,100 to 138,200 jobs)

Computer, ATM, and office machine repairers install, fix, and maintain many of the machines that businesses, households, and other consumers use. Employment growth is expected to be slower than average for all occupations in the decade ahead. Limited growth will be driven by the increasing dependence of business and individuals on computers and other sophisticated office machines. The need to maintain this equipment will create new jobs for repairers. At the same time, remote diagnostic software will result in repairers becoming more productive, limiting overall employment growth; the need for on-site service calls will decrease. In some cases, replacing computers or other office equipment will be more cost-effective than having them repaired.

Computer Network Architects

- **Annual Earnings:** $91,000 ($43.75 per hour)
- **Education/Training:** Bachelor's degree
- **Outlook:** Faster than average – 15% growth from 2012 to 2022 (from 143,400 to 164,300 jobs)

Computer network architects design and build data communication networks, including local area networks (LANs), wide area networks (WANs), and intranets. These networks range from a small connection between two offices to a multinational series of globally distributed communications systems. Demand for computer network architects will increase as firms continue to expand their use of wireless and mobile networks. Designing and building these new networks, as well as upgrading existing ones, will create opportunities for computer network architects. The expansion of health care information technology will also contribute to employment growth. Adoption of cloud computing, which allows users to access storage, software, and other computer services over the Internet, is likely to cause a decrease in the demand for computer network architects. Organizations will no longer have to design and build networks in-house; instead, firms that provide cloud services will do this. However, because architects at cloud providers can work on more than one organization's network, these providers will not have to employ as many architects as individual organizations do for the same amount of work.

Web Developers

- **Annual Earnings:** $62,500 ($30.05 per hour)
- **Education/Training:** Associate's degree
- **Outlook:** Faster than average – 20% growth from 2012 to 2022 (from 141,400 to 159,900 jobs)

Web developers design and create websites. They are responsible for the look of the site. They are also responsible for the site's technical aspects, such as performance and capacity, which are measures of a website's speed and how much traffic the site can handle. They also may create content for the site. Employment of web developers is projected to grow as e-commerce continues to expand. Online purchasing is expected to grow faster than the overall retail industry. As retail firms expand their online offerings, demand for web developers will increase. Additionally, an increase in the use of mobile devices to search the web will also lead to an increase in employment of web developers. Instead of designing a website for a desktop computer, developers will have to create sites that work on mobile devices with many different screen sizes, leading to more work. Because websites can be built from anywhere in the world, some web developer jobs may be moved to countries with lower wages, decreasing employment growth. However, this practice may decline because of a growing trend of firms hiring workers in low-cost areas of the U.S. instead of in foreign countries.

Health and Medical Care Jobs

Health and medical care jobs represent some of the fastest growing and best paying opportunities for people re-entering the workforce. This is an enormous industry, which consumes over $3 trillion a year in the U.S., representing nearly 20% of the gross domestic product! If you don't know what you want to do, seriously consider whether you would enjoy working in this field. Opportunities are numerous and the rewards are many. Entry into the medical field will most likely result in a satisfying long-term career.

If you don't have the necessary educational background and credentials to qualify for entering health and medical fields, you should survey various options for acquiring basic qualifications for breaking into these high-demand fields. Most jobs require some form of postsecondary education, training, or certification. Many jobs require two-year associate degrees provided by community or junior colleges, while other jobs only require on-the-job training or a nine- to 24-month training program offered by hospitals, vocational schools, or community colleges.

Seven of the 10 fastest growing jobs in the decade ahead are projected to be in the health care field. Altogether, over 18 million people work in the health care industry. While major restructuring of health care financing and services may negatively affect some jobs in this field, especially nurses in hospitals and physicians in private practice, medicine and health care are hot career fields for the decade ahead.

In general, jobs in the medical and health care industries pay better than in most other industries. They also offer good advancement opportunities for those who seek additional training and certification within or between related medical fields. The best paying jobs will go to those with high levels of education and specialized training, such as surgeons, radiologists, gynecologists, and anesthesiologists. These fields also will generate hundreds of thousands of lower paying entry-level support positions, especially for medical assistants, technicians, technologists, nursing aides, and home health aides, which require the least amounts of medical education and training.

Seven of the jobs appearing in this section are usually included on most lists of the "50 best jobs." While not necessarily the best paying jobs, they are in high demand and offer excellent entry into the expanding health care industry.

Athletic Trainers and Exercise Physiologists

- **Annual Earnings:** $42,690 ($20.52 per hour)
- **Education/Training:** Bachelor's degree
- **Outlook:** Faster than average – 19% growth from 2012 to 2022 (from 28,900 to 34,300 jobs)

Athletic trainers specialize in preventing, diagnosing, and treating muscle and bone injuries and illnesses. Exercise physiologists develop fitness and exercise programs that help patients recover from chronic diseases and improve cardiovascular function, body composition, and flexibility. As people become more aware of sports-related injuries at a young age, demand for athletic trainers is expected to increase, most significantly in colleges, universities, and youth leagues. Advances in injury prevention and detection and more sophisticated treatments are projected to increase the demand for athletic trainers. Growth in an increasingly active middle-aged and elderly population will likely lead to an increased incidence of athletic-related injuries, such as sprains. Sports programs at all ages and for all experience levels will continue to create demand for athletic trainers.

Dental Assistants

- **Annual Earnings:** $34,500 ($16.59 per hour)
- **Education/Training:** 1-2 year postsecondary
- **Outlook:** Much faster than average – 25% growth from 2012 to 2022 (from 303,200 to 377,600 jobs)

Dental assistants have many tasks, ranging from providing patient care and taking X-rays to recordkeeping and scheduling appointments. Their duties vary by state and by the dentist's offices where they work. Ongoing research linking oral health and general health will likely continue to increase the demand for preventive dental services. Dentists will continue to hire more dental assistants to complete routine tasks, allowing the dentists to see more patients in their practice and to spend their time on more complex procedures. As dental practices grow, more dental assistants will be needed. Federal health legislation is expected to expand the number of patients who have access to health insurance. People with new or expanded dental insurance coverage will be more likely to

visit a dentist than in the past. This will increase the demand for all dental services, including those performed by dental assistants.

Dental Hygienists

- **Annual Earnings:** $70,210 ($33.75 per hour)
- **Education/Training:** Associate degree
- **Outlook:** Much faster than average – 33% growth from 2012 to 2022 (from 192,000 to 257,000 jobs)

Dental hygienists clean teeth, examine patients for signs of oral diseases such as gingivitis, and provide other preventative dental care. They also educate patients on ways to improve and maintain good oral health. Ongoing research linking oral health and general health will continue to spur the demand for preventative dental services, which are often provided by dental hygienists. As their practices expand, dentists will hire more hygienists to perform routine dental care, allowing the dentist to see more patients. In addition, as the large baby-boom population ages and people keep more of their original teeth than previous generations did, the need to maintain and treat these teeth will continue to drive demand for dental care. Federal health legislation is expected to expand the number of patients who have access to health insurance. People with new or expanded dental insurance coverage will be more likely to visit a dentist than in the past. As a result, the demand for all dental services, including those performed by hygienists, will increase.

Diagnostic Medical Sonographers and Cardiovascular Technicians

- **Annual Earnings:** $60,350 ($29.02 per hour)
- **Education/Training:** Associate degree
- **Outlook:** Much faster than average – 39% growth from 2012 to 2022 (from 110,400 to 153,100 jobs)

Diagnostic medical sonographers and cardiovascular technologists and technicians, including vascular technologists, operate special imaging equipment to create images or conduct tests. The images and test results help physicians assess and diagnose medical conditions. Some technologists assist physicians and surgeons during surgical procedures. As their practices expand, dentists will hire more hygienists to perform routine dental care, allowing the dentist to see more patients. In addition, as the large baby-boom population ages and people keep more of their original teeth than previous generations did, the need to maintain and treat these teeth will continue to drive demand for dental care. Federal health legislation is expected to expand the number of patients who have access to health insurance. People with new or expanded dental insurance coverage will be more likely to visit a dentist than in the past. As a result, the demand for all dental services, including those performed by hygienists, will increase.

EMTs and Paramedics

- **Annual Earnings:** $31,020 ($14.91 per hour)
- **Education/Training:** 1-2 year postsecondary
- **Outlook:** Much faster than average – 23% growth from 2012 to 2022 (from 239,100 to 294,400 jobs)

Emergency medical technicians (EMTs) and paramedics care for the sick or injured in emergency medical settings. EMTs and paramedics respond to emergency calls, performing medical services and transporting patients to medical facilities. Emergencies, such as car crashes, natural disasters, or acts of violence, will continue to create demand for EMTs and paramedics. Demand for part-time, volunteer EMTs and paramedics in rural areas and smaller metropolitan areas will also continue. Growth in the middle-aged and elderly population will lead to an increase in the number of age-related health emergencies, such as heart attacks or strokes. This, in turn, will create greater demand for EMTs and paramedic services. An increase in the number of specialized medical facilities will require more EMTs and paramedics to transfer patients with specific conditions to these facilities for treatment.

Massage Therapists

- **Annual Earnings:** $35,970 ($17.29)
- **Education/Training:** 1-2 year postsecondary
- **Outlook:** Much faster than average – 23% growth from 2012 to 2022 (from 132,800 to 162,800 jobs)

Massage therapists treat clients by using touch to manipulate the soft-tissue muscles of the body. As such, they relieve pain, help rehabilitate injuries, improve circulation, relieve stress, increase relaxation, and aid in the general wellness of clients. Continued growth in the demand for massage services will lead to new openings for massage therapists. As an increasing number of states adopt licensing requirements and standards for therapists, the practice of massage is likely to be respected and accepted by more people as a way to treat pain and to improve overall wellness. Similarly, as more health care providers understand the benefits of massage, demand will increase as these services become part of treatment plans. Demand for massage services will grow as the baby-boom generation seeks these services as a way to help maintain their health as they age. Older people in nursing homes or assisted-living facilities also are finding benefits from massage, such as increased energy levels and reduced health problems. Demand for massage therapy should grow among older age groups because they increasingly are enjoying longer, more active lives.

Medical Assistants

- **Annual Earnings:** $29,370 ($14.12)
- **Education/Training:** 1-2 year postsecondary
- **Outlook:** Much faster than average – 29% growth from 2012 to 2022 (from 560,800 to 723,700 jobs)

Medical assistants complete administrative and clinical tasks in the offices of physicians, podiatrists, chiropractors, and other health practitioners. Their duties vary with the location, specialty, and size of the practice. The growth of the aging baby-boom population will continue to spur demand for preventive medical services, which are often provided by physicians. As their practices expand, physicians will hire more assistants to perform routine administrative and clinical duties, allowing the physicians to see more patients. An increasing number of group practices, clinics, and other health care facilities need support workers, particularly medical assistants, to do both administrative and clinical duties. Medical assistants work mostly in primary care, a steadily growing sector of the health care industry. In addition, federal health legislation will expand the number of patients who have access to health insurance, increasing patient access to medical care.

Medical Records and Health Information Technicians

- **Annual Earnings:** $34,160 ($16.42 per hour)
- **Education/Training:** 1-2 year postsecondary
- **Outlook:** Much faster than average – 22% growth from 2012 to 2022 (from 186,300 to 227,400 jobs)

Medical records and health information technicians organize and manage health information data. They ensure its quality, accuracy, accessibility, and security in both paper and electronic systems. They use various classification systems to code and categorize patient information for insurance reimbursement purposes, for databases and registries, and to maintain patients' medical and treatment histories. This occupational field should experience excellent job growth due to the rapid growth in the number of medical tests, treatments, and procedures that will be increasingly scrutinized by third-party payers, regulators, courts, and consumers. An aging population will need more medical tests, treatments, and procedures. This will mean more claims for reimbursement from insurance companies. Additional records, coupled with widespread use of electronic health records (EHRs) by all types of health care providers, could lead to an increased need for technicians to organize and manage the associated information in all areas of the health care industry. Cancer registrars are expected to continue to be in high demand. As the population ages, there will likely be more types of special-purpose registries because many illnesses are detected and treated later in life.

Medical Transcriptionists

- **Annual Earnings:** $34,020 ($16.36 per hour)
- **Education/Training:** 1-2 year postsecondary
- **Outlook:** As fast as average – 8% growth from 2012 to 2022 (from 84,100 to 90,500 jobs)

Medical transcriptionists listen to voice recordings that physicians and other health care professionals make and convert them into written reports. They may also review and edit medical documents created using speech recognition technology. Transcriptionists interpret medical terminology and abbreviations in preparing patients' medical histories, discharge summaries, and other documents. Federal health legislation will expand the number of patients who have access to health insurance, increasing patient access to medical care. The increasing volume of health care services will result in a growing number of medical tests and procedures, all of which will require transcription. At the same time, technological advances have changed the way medical transcription is done. Speech recognition software and other technological advances may make transcriptionists more productive and, therefore, limit employment growth.

Nuclear Medicine Technologists

- **Annual Earnings:** $70,180 ($33.74 per hour)
- **Education/Training:** Associate degree
- **Outlook:** Faster than average – 20% growth from 2012 to 2022 (from 20,900 to 25,100 jobs)

Nuclear medicine technologists use a scanner to create images of various areas of a patient's body. They prepare radioactive drugs and administer them to patients undergoing the scans. The radioactive drugs cause abnormal areas of the body to appear different from normal areas in the images. Nuclear medicine technologists work mostly with adult patients, although procedures may be performed on children. A larger aging population should lead to the need to diagnose and treat medical conditions that require imaging, such as heart disease. Nuclear medicine technologists will be needed to administer radioactive drugs and maintain the imaging equipment required for diagnosis. Federal health legislation will increase the number of patients who have access to health insurance, increasing patient access to medical care. This will increase the demand for medical imaging services, including those provided by nuclear medicine technologists.

Nursing Assistants and Orderlies

- **Annual Earnings:** $24,400 ($11.73 per hour)
- **Education/Training:** 1-2 year postsecondary
- **Outlook:** Faster than average – 21% growth from 2012 to 2022 (from 1,534,400 to 1,855,600 jobs)

Nursing assistants and orderlies help provide basic care for patients in hospitals and residents of long-term care facilities, such as nursing homes. As the baby-boom population ages, many nursing assistants and orderlies will be needed to care for elderly patients in long-term care facilities, such as nursing homes. In addition, growing rates of dementia and several chronic ailments will lead to increased demand for patient care. Job prospects for nursing assistants who have completed a state-approved education program and passed their state's competency exam should be good, particularly in home health care services and community-based care settings. Because of the emotional and physical demands of this occupation, many nursing assistants and orderlies choose to leave the profession to get more training or another job, and thus they create opportunities for job seekers.

Occupational Health and Safety Technicians

- **Annual Earnings:** $66,790 ($32.11 per hour)
- **Education/Training:** Bachelor's degree
- **Outlook:** Slower than average – 7% growth from 2012 to 2022 (from 62,900 to 67,100 jobs)

Occupational health and safety specialists analyze many types of work environments and work procedures. Specialists inspect workplaces for adherence to regulations on safety, health, and the environment. They also design programs to prevent disease or injury to workers and damage to the environment. Specialists will be needed to work in a wide variety of industries to ensure that employers are adhering to both existing and new regulations. For example, technological advances that allow manufacturing workers to use new machinery will require specialists to create and enforce procedures to ensure safe use of the machinery. The increased adoption of nuclear power as a source of energy may lead to job growth for specialists in that field. These specialists will be needed to maintain the safety of both the powerplant workers and the surrounding environment. Specialists also will be necessary because insurance and workers' compensation costs have become a concern for many employers and insurance companies. An aging population is remaining in the workforce longer than past generations, and older workers usually have a greater proportion of workers' compensation claims.

Occupational Therapists

- **Annual Earnings:** $65,470 ($36.25 per hour)
- **Education/Training:** Master's degree in occupational therapy
- **Outlook:** Much faster than average - 29% growth from 2012 to 2022 (from 113,200 to 146,000 jobs)

Occupational therapists treat injured, ill, or disabled patients through the therapeutic use of everyday activities. They help these patients develop, recover, and improve the skills needed for daily living and working. Occupational therapy will continue to be an important part of treatment for people with various illnesses and disabilities, such as Alzheimer's disease, cerebral palsy, autism, or the loss of a limb. The need for occupational therapists is expected to increase as the large baby-boom generation ages and people remain active later in life. Occupational therapists help senior citizens maintain their independence by recommending home modifications and strategies that make daily activities easier. Therapists also play a large role in the treatment of many conditions and ailments commonly associated with aging, such as arthritis and stroke. They will also be needed in a variety of health care settings to act as part of a health care team in treating patients with chronic conditions, such as diabetes. Patients will continue to seek noninvasive outpatient treatment for long-term disabilities and illnesses, either in their homes or in residential care environments.

Occupational Therapy Assistants and Aides

- **Annual Earnings:** $48,940 ($23.53 per hour)
- **Education/Training:** High school diploma and some college or technical school program
- **Outlook:** Much faster than average – 41% growth from 2012 to 2022 (from 38,600 to 54,500 jobs)

Occupational therapy assistants and aides help patients develop, recover, and improve the skills needed for daily living and working. Occupational therapy assistants are directly involved in providing therapy to patients, while occupational therapy aides typically perform support activities. Both assistants and aides work under the direction of occupational therapists. Demand for occupational therapy is expected to rise significantly over the coming decade in response to the health needs of the aging baby-boom generation and a growing elderly population. Older adults are more prone than younger people to conditions and ailments such as arthritis and stroke. These conditions can affect the ability to perform a variety of everyday activities. Occupational therapy assistants and aides will be needed to help occupational therapists in caring for these people. Occupational therapy will also continue to be used for treating children and young adults with developmental disabilities such as autism. Demand for occupational therapy assistants is also expected to stem from health care providers employing more assistants to reduce the cost of occupational therapy services. After the therapist has evaluated a patient and designed a treatment plan, the occupational therapy assistant can provide many aspects of the treatment that the therapist prescribed.

Opticians, Dispensing

- **Annual Earnings:** $33,330 ($16.03 per hour)
- **Education/Training:** High school diploma or equivalent
- **Outlook:** Much faster than average – 23% increase from 2012 to 2022 (from 67,600 to 83,400 jobs)

Dispensing opticians help fit eyeglasses and contact lenses, following prescriptions from ophthalmologists and optometrists. They also help customers decide which eyeglass frames or contact lenses to buy. The growth in the older population is anticipated to lead to greater demand for eye care services. Because people usually have eye problems more frequently as they age, the need for opticians is expected to grow with the increase in the number of older people. Increasing rates of chronic diseases such as diabetes may also increase demand for optical services because some chronic diseases cause vision problems. Additional opticians will be needed to fill prescriptions for corrective eyewear for individuals with conditions that damage their eyesight. A growing proportion of opticians are expected to find employment in group medical practices. Optometrists and ophthalmologists are increasingly offering glasses

and contact lenses to their patients as a way to expand their businesses, leading to a greater need for opticians in those settings.

Personal Care Aides

- **Annual Earnings:** $19,910 ($9.57 per hour)
- **Education/Training:** Less than high school
- **Outlook:** Much faster than average – 49% increase from 2012 to 2012 (from 1,190,600 to 1,771,400 jobs)

Personal care aides help clients with self-care and everyday tasks, and provide companionship. As the baby-boom population ages, there will be an increase in the number of clients requiring assistance or companionship. As clients age, they often develop health or mobility problems and require assistance with daily tasks. The demand for the services that personal care aides provide will continue to rise. Elderly and disabled clients who do not require medical care are increasingly choosing home care instead of entering nursing homes or hospitals. Home care is often a less expensive and more personal experience for the client. Because personal care aides do not provide any medical services, they are a less expensive option for families or clients who seek someone to perform light household chores or provide companionship.

Phlebotomists

- **Annual Earnings:** $29,730 ($14.29 per hour)
- **Education/Training:** 1-2 year postsecondary
- **Outlook:** Much faster than average – 27% increase from 2012 to 2022 (from 101,300 to 128,400 jobs)

Phlebotomists draw blood for tests, transfusions, research, or blood donations. Some explain their work to patients and provide assistance when patients have adverse reactions after their blood is drawn. Hospitals, diagnostic laboratories, blood donor centers, and other locations will need phlebotomists to perform blood work. Blood analysis remains an essential function in medical laboratories and hospitals. Demand for phlebotomists will remain high as doctors and other health care professionals require blood work for analysis and diagnoses. However, federal health legislation will expand the number of patients who have access to health insurance, increasing patient access to medical care. As hospitals and medical laboratories evaluate their staffing needs, phlebotomists may be replaced by other more skilled health care workers.

Physical Therapy Assistants and Aides

- **Annual Earnings:** $39,430 ($18.96 per hour)
- **Education/Training:** Associate degree from an accredited physical therapist assistant program.
- **Outlook:** Must faster than average – 41% increase from 2012 to 2022 (from 121,400 to 170,800 jobs)

Physical therapist assistants (sometimes called PTAs) and physical therapist aides work under the direction and supervision of physical therapists. They help patients who are recovering from injuries and illnesses regain movement and manage pain. Demand for physical therapy services is expected to increase in response to the health needs of an aging population, particularly the large baby-boom generation. This group is staying more active later in life than previous generations. However, many baby boomers also are entering the prime age for heart attacks and strokes, increasing the demand for cardiac and physical rehabilitation. Older people are particularly vulnerable to a number of chronic and debilitating conditions that require therapeutic services. These patients often need additional help in their treatment, making the roles of physical therapist assistants and aides vital. In addition, the incidence of chronic conditions such as diabetes and obesity is growing. More physical therapist assistants and aides will be needed to help patients maintain their mobility and manage the effects of such conditions.

Physician Assistants

- **Annual Earnings:** $90,930 ($43.72 per hour)
- **Education/Training:** Master's degree
- **Outlook:** Much faster than average – 38% increase from 2012 to 2022 (from 86,700 to 112,000 jobs)

Physician assistants (PAs) practice medicine on a team under the supervision of physicians and surgeons. They are formally educated to examine patients, diagnose injuries and illnesses, and provide treatment. Demand for health care services will increase because of the growing and aging population. More people means more need for health care specialists, and as the large baby-boom generation ages, it will require more health care. This, coupled with an increase in several chronic diseases such as diabetes, will drive the need for physician assistants to provide preventive care and treat those who are sick. Physician assistants, who can perform many of the same services as doctors, are expected to have a larger role in giving routine care because they are more cost effective than physicians. As more physicians retire or enter specialty areas of medicine, more physician assistants are expected to take on the role of primary care provider. Furthermore, the number of individuals who have access to primary care services will increase as a result of federal health insurance reform. The role of physician assistants is expected to expand as states continue to allow assistants to do more procedures and as insurance companies expand their coverage of physician assistant services.

Radiologic and MRI Technologists

- **Annual Earnings:** $55,910 ($26.88 per hour)
- **Education/Training:** Associate degree
- **Outlook:** Faster than average – 21% increase from 2012 to 2022 (from 229,300 to 277,900 jobs)

Radiologic technologists perform diagnostic imaging examinations, such as X-rays, on patients. MRI technologists operate magnetic resonance imaging (MRI) scanners to create diagnostic images. As the population grows older, there will be an increase in medical conditions, such as breaks and fractures caused by osteoporosis, which can require imaging to diagnose them. Radiologic and MRI technologists will be needed to maintain and use the diagnostic equipment. In addition, federal health legislation will expand the number of patients who have access to health insurance, increasing patient access to medical care. Although hospitals will remain the main employer of radiologic and MRI technologists, a number of new jobs will be in physicians' offices and in outpatient imaging centers. Employment in these health care settings is expected to increase because of the shift toward outpatient care whenever possible. Outpatient care is encouraged by third-party payers as a cost-saving measure and is made possible by technological advances, such as less expensive equipment, that allow for more procedures to be done outside of hospitals.

Registered Nurses

- **Annual Earnings:** $65,470 ($31.48 per hour)
- **Education/Training:** Associate degree
- **Outlook:** Faster than average – 19% increase from 2012 to 2022 (from 2,711,500 to 3,238,300 jobs)

Registered nurses (RNs) provide and coordinate patient care, educate patients and the public about various health conditions, and provide advice and emotional support to patients and their family members. Demand for health care services will increase because of the aging population, since older people typically have more medical problems than younger people. Nurses also will be needed to educate and to care for patients with various chronic conditions, such as arthritis, dementia, diabetes, and obesity. In addition, the number of individuals who have access to health care services will increase, as a result of federal health insurance reform. More nurses will be needed to care for these patients. The financial pressure on hospitals to discharge patients as soon as possible may result in more people admitted to long-term care facilities, outpatient care centers, and greater need for home health care. Job growth is expected in facilities that provide long-term rehabilitation for stroke and head injury patients, as well as facilities that treat people with Alzheimer's disease. In addition, because many older people prefer to be treated at home or in residential care facilities, registered nurses will be in demand in those settings. Growth is also expected to be faster than average in outpatient care centers where patients do not stay overnight, such as those that provide same-day chemotherapy, rehabilitation, and surgery. In addition, an increased number of procedures, as well as more sophisticated procedures previously done only in hospitals, are performed in ambulatory care settings and physicians' offices.

Respiratory Therapists

- **Annual Earnings:** $55,870 ($26.86 per hour)
- **Education/Training:** Associate degree
- **Outlook:** Faster than average – 19% growth from 2012 to 2022 (from 119,300 to 142,000 jobs)

Respiratory therapists care for patients who have trouble breathing – for example, from a chronic respiratory disease, such as asthma or emphysema. Their patients range from premature infants with undeveloped lungs to elderly patients who have diseased lungs. They also provide emergency care to patients suffering from heart attacks, drowning, or shock. Growth in the middle-aged and elderly population will lead to an increased incidence of respiratory conditions such as emphysema, chronic bronchitis, pneumonia, and other disorders that can permanently damage the lungs or restrict lung function. These factors will in turn lead to an increased demand for respiratory therapy services and treatments, mostly in hospitals and nursing homes. In addition, advances in preventing and detecting disease, improved medications, and more sophisticated treatments will increase the demand for respiratory therapists. Other conditions affecting the general population, such as smoking, air pollution, and respiratory emergencies, will continue to create demand for respiratory therapists.

Surgical Technologists

- **Annual Earnings:** $41,790 ($20.09 per hour)
- **Education/Training:** 1-2 year postsecondary
- **Outlook:** Much faster than average – 30% increase from 2012 to 2022 (from 98,500 to 127,800 jobs)

Surgical technologists, also called operating room technicians, assist in surgical procedures. They prepare operating rooms, arrange equipment, and help doctors during surgeries. Advances in medical technology have made surgery safer, and more operations are being done to treat a variety of illnesses and injuries. The aging of the large baby-boom generation also is expected to increase the need for surgical technologists because older people usually require more operations. Moreover, as these individuals age, they may be more willing than those in previous generations to seek medical treatment to improve their quality of life. For example, an individual may decide to have a knee replacement operation in order to maintain an active lifestyle. Hospitals will continue to employ surgical technologists to work in operating rooms because they are more cost-effective than higher-paid registered nurses.

Veterinary Assistants and Laboratory Animal Caretakers

- **Annual Earnings:** $23,130 ($11.12 per hour)
- **Education/Training:** High school diploma or equivalent
- **Outlook:** As fast as average – 10% increase from 2012 to 2022 (from 74,600 to 81,700 jobs)

Veterinary assistants and laboratory animal caretakers look after animals in laboratories, animal hospitals, and clinics. They care for the well-being of animals by performing routine tasks under the supervision of veterinarians, scientists, and veterinary technologists and technicians. Although veterinary assistants and laboratory animal caretakers will be needed to assist veterinarians and other veterinary care staff, many veterinary practices are expected to increasingly replace veterinary assistants with higher-skilled veterinary technicians and technologists, thus requiring fewer veterinary assistants. However, there will be demand for laboratory animal caretakers in areas such as public health, food and animal safety, national disease control, and biomedical research on human health problems.

Veterinary Technologists and Technicians

- **Annual Earnings:** $30,290 ($14.56 per hour)
- **Education/Training:** Associate degree
- **Outlook:** Much faster than average – 30% increase from 2012 to 2022 from 84,800 to 109,800 jobs)

Veterinary technologists and technicians perform medical tests under the supervision of a licensed veterinarian to help diagnose the illnesses and injuries of animals. Because veterinarians perform specialized tasks, clinics and animal hospitals are increasingly using veterinary technologists and technicians to provide more general care and perform more laboratory work. Furthermore, veterinarians will continue to prefer higher skilled veterinary technologists and technicians over veterinary assistants for more complex work. There will also be demand for veterinary technicians in areas such as public health, food and animal safety, national disease control, and biomedical research on human health problems.

Sales and Related Jobs

Many people re-entering the workforce can look toward a variety of sales positions to start new careers. These are some of the most recession-proof jobs. After all, even in tough times, companies are always looking to maintain and expand their market shares through good sales representatives. These jobs also are ideal for people who prefer flexible work schedules or enjoy operating as independent contractors. However, you'll need to check to see if you might be barred from any sales jobs because of past convictions, especially any that relate to drugs (pharmaceuticals) and finances (banks, insurance, investments).

Are you born to sell? Not many people are, but you may find you have many hidden talents that would be perfect for re-entering the job market as a salesperson. If, for example, you are self-motivated and goal-oriented, enjoy meeting strangers, can handle rejections, and are good at persuading others to buy a product or perform a service, a job or career in one of many sales fields may be right for you. While a college degree is often a plus for individuals who deal with highly technical and scientific products and services, such as pharmaceuticals, computers, weapons systems, and financial services, many sales fields, such as automotive, real estate, and insurance, are open to anyone who has demonstrated the ability to learn about a product, network for clients, and present and close deals. Regardless of their educational backgrounds, talented salespeople working in commission-based fields selling high-ticket items can realize substantial annual earnings.

You don't need formal education credentials to be a good and productive salesperson. Effective selling skills often center on attitude, personality, communication, prospecting, perseverance, organization, and follow-through. Good salespeople can often transfer their skills from one occupational field to another because of the generic nature of their skills. For example, an individual who starts out selling automobiles may later move into insurance and real estate.

Earnings for salespeople can vary considerably depending on the economy, their industry, their products/services, and their talent. The least compensated tend to be part-time salespeople in retail establishments, especially in clothing and merchandising. The best compensated are generally salespeople in the financial and pharmaceutical industries.

Since most salespeople receive a base salary plus commission, their income largely depends on a combination of factors that may or may not be within their control, such as the state of the economy and their industry. Many real estate agents, for example, realized substantial increases in incomes during the hot real estate market of 2003-2005. That situation changed dramatically during 2007-2012 when the real estate market cooled down and declined substantially.

Nonetheless, sales is a very talent-driven type of occupation involving a great deal of hard work, self-motivation, and persistence. If you are born to sell, you'll most likely do very well in any sales field. You will be sought after by many employers who readily seek such talent that immediately contributes to increasing their company's bottom line. Better still, employers will overlook your past record if you can produce a stellar sales record!

Advertising Sales Agents

- **Annual Earnings:** $46,290 ($22.26 per hour)
- **Education/Training:** High school diploma or equivalent
- **Outlook:** Little or no change – 1% decline from 2012 to 2022 (from 154,600 to 153,600 jobs)

Advertising sales agents sell advertising space to businesses and individuals. They contact potential clients, make sales presentations, and maintain client accounts. Media companies will continue to rely on advertising revenue for profitability, driving growth in the advertising industry as a whole. Employment growth of advertising sales agents will largely follow broader industry trends. For example, although newspaper print advertising is expected to decline, some of this decline will be offset by the sale of ad space on newspaper websites. Therefore, although employment of advertising sales agents is projected to decline in the newspaper publishing industry, it is not projected to decline as fast as other occupations in that industry. However, an increasing amount of advertising is expected to be concentrated in digital media, including digital ads intended for cell phones, tablet-style computers, and online radio stations. Digital advertising allows companies to directly target potential consumers because websites are usually associated with the types of products that possible customers would like to buy. Digital advertising can be done without an advertising sales agent. For example, in some cases it can be done through a software application or search engine program. Therefore, an increase in digital advertising expenditures will not necessarily result in increased demand for advertising sales agents.

Insurance Sales Agents

- **Annual Earnings:** $48,150 ($23.15 per hour)
- **Education/Training:** High school diploma or equivalent
- **Outlook:** As fast as average – 10% growth from 2012 to 2022 (from 443,400 to 489,300 jobs)

Insurance sales agents help insurance companies generate new business by contacting potential customers and selling one or more types of insurance. Insurance sales agents explain various insurance policies and help clients choose plans that suit them. The insurance industry generally grows with the economy as a whole. Overall economic growth will continue to create demand for insurance policies. Direct online purchases of insurance are not expected to negatively affect employment of traditional sales agents, because they will continue to have a critical role in the insurance industry. Because the profitability of insurance companies depends on a steady stream of new customers, the demand for insurance sales agents is expected to continue. Employment growth will likely be strongest for independent sales agents, as insurance companies rely more on brokerages and less on captive agents as a way to control costs. Many clients do their own Internet research and purchase insurance online. This somewhat reduces demand for insurance sales agents, as many purchases can be made without their services. Agents are still needed to interact with clients regarding more complicated policies, however. Also, many people lack the time or expertise to study the different types of insurance to decide what they need. These clients will continue to rely on the advice from insurance sales agents.

Employment growth should be stronger for agents selling health and long-term care insurance. As the population ages over the next decade, demand will likely increase for packages that cover long-term care. The number of individuals who have access to health insurance will increase due to federal health insurance reform legislation. Insurance companies will rely on sales agents to enroll people from this new customer base.

Real Estate Brokers and Sales Agents

- **Annual Earnings:** $41,990 ($20.19 per hour)
- **Education/Training:** High school diploma or equivalent
- **Outlook:** As fast as average – 11% increase from 2012 to 2022 (from 422,000 to 468,600 jobs)

Real estate brokers and sales agents help clients buy, sell, and rent properties. Although brokers and agents do similar work, brokers are licensed to manage their own real estate businesses. Sales agents must work with a real estate broker. Employment will grow as the real estate market improves. Population growth and mobility also will continue to stimulate the need for new brokers and agents. In addition to first-time home buyers, people will need brokers and agents when looking for a larger home, relocating for a new job, and other reasons. In addition, an improving job market and rising consumer spending will drive demand for brokers and agents to handle commercial, retail, and industrial real estate transactions.

Retail Sales Workers

- **Annual Earnings:** $21,410 ($10.29 per hour)
- **Education/Training:** Less than high school
- **Outlook:** As fast as average – 10% growth from 2012 to 2022 (from 4,668,300 to 5,118,500 jobs)

Retail sales workers include both those who sell retail merchandise, such as clothing, furniture, and automobiles, and those who sell spare and replacement parts and equipment, especially car parts. Both types of workers help customers find the products they want and process customers' payments. Employment of retail salespersons has traditionally grown with the overall economy, and this trend is expected to continue. Online sales have had a detrimental effect on certain in-store retailers, primarily book and media stores. However, other retail segments, such as automobile dealers and clothing stores, have seen much less of an impact. In general, although consumers are increasing their online retail shopping, they will continue to do the vast majority of their retail shopping in stores. Retail salespersons will be needed in stores to help customers and complete sales. Among the various retail industries, other general merchandise stores, which include warehouse clubs and supercenters, are expected to see strong job growth. These large stores sell a wide range of goods from a single location. Thus, employment of retail salespersons in this industry is projected to grow 28% during the next decade. However, employment of these workers in department stores is projected to grow only 5%.

Sales Representatives, Wholesale and Manufacturing

- **Annual Earnings:** $57,870 ($27.82 per hour)
- **Education/Training:** High school diploma or equivalent
- **Outlook:** As fast as average – 9% increase from 2012 to 2022 (from 1,863,000 to 2,032,300 jobs)

Wholesale and manufacturing sales representatives sell goods for wholesalers or manufacturers to businesses, government agencies, and other organizations. They contact customers, explain product features, answer any questions that their customers may have, and negotiate prices. Employment growth for wholesale and manufacturing sales representatives will largely follow growth of the overall economy. Employment growth is expected to be strongest for sales representatives working at independent sales agencies. Companies are increasingly giving their sales activities to independent companies as a way to cut costs and boost revenue. These independent companies do not buy and hold the products they are selling. Instead, they operate on a fee or commission basis in representing the product manufacturer. Job prospects for wholesale sales representatives will be better than those for manufacturing sales representatives because manufacturers are expected to continue contracting out sales duties to independent agents rather than using in-house or direct sales personnel.

Sports, Entertainment, and Media Jobs

Few job and career fields have such a mass appeal as sports, entertainment, and the media. Many people would love to get paid playing their favorite sport, starring in a movie, or being in front of the television camera. Others would like to become a famous artist, musician, singer, or designer. And still others dream of working behind the scenes, where they put together and market productions.

In many respects, these fields generate a disproportionate number of glamour jobs that place primary emphasis on special skills and demonstrated talents rather than education credentials. Talented and entrepreneurial individuals, who demonstrate a great deal of creativity and imagination, will find many opportunities in these fields.

Be forewarned, however, that jobs in sports, entertainment, and the media often pay much less than expected. While the top talent in these fields earn top dollar, many others working in these fields struggle for years on a part-time basis as they attempt to acquire experience and connections for making a rewarding career in a field that allows them to pursue their passions. If you have the necessary talent and drive, you'll find numerous jobs opportunities in these exciting fields.

Actors

- **Earnings:** $20.26 per hour
- **Education/Training:** Some college, no degree
- **Outlook:** Slower than average – 4% increase from 2012 to 2022 (from 79,800 to 83,100 jobs)

Actors express ideas and portray characters in theater, film, television, and other performing arts media. They also work at theme parks or other live events. They interpret a writer's script to entertain or inform an audience. Job growth in the motion picture industry will stem from continued strong demand for new movies and television shows. However, employment is not expected to keep pace with that demand. Production companies are experimenting with new content delivery methods, such as video on demand and online television, which may lead to more work for actors in the future. However, these delivery methods are still in their early stages, and it remains to be seen how successful they will be. Actors who work in performing arts companies are expected to see slower job growth than those in film. Many small and medium-size theaters have difficulty getting funding. As a result, the number of performances is expected to decline. Large theaters, with their more stable sources of funding, should provide more opportunities.

Broadcast and Sound Engineering Technicians

- **Annual Earnings:** $41,200 ($19.81 per hour)
- **Education/Training:** 1-2 year postsecondary or certificate

- **Outlook:** As fast as average – 9% increase from 2012 to 2022 (from 121,400 to 131,400 jobs)

Broadcast and sound engineering technicians set up, operate, and maintain the electrical equipment for radio and television broadcasts, concerts, sound recordings, movies, and in office and school buildings. Competition for jobs will be strong. This occupation attracts many applicants who are interested in working with the latest technology and electronic equipment. Many applicants also are attracted to working in the radio and television industry. Those looking for work in this industry will have the most job opportunities in smaller markets or stations. Those with hands-on experience with complex electronics and software, or with work experience at a radio or television station, will have the best job prospects. In addition, technicians should be versatile since they set up, operate, and maintain equipment, whereas previously technicians typically specialized in one area. An associate's or bachelor's degree in broadcast technology, broadcast production, computer networking, or a related field will also improve job prospects for applicants.

Craft and Fine Artists

- **Annual Earnings:** $44,380 ($21.34 per hour)
- **Education/Training:** High school diploma or equivalent
- **Outlook:** Slower than average – 3% increase from 2012 to 2022 (from 51,400 to 52,700 jobs)

Craft and fine artists use a variety of materials and techniques to create art for sale and exhibition. Craft artists create handmade objects, such as pottery, glassware, textiles or other objects that are designed to be functional. Fine artists, including painters, sculptors, and illustrators, create original works of art for their aesthetic value, rather than for a functional one. Competition for jobs as craft and fine artists is expected to be strong, because there are more qualified candidates than available jobs. Only the most successful craft and fine artists receive major commissions for their work. Despite the competition, studios, galleries, and individual clients are always on the lookout for artists who display outstanding talent, creativity, and style. Talented individuals who have developed a mastery of artistic techniques and marketing skills will have the best job prospects. Competition among artists for the privilege of being shown in galleries is expected to remain intense, as will competition for grants from funders, such as private foundations, state and local arts councils, and the National Endowment for the Arts.

Film and Video Editors and Camera Operators

- **Annual Earnings:** $46,280 ($22.25)
- **Education/Training:** Bachelor's degree
- **Outlook:** Slower than average – 3% increase from 2012 to 2022 (from 49,500 to 50,900 jobs)

Film and video editors and camera operators manipulate images that entertain or inform an audience. Job growth is expected to be slow in broadcasting because automatic camera systems reduce the need for camera operators at many TV stations. Because of the public's continued strong demand for new movies and TV shows, companies are hiring more people as the motion picture industry becomes more productive. Production companies and video freelancers are working within new content delivery methods, such as mobile and online TV, which has led to more work for operators and editors. These delivery methods are still in their early stages, yet they provide an opportunity for operators and editors to showcase their work. Job openings are projected to be in entertainment hubs such as New York and Los Angeles because specialized editing jobs are needed there. Still, film and video editors and camera operators will face strong competition for jobs. Those with more experience at a TV station or on a film set should have the best prospects.

Fitness Trainers and Instructors

- **Annual Earnings:** $31,720 ($15.25 per hour)
- **Education/Training:** High school diploma or equivalent
- **Outlook:** As fast as average – 13% growth from 2012 to 2022 (from 267,000 to 300,500 jobs)

Fitness trainers and instructors lead, instruct, and motivate individuals or groups in exercise activities, including cardiovascular exercise (exercises for the heart and blood system), strength training, and stretching. They work with people of all ages and skill levels. As businesses, government, and insurance organizations continue to recognize the benefits of health and fitness programs for their employees, incentives to join gyms or other types of health clubs is expected to increase the need for fitness trainers and instructors. Some businesses may even decide to open their own onsite facility to decrease the need for their employees to travel for exercise. As baby boomers age, many remain active to help prevent injuries and illnesses associated with aging. With the increasing number of older residents in nursing homes or residential care facilities and communities, jobs for fitness trainers and instructors are expected to rise in the fitness centers in these locations. Participation in yoga and Pilates is expected to continue to increase, driven partly by older adults who want low-impact forms of exercise and relief from arthritis and other ailments. Job prospects should be best for workers with professional certification or increased levels of formal education in health or fitness. Jobs for fitness workers are expected to increase much faster than the average. Fitness workers should have good opportunities due to the rapid job growth in health clubs, fitness facilities, and other settings where fitness workers are concentrated.

Gaming Services Occupations

- **Annual Earnings:** $20,210 ($9.71 per hour)
- **Education/Training:** High school diploma or equivalent
- **Outlook:** As fast as average – 10% increase from 2012 to 2022 (from 182,200 to 200,100 jobs)

Gaming services workers serve customers in gambling establishments, such as casinos or racetracks. Some workers tend slot machines deal cards, or oversee other gaming activities such as keno or bingo. Others take bets or pay out winnings. Still others supervise or manage gaming workers and operations. These occupations will be driven by the increasing popularity of gambling establishments such as Native American casinos and regional casinos. Because states benefit from some casinos in the form of tax revenues, additional states may expand the number of gambling establishments over the next decade. Many jurisdictions that currently allow only slot machines are expected to begin allowing table games for the additional money they bring. However, new electronic table games, which eliminate the need for a dealer, may moderate employment growth.

Graphic Designers

- **Annual Earnings:** $44,150 ($21.22 per hour)
- **Education/Training:** Bachelor's degree
- **Outlook:** Slower than average – 7% growth from 2012 to 2022 (from 259,500 to 277,900 jobs)

Graphic designers create visual concepts, by hand or using computer software, to communicate ideas that inspire, inform, or captivate consumers. They develop the overall layout and production design for advertisements, brochures, magazines, and corporate reports. The change in employment of graphic designers from 2012 to 2022 is projected to vary by industry. Employment of graphic designers in newspaper, periodical, book, and directory publishers is projected to decline 16% from 2012 to 2022. However, employment of graphic designers in computer systems design and related services is projected to grow 35% over the same period. With the increased use of the Internet, graphic designers will be needed to create designs and images for portable devices, websites, electronic publications, and video entertainment media.

Musicians and Singers

- **Earnings:** $23.50 per hour
- **Education/Training:** High school diploma or equivalent
- **Outlook:** Slower than average – 5% increase from 2012 to 2022 (from 167,400 to 176,100 jobs)

Musicians and singers play instruments or sing for live audiences and in recording studios. Growth will be due to increases in demand for musical performances. Digital downloads and streaming platforms make it easier for fans to listen to recordings and view performances. Easier access to recordings gives musicians more publicity and grows interest in their work, and concert goers may become interested in seeing them perform live. There will be additional demand for musicians to serve as session musicians and backup artists for recordings and to go on tour. Singers will be needed to sing backup and to make recordings for commercials, films, and television. However, employment growth will likely be limited in orchestras, opera companies, and other musical groups because they can have difficulty getting funding. Some musicians and singers work for nonprofit organizations that rely on donations, government funding, and corporate sponsorships in addition to ticket sales to fund their work. During economic downturns, these organizations may have trouble finding enough funding to cover their expenses.

Photographers

- **Annual Earnings:** $28,490 ($13.70 per hour)
- **Education/Training:** High school diploma or equivalent
- **Outlook:** Slower than average – 4% increase from 2012 to 2022 (from 136,300 to 142,200 jobs)

Photographers use their technical expertise, creativity, and composition skills to produce and preserve images that visually tell a story or record an event. Photographers will face strong competition for most jobs. Because of reduced barriers to entry, there will be many qualified candidates for relatively few positions. In addition, salaried jobs may be more difficult to obtain as companies increasingly contract with freelancers rather than hire their own photographers. Job prospects will be best for candidates who are multitalented and possess related skills such as picture editing and capturing digital video.

Public Relations Specialists

- **Annual Earnings:** $54,170 ($26.04 per hour)
- **Education/Training:** Bachelor's degree
- **Outlook:** As fast as average – 12% increase from 2012 to 2022 (from 229,100 to 256,500 jobs)

Public relations specialists create and maintain a favorable public image for the organization they represent. They design media releases to shape public perception of their organization and to increase awareness of its work and goals. Increased use of social media also is expected to increase employment for public relations specialists. These media outlets will create more work for public relations specialists as they try to appeal to consumers and the general public in new ways. Public relations specialists will be needed to help their clients use these new types of social media effectively. Candidates can expect particularly strong competition at advertising firms, organizations with large media exposure, and at prestigious public relations firms.

The industries employing the most public relations specialists are religious, grant making, civic, and professional (20%); advertising, public relations, and related services (14%); educational services (12%); government (9%); and health care and social assistance (8%). Public relations specialists usually work in offices, but they also deliver speeches, attend meetings and community activities, and occasionally travel.

Umpires, Referees, and Other Sports Officials

- **Annual Earnings:** $23,290
- **Education/Training:** High school diploma or equivalent
- **Outlook:** As fast as average – 8% increase from 2012 to 2022 (from 17,500 to 18,800 jobs)

Umpires, referees, and other sports officials preside over competitive athletic or sporting events to help maintain standards of play. They detect infractions and decide penalties according to the rules of the game. Overall job prospects for umpires, referees, and sports officials are expected to be good at the youth and high school levels. Those with prior officiating experience will have the best job opportunities. However, competition is expected to be strong for the college and professional levels. Many people are attracted to working in sports, and the collegiate and professional levels typically have few job openings and low turnover.

Office and Administrative Support Jobs

Numerous job opportunities are available in office and administrative support occupations that would be appropriate for ex-offenders. Many of these jobs encompass back-office operations that large corporations have been increasingly outsourced to cheap labor markets abroad. Some of the best opportunities in these occupational fields will be found with small businesses that employ fewer than 100 individuals. These companies tend to rely on in-house personnel rather than outsource such jobs abroad. Most of the jobs profiled in this section require a high school diploma and some additional training.

Bill and Account Collectors

- **Annual Earnings:** $32,480 ($15.61 per hour)
- **Education/Training:** High school diploma or equivalent
- **Outlook:** Faster than average – 15% increase from 2012 to 2022 (from 397,400 to 455,600 jobs)

Bill and account collectors, sometimes called collectors, try to recover payment on overdue bills. They negotiate repayment plans with debtors and help them find solutions to make paying their overdue bills easier. Fast job growth is expected for collectors in medical industries. As the cost of health care increases, the amount of medical debt that people incur is likely to rise as well. Employment of bill and account collectors is projected to grow 30% in offices of health practitioners from 2012 to 2022. In addition, credit card companies are more commonly selling their debts to third-party agencies, likely also increasing job growth in the collections industry. From 2012 to 2022, employment of bill and account collectors is projected to grow 20% in business support services, which includes collection agencies.

Bookkeeping, Accounting, and Auditing Clerks

- **Annual Earnings:** $35,170 ($16.91 per hour)
- **Education/Training:** High school diploma or equivalent
- **Outlook:** As fast as average – 11% increase from 2012 to 2022 (from 1,799,800 to 2,004,400 jobs)

Bookkeeping, accounting, and auditing clerks produce financial records for organizations. They record financial transactions, update statements, and check financial records for accuracy. Job growth for these workers is largely driven by overall economic growth. As the number of organizations increases, more bookkeepers will be needed to keep these organizations' books. In addition, in response to the recent financial crisis, investors will pay increased attention to the accuracy of corporate books. Stricter regulation in the financial sector will create demand for accounting services, creating opportunities for accounting clerks. Some tasks that these clerks perform have been affected by technological changes. For example, electronic banking and bookkeeping software has reduced the need for bookkeepers and clerks to send and receive checks. However, when checks are sent or received, these workers are still needed to update statements and check for accuracy. Rather than reduce the need for these workers, these technological changes are expected to help bookkeeping, accounting, and auditing clerks do their jobs.

Customer Service Representatives

- **Annual Earnings:** $30,580 ($14.70 per hour)
- **Education/Training:** High school diploma or equivalent
- **Outlook:** As fast as average – 13% increase from 2012 to 2022 (from 2,362,800 to 2,661,500 jobs)

Customer service representatives handle customer complaints, process orders, and provide information about an organization's products and services. Overall employment growth should result from growing industries that specialize in handling customer service. Specifically, telephone call centers, also known as customer contact centers, are expected to add the most new jobs for customer service representatives. Employment of representatives in these centers is projected to grow 38% from 2012 to 2022, much faster than the average for all occupations. Some businesses are increasingly contracting out their customer service operations to telephone call centers as they provide consolidated sales and customer service functions. Job prospects for customer service representatives are expected to be good due to employment growth and the need to replace workers who leave the occupation each year. Job opportunities should be best in telephone call centers. There will be greater competition for in-house

customer service jobs in the insurance and finance sectors – which often have higher pay – than for jobs in the telephone call center industry. Candidates with good customer service and computer skills should have the best job prospects.

General Office Clerks

- **Annual Earnings:** $27,470 ($13.21 per hour)
- **Education/Training:** High school diploma or equivalent
- **Outlook:** Slower than average – 6% increase from 2012 to 2022 (from 2,983,500 to 3,167,600 jobs)

General office clerks perform a variety of administrative tasks, including answering telephones, typing or word processing, making copies of documents, and maintaining records. Employment growth of office clerks should moderate as technology makes them more productive. For example, many organizations maintain electronic documents or use automated phone systems, reducing the need for general office clerks. Job prospects are expected to be good due to employment growth and the need to replace workers who leave the occupation. Job opportunities in health care facilities should be best, while opportunities in schools and government are expected to be less favorable. Candidates who have a combination of work experience and computer software skills should have the best job prospects.

Information Clerks

- **Annual Earnings:** $30,650 ($14.74 per hour)
- **Education/Training:** High school diploma or equivalent
- **Outlook:** Little or no change – 2% increase from 2012 to 2022 (from 1,567,100 to 1,599,900 jobs)

Information clerks perform routine clerical duties such as maintaining records, collecting data, and providing information to customers. A growing population's need for travel-related services, government services, and health care will drive overall demand for information clerks. Increased travel is expected to result in the demand for new hotels and other lodging establishments. Because customer service and personal services are not easily automated, hotels will continue to use clerks to provide guest services. As more baby boomers become eligible for Social Security and Medicare, demand for clerical support to handle eligibility requests will increase. In addition, the number of individuals who have access to health insurance will increase due to federal health insurance reform legislation, resulting in a greater need for office staff in health care facilities. However, overall employment growth of information clerks is expected to be limited as organizations and businesses automate and consolidate their administrative functions. For example, many businesses increasingly use online applications for benefits and employment, thereby streamlining the process. Increased use of online ordering and reservations systems and self-service ticketing kiosks will result in the need for fewer clerks to process orders and maintain files. In some businesses, including medical offices, receptionists and other workers are increasingly performing the tasks that clerks used to do. Despite little or no change in employment, overall job prospects should be good because of the need to replace workers who leave the occupation each year. Job opportunities should be best in hotels and other lodging establishments. Clerks with some college education and good computer software skills should have the best job prospects

Police, Fire, and Ambulance Dispatcher

- **Annual Earnings:** $36,300 ($17.45 per hour)
- **Education/Training:** High school diploma or equivalent
- **Outlook:** As fast as average – 8% growth from 2012 to 2022 (from 98,500 to 116,100 jobs)

Police, fire, and ambulance dispatchers, also called **9-1-1 operators** or **public safety telecommunicators**, answer emergency and non-emergency calls. The prevalence of cellular phones has increased the number of calls that dispatchers receive, and this trend is expected to continue. A growing elderly population should also result in more emergency calls, requiring more dispatchers. It is expected that Next Generation 9-1-1 – a service that allows people to communicate through text and video messages with emergency dispatchers – will be implemented in the coming years. This development should also increase demand for dispatchers as emergency call centers will take in more information. However,

most police, fire, and ambulance dispatchers are employed by local and state governments. Therefore, any future budget constraints will likely limit the number of dispatchers hired in the coming decade. Overall job prospects should be favorable because the work of a dispatcher remains stressful and demanding, leading some applicants to seek other types of work. Although employment growth will generate some job openings, the majority of positions will come from the need to replace the large number of dispatchers expected to transfer to other occupations or leave the labor force. Those with good communication and computer skills should have the best job prospects.

Receptionists

- **Annual Earnings:** $25,990 ($12.49 per hour)
- **Education/Training:** High school diploma or equivalent
- **Outlook:** As fast as average – 14% increase between 2012 and 2022 (from 1,006,700 to 1,142,600 jobs)

Receptionists perform administrative tasks, such as answering phones, receiving visitors, and providing general information about their organization to the public and customers. Employment growth for receptionists will result mainly from a growing health care industry. Specifically, offices of physicians and dentists are expected to add the most receptionist jobs as an aging population demands more medical services. In addition, the number of individuals who have health insurance is expected to increase due to federal health insurance reform legislation, resulting in a greater need for office staff in health care facilities. Some receptionists' tasks, such as checking patients in and coordinating patient care, are not easily automated. Employment growth of receptionists in most other industries should be slower than the average for all occupations as organizations continue to automate or consolidate administrative functions, such as using computer software to interact with the public or customers. In addition, technology will continue to make organizations more productive with the use of automated phone systems, further reducing the need for receptionists. Overall job prospects should be good, with the best job opportunities in the health care industry.

Secretaries and Administrative Assistants

- **Annual Earnings:** $35,330 ($16.99 per hour)
- **Education/Training:** High school diploma or equivalent
- **Outlook:** As fast as average – 12% increase from 2012 to 2022 (from 3,947,100 to 4,426,600 jobs)

Secretaries and administrative assistants perform routine clerical and administrative duties. They organize files, draft messages, schedule appointments, and support other staff. But these jobs are undergoing changes. For example, many companies are replacing executive secretaries with lower-cost administrative assistants. Many administrative assistants can also support more than one manager in an organization. In addition, many managers now perform work that was previously done by their executive secretaries. For example, they often type their own correspondence or schedule their own travel and meetings. Employment of medical secretaries is projected to grow 36% from 2012 to 2022, much faster than the average for all occupations. Federal health legislation will expand the number of patients who have access to health insurance, increasing patient access to medical care. In addition, the aging population will have increased demand for medical services. As a result, medical secretaries will be needed to handle administrative tasks related to billing and insurance processing. Employment of legal secretaries is projected to decline 3% from 2012 to 2022. In order to cut costs, a growing number of legal firms are having paralegals and legal assistants perform work normally done by legal secretaries. Employment of secretaries, except legal, medical, and executive, is projected to grow 13% from 2012 to 2022, about as fast as the average for all occupations. Many secretarial and administrative duties are of a personal, interactive nature. Because technology cannot substitute for interpersonal skills, secretaries and administrative assistants will continue to play a role in most organizations. Many job openings are expected to come from the need to replace secretaries and administrative assistants who leave the occupation. Those with a combination of related work experience and computer skills should have the best job prospects.

Military, Government, and Nonprofit Jobs

The military, government, and nonprofit organizations offer millions of jobs that crosscut many of the possible opportunities outlined throughout this book. Ex-offenders should be aware of the following employment opportunities related to this very large and exciting complex of organizations:

1. **The military occasionally hires ex-offenders.** As I noted earlier in Chapter 3, felons are prohibited from becoming members of the military. However, in the recent past (2003-2006) the military was generous in issuing over 100,000 "moral waivers," which allowed them to recruit ex-offenders, including felons, in order to meet mission requirements for the wars in Iraq and Afghanistan. But in 2012, the military suspended its moral waivers policy, and it now no longer accepts new recruits who have a history of drug or alcohol abuse or any kind of misconduct conviction. As in the past, this situation can change, depending on recruitment needs.

2. **Government employment is restricted for ex-offenders but by no means closed.** Most prohibitions to hiring ex-offenders in government relate to police and security jobs. Some federal, state, and local governments agencies may have a blanket prohibition on hiring ex-offenders, but these prohibitions are by no means uniform. You need to know the hiring practices of various government agencies. If, for example, you want to become an FBI agent, it's best to move on with your dreams since employment is very restrictive and selective with this high-profile agency. At the same time, many city, county, and state governments, which literally employ most public servants (20+ million), do hire ex-offenders for certain positions. For example, at the state level, many departments of corrections are open to hiring ex-offenders for non-security-related positions (see the

brief discussion and accompanying chart on pages 25-26). Many local governments will hire ex-offenders for public works and social welfare positions. Indeed, many transitional work experiences (see discussion on pages 15-20) are sponsored by local governments, especially in the public works departments. Do check out **contracting opportunities** with private firms that do business with government agencies. Many of these semi-public organizations hire ex-offenders.

3. **Many nonprofit organizations regularly hire ex-offenders.** Many organizations within the nonprofit sector (which employs 10+ million people) regularly hire ex-offenders. These include faith-based, drug and alcohol rehabilitation, housing/homeless, family, health, HIV/AIDS, social welfare, and mental health organizations – in other words, nonprofit organizations that are closely associated with the corrections system and related recovery and re-entry issues. Well-known nonprofits, such as The Salvation Army and Goodwill Industries, regularly work with and employ ex-offenders. Local United Way agencies help fund many of the nonprofits that also employ ex-offenders. Some ex-offenders end up working for nonprofits that relate to their own addictions – the classic "major in your own problem" career choice phenomenon. When considering a career with nonprofits, keep in mind that many of these organizations are very poor and thus pay little; they are constantly looking for resources to keep in operation. In other words, many are struggling organizations that mirror many of the struggles their targeted constituents are dealing with on a daily basis. For more information on employment with nonprofits, check out these excellent gateway websites, which focus on jobs with the nonprofit sector:

▪ **Action Without Borders**	www.idealist.org
▪ **NonProfitJobs.org**	www.nonprofitjobs.org
▪ **Foundation Center**	www.foundationcenter.org
▪ **Independent Sector**	www.independentsector.org
▪ **Nonprofit Charitable Organizations**	http://nonprofit.about.com
▪ **Nonprofit Jobs**	www.opportunityknocks.org
▪ **GuideStar**	www.guidestar.org

Start Your Own Business

While most of this book focuses on jobs with other people's organizations, you may also be interested in working for yourself. Indeed, each year nearly seven percent of Americans strike out on their own to start their own business. They do so for a variety of positive and negative reasons. Like many other ex-offenders who seek true freedom, you may want to become your own boss as you pursue dreams of operating your own business.

The fact that you may have little or no business experience should not dissuade you from considering an entrepreneurial option to employment. If you have the right combination of skills, some great ideas, and the necessary drive to be an entrepreneur, you should consider working for yourself.

While nearly 900,000 new businesses are started each year, another 700,000 to 800,000 businesses fail each year; 50% fail within the first 38 months; and nearly 90% fail within 10 years. Unfortunately, starting your own business is risky; the statistical odds are against becoming a successful entrepreneur.

You should approach business opportunities the same way you approach the job market: do research, develop networks, and conduct informational and referral interviews. Most business people will tell you similar stories about the realities of running one's own business. Do your market research, work long hours, plan, and be persistent. They also will give you advice on businesses to avoid and essential business routines.

Many service and high-tech businesses will be growing in the decade ahead. Given major issues, such as energy, the environment, health care, fitness, and leisure, and the changing demographic structure (fewer young people, more elderly, the two-career family) numerous opportunities are arising for small personal-service businesses to meet the needs of the elderly and career-oriented families. Businesses relating to restaurants, home maintenance, health care, housing for the elderly, green technologies, energy, the environment, and mortuaries and cemeteries should expand considerably in the future.

Opportunities are also available for inventive business people who can make more productive use of busy people's time – for example, fast food, financial planning, and mail-order Internet and catalog shopping. The information and high-tech revolutions are taking place at the same time two-career families do not have time to waste standing in lines at banks, grocery stores, and department stores. Mail-order or Internet-based home and office-based shopping should increase dramatically during the next decade.

A service business is especially attractive. It's easy to establish; many require a small initial investment; and the accounting is often simple. You may be able to operate from your home and thus keep the costs of operation down.

If you decide to go into business, make sure you choose the right business for your particular skills, abilities, motivation, and interests. A good starting point is the Small Business Administration's website, especially the useful section on determining whether or not you are best suited for the entrepreneurial life:

www.sba.gov/category/navigation-structure/starting-managing-business

You also should visit this section of their website, which includes a listing of several free online courses on starting a business:

www.sba.gov/tools/sba-learning-center/search/trainingtool

One of the most popular and useful such courses recommended by the Small Business Administration is entitled "Entrepreneurship: Starting and Managing Your Business":

www.myownbusiness.org/course_sba.html

Available in 13 sessions, it's offered as both a free or enhanced fee-based course. Whatever you do, make sure you take this course.

Several other websites also can provide useful assistance on how to start and run a successful business:

■ **Small Business Administration**	www.sba.gov
■ **BizMove.com**	http://bizmove.com
■ **Business Know-How**	http://businessknowhow.com
■ **AllBusiness**	www.allbusiness.com
■ **Business Owner's Toolkit**	http://toolkit.com
■ **CEO Business Express**	www.ceoexpress.com
■ **Entrepreneur.com**	www.entrepreneur.com
■ **Entrepreneurship**	www.entrepreneurship.org

The 101 Best Jobs –
Summary Index, Education, Salary

Job	Page	Education	Salary
▪ Nuclear Medicine Technologists	114	Associate	$70,180
▪ Nursing Assistants and Orderlies	114	Postsecondary	$24,400
▪ Occupational Health and Safety Technicians	115	Bachelor	$66,790
▪ Occupational Therapists	115	Master	$65,470
▪ Occupational Therapy Assistants and Aides	115	HS diploma	$48,940
▪ Opticians, Dispensing	116	HS diploma	$33,330
▪ Personal Care Aides	116	Less than HS	$19,910
▪ Phlebotomists	116	Postsecondary	$29,730
▪ Physical Therapy Assistants and Aides	116	Associate	$39,430
▪ Physician Assistants	117	Master	$90,930
▪ Radiologic and MRI Technologists	117	Associate	$55,910
▪ Registered Nurses	118	Associate	$65,470
▪ Respiratory Therapists	118	Associate	$55,870
▪ Surgical Technologists	118	Postsecondary	$41,790
▪ Veterinary Assistants and Laboratory Animal Caretakers	119	HS diploma	$23,130
▪ Veterinary Technologists and Technicians	119	Associate	$30,290

Installation, Maintenance, and Repair Occupations

Job	Page	Education	Salary
▪ Aircraft and Avionics Equipment Mechanics and Service Technicians	54	Trade school	$55,230
▪ Automotive Body and Glass Repairers	56	HS diploma	$37,680
▪ Automotive Service Technicians and Mechanics	57	HS diploma	$36,610
▪ General Maintenance and Repair Workers	59	HS diploma	$35,210
▪ Heating, Air-Conditioning, and Refrigeration Mechanics and Installers	60	Postsecondary	$43,640
▪ Line Installers and Repairers	62	HS diploma	$58,210
▪ Small Engine Mechanics	64	HS diploma	$32,640

Office and Administrative Support Jobs

Job	Page	Education	Salary
▪ Bill and Account Collectors	125	HS diploma	$32,480
▪ Bookkeeping, Accounting, and Auditing Clerks	125	HS diploma	$35,170
▪ Customer Service Representatives	126	HS diploma	$30,580
▪ General Office Clerks	126	HS diploma	$27,470
▪ Information Clerks	126	HS diploma	$30,650
▪ Police, Fire, and Ambulance Dispatcher	127	HS diploma	$36,300
▪ Receptionists	127	HS diploma	$25,990
▪ Secretaries and Administrative Assistants	128	HS diploma	$35,330

Production Occupations

Job	Page	Education	Salary
▪ Machinists and Tool and Die Makers	77	HS diploma	$40,910
▪ Painting and Coating Workers	79	Less than HS	$32,850
▪ Welders, Cutters, Solderers, and Brazers	80	HS diploma	$36,300

Sales and Related Jobs

Job	Page	Education	Salary
▪ Advertising Sales Agents	120	HS diploma	$46,290
▪ Insurance Sales Agents	120	HS diploma	$48,150
▪ Real Estate Brokers and Sales Agents	121	HS diploma	$41,990
▪ Retail Sales Workers	121	Less than HS	$21,410
▪ Sales Representatives, Wholesale and Manufacturing	121	HS diploma	$57,870

Re-Entry Success Resources

THE FOLLOWING RE-ENTRY RESOURCES are available from Impact Publications. Full descriptions of each as well as downloadable catalogs and video clips can be found at www. impactpublications.com. Complete the following form or list the titles, include shipping (see formula at the end), enclose payment, and send your order to:

IMPACT PUBLICATIONS
9104 Manassas Drive, Suite N
Manassas Park, VA 20111-5211
1-800-361-1055 (orders only)
Tel. 703-361-7300 or Fax 703-335-9486
Email: query@impactpublications.com
Quick & easy online ordering: www.impactpublications.com

Orders from individuals must be prepaid by check, money order, or major credit card. We accept telephone, fax, and email orders. Since prices may change, please verify online www. impactpublications.com before ordering.

Qty.	TITLES	Price	TOTAL
Featured Title			
_____	Best Jobs For Ex-Offenders	$11.95	_____
Re-Entry Pocket Guides (quantity discounts featured on inside cover page)			
_____	The Anger Management Pocket Guide	$2.95	_____
_____	Re-Entry Employment & Life Skills Pocket Guide	2.95	_____
_____	Re-Entry Personal Finance Pocket Guide	2.95	_____
_____	Re-Entry Start-Up Pocket Guide	2.95	_____
_____	Re-Imagining Life on the Outside Pocket Guide	2.95	_____
Re-Entry and Survival for Ex-Offenders			
_____	9 to 5 Beats Ten to Life	$20.00	_____
_____	99 Days and a Get Up	9.95	_____
_____	99 Days to Re-Entry Success	4.95	_____
_____	Best Jobs for Ex-Offenders	11.95	_____
_____	Best Resumes and Letters for Ex-Offenders	19.95	_____
_____	Beyond Bars	13.95	_____
_____	Chicken Soup for the Prisoner's Soul	14.95	_____
_____	The Dedicated Ex-Prisoner's Life and Success on the Outside	19.95	_____
_____	Ex-Offender's 30/30 Job Solution	11.95	_____
_____	Ex-Offender's Re-Entry Assistance Directory	29.95	_____
_____	Ex-Offender's Guide to a Responsible Life	15.95	_____
_____	Ex-Offender's Job Interview Guide	11.95	_____
_____	Ex-Offender's New Job Finding and Survival Guide	19.95	_____
_____	Ex-Offender's Quick Job Hunting Guide	11.95	_____
_____	Ex-Offender's Re-Entry Assistance Directory	29.95	_____
_____	Ex-Offender's Re-Entry Success Guide	11.95	_____
_____	Houses of Healing	15.00	_____
_____	How to Do Good After Prison	19.95	_____
_____	Jobs for Felons	7.95	_____
_____	Letters to an Incarcerated Brother	16.00	_____
_____	Life Beyond Loss	20.00	_____

_____	Life Without a Crutch	7.95	_____
_____	Man, I Need a Job	7.95	_____
_____	A Map Through the Maze	11.95	_____
_____	No One is Unemployable	29.95	_____
_____	Picking Up the Pieces (for Women)	20.00	_____
_____	Quick Job Search for Ex-Offenders	7.95	_____
_____	Re-Entry Support Programs for Ex-Offenders	40.00	_____
_____	Serving Productive Time	14.95	_____

Personal Finance Guides

_____	The Total Money Makeover	$24.99	_____
_____	The Truth About Money	21.99	_____

Attitude, Motivation, and Inspiration

_____	7 Habits of Highly Effective People	$17.00	_____
_____	30 Lessons for Living	16.00	_____
_____	100 Ways to Motivate Yourself	15.99	_____
_____	The Art of Doing	16.00	_____
_____	Attitude Is Everything	16.99	_____
_____	Awaken the Giant Within	17.99	_____
_____	Breaking the Habit of Being Yourself	16.95	_____
_____	The Bounce Back Book	12.95	_____
_____	Bouncing Back: Rewiring Your Brain	17.95	_____
_____	Can I Get a Do Over?	14.95	_____
_____	Change Your Attitude	16.99	_____
_____	Change Your Thinking, Change Your Life	22.00	_____
_____	Create Your Own Future	21.00	_____
_____	Eat That Frog!	15.95	_____
_____	The Element: How Finding Your Passion Changes Everything	16.00	_____
_____	Finding Your Own North Star	15.00	_____
_____	Free At Last: Daily Meditations By and For Ex-Offenders	15.95	_____
_____	Get Out of Your Own Way: Overcoming Self-Defeating Behavior	15.00	_____
_____	Get the Life Your Want	19.95	_____
_____	Goals!	19.95	_____
_____	Healing is a Choice	18.99	_____
_____	How to Save Your Own Life	14.00	_____
_____	How to Win Friends and Influence People	16.95	_____
_____	The Last Lecture	21.95	_____
_____	Magic of Thinking Big	15.99	_____
_____	Making Good Habit, Breaking Bad Habits	19.99	_____
_____	Making Hope Happen	26.00	_____
_____	The Power of Habit	16.00	_____
_____	The Power of Positive Thinking	15.99	_____
_____	Reinventing Your Life	17.00	_____
_____	The Secret	23.95	_____
_____	The Success Principles	18.99	_____
_____	Think and Grow Rich	18.95	_____
_____	What Should I Do With My Life?	16.00	_____
_____	What You're Really Meant to Do	25.00	_____
_____	Wishcraft: How to Get What You Really Want	15.00	_____

Reimagining Your Life With Purpose

_____	Claiming Your Place At the Fire	$16.95	_____
_____	From Age-ing to Sage-ing	15.00	_____
_____	Life Reimagined: Discovering Your New Life Possibilities	16.95	_____
_____	Man's Search for Meaning	9.99	_____
_____	The Power of Purpose	17.95	_____
_____	Repacking Your Bags	17.95	_____

_____	Something to Live For	16.95 _____
_____	Your Best Life Ever	21.99 _____
_____	Your Life Calling: Reimagining the Rest of Your Life	16.00 _____

Mindfulness

_____	The Gifts of Imperfection	$14.95 _____
_____	Mindfulness: A Practical Guide to Awakening	25.95 _____
_____	Mindfulness for Beginners	21.95 _____
_____	Mindfulness for Dummies	26.99 _____
_____	The Mindfulness Solution	16.95 _____
_____	One-Minute Mindfulness	15.95 _____
_____	The Power of Now	15.00 _____
_____	Spiritual Solutions: Answers to Life's Greatest Challenges	22.00 _____
_____	Stillness Speaks	17.00 _____
_____	Super Brain	15.00 _____
_____	Thrive	26.00 _____

Assessment Instruments (packages of 25)

_____	Barriers to Employment Success Inventory	$57.95 _____
_____	Job Survival and Success Scale	53.95 _____
_____	Offender Reintegration Scale	47.95 _____
_____	Transition-to-Work Inventory	54.95 _____

Career Exploration

_____	50 Best Jobs for Your Personality	$17.95 _____
_____	150 Best Jobs for a Secure Future	17.95 _____
_____	150 Best Jobs for Your Skills	17.95 _____
_____	150 Best Low-Stress Jobs	16.95 _____
_____	200 Best Jobs for Introverts	16.95 _____
_____	200 Best Jobs Through Apprenticeships	24.95 _____
_____	250 Best-Paying Jobs	17.95 _____
_____	300 Best Jobs Without a Four-Year Degree	18.95 _____
_____	Best Jobs for the 21st Century	19.95 _____
_____	Occupational Outlook Handbook	19.95 _____
_____	Top 100 Health-Care Careers	25.95 _____

Finding Jobs and Getting Hired

_____	The 2-Hour Job Search	$12.99 _____
_____	Guerrilla Marketing for Job Hunters 3.0	21.95 _____
_____	Job Hunting Tips for People With Hot and Not-So-Hot Backgrounds	17.95 _____
_____	Knock 'Em Dead: The Ultimate Job Search Guide	16.99 _____
_____	No One Will Hire Me!	15.95 _____
_____	Overcoming Barriers to Employment	17.95 _____
_____	Unemployed, But Moving On!	13.95 _____
_____	What Color is Your Parachute? (annual edition)	18.99 _____

Career Assessment

_____	Career Match	$15.00 _____
_____	Discover What You're Best At	15.99 _____
_____	Do What You Are	18.99 _____
_____	Everything Career Tests Book	15.99 _____
_____	Gifts Differing	18.95 _____
_____	Go Put Your Strengths to Work	16.00 _____
_____	I Don't Know What I Want, But I Know It's Not This	15.00 _____
_____	I Want to Do Something Else, But I 'm Not Sure What It Is	15.95 _____
_____	Pathfinder	17.95 _____
_____	What Color Is Your Parachute Workbook	12.99 _____
_____	What Type Am I?	17.00 _____

Resumes and Cover Letters

_____	100 Best Resumes	$20.00 _____
_____	201 Dynamite Job Search Letters	19.95 _____
_____	Best KeyWords for Resumes, Cover Letters, and Interviews	17.95 _____
_____	Best Resumes for People Without a Four-Year Degree	19.95 _____
_____	Blue-Collar Resume and Job Hunting Guide	15.95 _____
_____	Damn Good Resume Guide	11.99 _____
_____	Gallery of Best Resumes for People Without a Four-Year Degree	18.95 _____
_____	Haldane's Best Cover Letters for Professionals	15.95 _____
_____	High Impact Resumes and Letters	19.95 _____
_____	Knock 'Em Dead Cover Letters	14.99 _____
_____	Knock 'Em Dead Resumes	14.99 _____
_____	Nail the Cover Letter	17.95 _____
_____	Nail the Resume!	17.95 _____
_____	The Resume Catalog	19.99 _____
_____	Resumes for Dummies	18.99 _____

Networking and Social Media

_____	Branding Yourself	$24.99 _____
_____	How to Find a Job on LinkedIn, Facebook, Twitter, and Google+	20.00 _____
_____	Job Searching With Social Media for Dummies	19.99 _____
_____	Know 'Em Dead Social Networking	15.99 _____
_____	Networking for People Who Hate Networking	16.95 _____
_____	The Power Formula for LinkedIn Success	16.95 _____
_____	Savvy Networker	16.95 _____
_____	Social Networking for Career Success	20.00 _____

Interviewing

_____	101 Dynamite Questions to Ask At Your Job Interview	$13.95 _____
_____	101 Great Answers to the Toughest Interview Questions	12.99 _____
_____	Best Answers to 202 Job Interview Questions	17.95 _____
_____	I Can't Believe They Asked Me That!	17.95 _____
_____	Job Interview Tips for People With Not-So-Hot Backgrounds	14.95 _____
_____	KeyWords to Nail Your Job Interview	17.95 _____
_____	Knock 'Em Dead Job Interviews	14.95 _____
_____	Nail the Job Interview	17.95 _____
_____	Job Interview for Dummies	17.99 _____
_____	Savvy Interviewing	10.95 _____
_____	Sweaty Palms	13.95 _____
_____	Win the Interview, Win the Job	15.95 _____
_____	You Should Hire Me!	15.95 _____

Salary Negotiations

_____	Get a Raise in 7 Days	$16.95 _____
_____	Give Me More Money!	17.95 _____
_____	Salary Negotiation Tips for Professionals	16.95 _____

Job Keeping and Revitalization

_____	How to Be a Star At Work	$15.00 _____
_____	Love 'Em or Lose 'Em	24.95 _____
_____	Who Gets Promoted, Who Doesn't, and Why	14.95 _____

Start and Manage a Business

_____	The $100,000 Entrepreneur	$19.95 _____
_____	Small Business Start-Up Kit	29.99 _____
_____	Start Your Own Business	24.95 _____

Addiction

_____	12 Hidden Rewards of Making Amends	$14.95 _____
_____	12 Smart Things to Do When the Booze and Drugs Are Gone	14.95 _____
_____	12 Stupid Things That Mess Up Recovery	14.95 _____
_____	Chicken Soup for the Recovering Soul	14.95 _____
_____	Clean: Overcoming Addiction and Ending America's Greatest Tragedy	25.00 _____
_____	Denial Is Not a River in Egypt	13.95 _____
_____	Ending Addiction for Good	14.95 _____
_____	How to Get and Stay Sober	14.95 _____
_____	The Life Recovery Bible	19.99 _____
_____	Life Without a Crutch	7.95 _____
_____	Now What? An Insider's Guide to Addiction and Recovery	14.95 _____
_____	Painkillers, Heroin, and the Road to Sanity	14.95 _____
_____	Passages Through Recovery	14.95 _____
_____	Recover to Live	25.95 _____
_____	The Recovery Book	15.95 _____
_____	Rein in Your Brain	14.95 _____
_____	Stop the Chaos	14.95 _____
_____	The Truth About Addiction and Recovery	16.00 _____
_____	Understanding the Twelve Steps	15.00 _____
_____	You Need Help!	14.95 _____

Anger Management

_____	Anger Control Workbook	$21.95 _____
_____	Anger Management for Dummies	22.99 _____
_____	Anger Management Sourcebook	18.95 _____
_____	Angry Men	14.95 _____
_____	Angry Women	14.95 _____
_____	Beyond Anger: A Guide for Men	15.99 _____
_____	Cage Your Rage for Women	20.00 _____
_____	Cage Your Rage Workbook	25.00 _____
_____	Forgiveness	17.95 _____
_____	Healthy Anger	24.95 _____
_____	Letting Go of Anger	16.95 _____
_____	Managing Teen Anger and Violence	19.95 _____
_____	Pathways to Peace Anger Management Workbook	29.95 _____
_____	Teen Anger Workbook	49.95 _____
_____	Violent No More	24.95 _____

Special Value Kits

_____	71 Re-Entry Success Books for Ex-Offenders	$1,149.95 _____
_____	Anger, Rage, and Recovery Kit	848.00 _____
_____	Discover What You're Best At Kit	429.95 _____
_____	Ex-Offender's Re-Entry Success Library	330.95 _____
_____	Helping Ex-Offenders Achieve Re-Entry Success	373.95 _____
_____	Job Finding With Social Media and Technology Kit	282.95 _____
_____	Learning From Successes and Failures Kit	1,069.95 _____
_____	Mindfulness for Refocusing Your Life Kit	297.95 _____
_____	New Attitudes, Goals, and Motivations Kit	411.95 _____
_____	Overcoming Self-Defeating Behaviors and Bouncing Back Kit	245.95 _____
_____	Reimagining Life: Discovering Your Meaning and Purpose in Life Kit	203.95 _____
_____	Start Your Own Business Kit	316.95 _____
_____	Substance Abuse, Addictive Behaviors, and Recovery Kit	899.95 _____
_____	Tony Robbins "Transform Your Life" Collection	189.95 _____

Survival and Re-Entry Curriculum Programs

_____	99 Days and a Get Up Training Program	$2,500.00 _____
_____	From the Inside Out Curriculum	599.00 _____
_____	Co-occurring Disorders Program (CDP)	829.00 _____

_____ Life Skills Series for Parolees and Inmates	1,239.00	_____
_____ Life Without a Crutch Training Program	995.00	_____
_____ Map Through the Maze Program	389.95	_____
_____ A New Direction for Ex-Offenders: A Curriculum	4,695.00	_____
_____ Ultimate Re-Entry Success Curriculum Starter Kit	1,795.00	_____

Re-Entry and Survival DVDs

_____ 9 to 5 Beats Ten to Life	$95.00	_____
_____ After Prison	149.00	_____
_____ Breaking and Entering...Into a Better Life	199.95	_____
_____ Countdown to Freedom (for men or women)	695.00	_____
_____ Down But Not Out	149.00	_____
_____ Ex-Offenders CAN Ace the Job Interview	179.00	_____
_____ Ex-Offender's Guide to Job Fair Success	129.00	_____
_____ From Prison to Home	`169.95	_____
_____ From Parole to Payroll (3 DVDs)	299.85	_____
_____ From Prison to Paycheck (8 DVDs)	999.00	_____
_____ Life After Prison	99.95	_____
_____ Living Free	149.00	_____
_____ Parole: Getting Out and Staying Out	69.95	_____
_____ Putting the Bars Behind You	99.00	_____
_____ Starting Fresh With a Troubled Background Series	299.95	_____
_____ Stop Recidivism, Now! (3 DVDs)	275.00	_____
_____ Why Bother? Finding the Will to Go On	119.95	_____

Life Skills/Personal Finance DVD/CD Programs

_____ Buying the Basics	$199.00	_____
_____ Effectively Managing Your Money and Work Program	1,170.00	_____
_____ Life Skills for Independent Living CD Program	1,319.00	_____
_____ Life Steps DVD Series	799.95	_____
_____ Managing Your Personal Finances	540.00	_____
_____ On Your Own: Independent Living Skills	99.95	_____

Addiction, Recovery, and Relapse Programs

_____ Addiction Recovery for Ex-Offenders DVD Series	$999.00	_____
_____ Co-Occurring Disorders Program	1,395.00	_____
_____ Substance Abuse and Addictive Behaviors Kit	557.95	_____

TERMS: Individuals must prepay; approved accounts are billed net 30 days. All orders under $100.00 should be prepaid.

RUSH ORDERS: fax, call, or email for more information on any special shipping arrangements and charges.

SUBTOTAL _____

Virginia residents add 6% sales tax _____
California residents add ___% sales tax _____

Shipping ($5 +8% of SUBTOTAL) _____

TOTAL ORDER _____

Bill To:

Name_____ Title _____
Address _____
City _____ State/Zip _____
Phone (   )_____(daytime)
Email _____

Ship To: (if different from "Bill To;" include street delivery address) :

Name_____ Title _____
Address _____
City _____ State/Zip _____
Phone (   )_____(daytime)
Email _____

PAYMENT METHOD: ❑ **Purchase Order #_____** *(attach or fax with this order form)*
  ❑ **Check** – Make payable to IMPACT PUBLICATIONS
  ❑ **Credit Card**:   ❑ Visa   ❑ MasterCard   ❑ AMEX   ❑ Discover

Card #											Expiration Date		
Signature							Name on Card (print)						

Re-Entry Companion Guides

The Ex-Offender's New Job Finding and Survival Guide: 10 Steps for Successfully Re-Entering the Work World (2nd Edition)

Ronald L. Krannich, Ph.D.

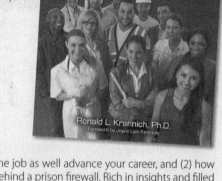

#9218 What should ex-offenders do in order to land a good job? This book provides important answers to many re-entry questions facing ex-offenders. Beginning with an examination of 20 myths/realities and 22 principles for success, it reveals 10 steps to job and career success:

1. Examine and change your attitudes
2. Seek assistance and become proactive
3. Select appropriate job search approaches
4. Assess your skills and identify your motivational pattern
5. State a powerful objective
6. Conduct research on jobs and communities
7. Write effective resumes and letters
8. Network for information, advice, and referrals
9. Develop winning job interview skills
10. Negotiate salary and benefits like a pro

Includes two special chapters – (1) how to survive and prosper on the job as well advance your career, and (2) how to best navigate the electronic world after spending so much time behind a prison firewall. Rich in insights and filled with practical examples, exercises, self-tests, and resources. 240 pages. Copyright © 2016. ISBN 978-1-57023-362-3. **$19.95. SPECIALS: 10 copies for $159.60; 100 copies for $998.00; 1,000 copies for $7,980.00.**

99 Days to Re-Entry Success Journal:
Your Weekly Planning and Implementation Tool for Staying Out for Good! (2nd Edition)

Ronald L. Krannich, Ph.D.

#7679 This handy journal assists ex-offenders in dealing with key transition issues during their first 99 days, or 14 weeks, in the free world. It requires users to:

♦ specify three major objectives each week
♦ identify specific supporting daily activities
♦ anticipate related outcomes
♦ evaluate their progress at the end of each week
♦ make key adjustments for the next week

Users record exactly what they plan to do each day (a daily "To Do" list) and then evaluate their progress on a scale of 1 to 10 in accomplishing their goals for the week. The journal also includes important sections on:

♦ commitment
♦ key contacts
♦ appointments
♦ financial planning
♦ budgeting
♦ personal information
♦ documentation
♦ re-entry resources

Helps ex-offenders focus on those things they need to do on a daily basis to develop a new pattern of behavior for achieving success in the free world. 64 pages. Copyright © 2016. ISBN 978-1-57023-372-2. **$4.95. SPECIALS: 10 copies for $39.80; 100 copies for $297.00; 1,000 copies for $2,227.00.**

The Re-Entry Start-Up Pocket Guide:
Mapping Your Way Through the Free World Maze

Ronald L. Krannich, Ph.D.

#5512 Jam-packed with the author's signature self-tests, checklists, and exercises, this pocket guide is designed to help ex-offenders make wise re-entry decisions in any community relating to:

♦ documentation
♦ housing
♦ employment
♦ transportation
♦ food
♦ clothing
♦ health/wellness
♦ mental health
♦ substance abuse
♦ recreation/leisure
♦ education
♦ finance/banking
♦ mentoring
♦ veterans' services

Includes special sections on rap sheets, references, forgiveness letters, community networks, and gateway re-entry resources. Insightful, unconventional, and interactive, this is one of the most thoughtful guides to making it on the outside. 64 pages. **$2.95. SPECIALS: 10 copies for $23.60; 100 copies for $147.50; 1,000 copies for $1,180.00.**

Re-Entry Companion Guides: #6454 All three books (*The Ex-Offender's New Job Finding and Survival Guide, 99 Days to Re-Entry Success,* and *The Re-Entry Start-Up Pocket Guide*) for **$25.95. SPECIALS: 10 sets (30 books) for $222.95; 100 sets (300 books) for $1,395.95.**

**Quick & easy online ordering:
www.impactpublications.com**